Motivational Nudges to Empower Your Life

Plus InnerTalk® Resource Guide

Eldon Taylor, Ph.D.
and Ravinder Taylor

With eternal love and gratitude to Roy and Lois Bey.

Your incredible friendship and support made InnerTalk possible.

CONTENTS

Prologue by Eldon Taylor vii

Part One: Why We Need a Self-Improvement Strategy 1
   Chapter One: What Everyone Wants to Know 3
   Chapter Two: Behaviors to Change 6
   Chapter Three: Free Will? 9
   Chapter Four: Hurtful Words Damage the Brain 12
   Chapter Five: Hope 15
   Chapter Six: Power of Optimism 18
   Chapter Seven: Self-Sabotage 20
   Chapter Eight: The Gains in Self-Sabotage? 23

Part Two: A Few Ideas to Consider 27
   Chapter Nine: Your Personal Master Plan 29
   Chapter Ten: The Rehearsal That Makes a Lifetime Difference 32
   Chapter Eleven: The Impostor Syndrome 35
   Chapter Twelve: Using Different Forms of Mindfulness 38
   Chapter Thirteen: Change Your Mental Group 40
   Chapter Fourteen: Thoughts That Manipulate Matter 43
   Chapter Fifteen: Pollyanna and Pragmatics 47
   Chapter Sixteen: Control 52
   Chapter Seventeen: Our Identities 54
   Chapter Eighteen: Relationships 56
   Chapter Nineteen: Cookie Keepers 58
   Chapter Twenty: True Self-Responsibility 62
   Chapter Twenty-One: What Is an Authentic Life? 66
   Chapter Twenty-Two: Blessing Success and Money 69
   Chapter Twenty-Three: Choosing Perception 72

Part Three: InnerTalk® 75
   Chapter Twenty-Four: It Begins With a Story 77
   Chapter Twenty-Five: Why Self-Help 80

Chapter Twenty-Six: The Foundation Stone for
    All Forms of Self-Help 82
Chapter Twenty-Seven: What's in a Subliminal Program? 84
Chapter Twenty-Eight: A Beginner's Guide 85
Chapter Twenty-Nine: Different Ways to Use
    Your InnerTalk Programs 90
Chapter Thirty: Your Personal Coach 94
Chapter Thirty-One: The Missing Element 97
Chapter Thirty-Two: The Science Behind InnerTalk® 100
Chapter Thirty-Three: What You Can Expect 105

Part Four: Resource Guide 111
    How to Use This Resource Guide 113
    Libraries 119
    Collections 142
    Sets 149
    Subliminal 152
        Success 152
        Better Life 184
        Relationships 230
        Health and Wellness 241
        Habits and Addictions 266
        Body Image 273
        Sports and Fitness 279
        Children, Parenting, and Childbirth 291
        Learning 303
        Spirituality 312
    Power Imaging 333
    OZO and Echo-Tech 336
    Power Sets 341
    Platinum Plus Series 343
    Video Entrainment 346
    Further Education: Books and DVDs by Eldon Taylor 350
    Frequently Asked Questions 358
    Further Information 369

PROLOGUE

by Eldon Taylor

There is an old Sufi saying that, paraphrased, goes like this, "It's not what the book says, but what the book does that matters." Ravinder and I believe that self-realization is a journey that naturally leads to the question, "How high is up?" This work is dedicated to the proposition that there is always more to be accomplished, another goal to achieve, and to that end, the words that follow are designed to motivate the "do" in what the book does.

Ravinder and I have worked together for more than thirty years. Our ultimate ambition is to provide tools and technology that empower each and every individual. That said, tools can be problematic if not understood. For example, imagine a Neanderthal who stumbles upon a hard silver box that opens, has a number of strange white figures on black buttons, and has a silhouette of an apple on the outside. What do you think our Neanderthal would do with this newfound item?

InnerTalk® is a patented dichotic masking technology that has been repeatedly demonstrated effective in the most rigorous of scientific research designs and across many different domains. These domains range from ADHD to clinical depression, from examination anxiety to increasing reflectivity while lowering hostility and aggression in an incarcerated environment, and much more. Indeed, more than two dozen studies have demonstrated the efficacy of InnerTalk—yet there are many who don't understand how it works, when and where to use it, and why.

We have done our best to clarify the whys, whats, and hows that undergird the success you can expect when using InnerTalk. Ravinder and I have both contributed to this book in our own voices based on more than sixty years of combined experience working with InnerTalk. Each chapter is designed to be brief and provocative in order to promote introspection. Read what follows like a book or read it a chapter at a time, resting between chapters to contemplate the possible impact on your own life. Indeed, one of our readers noted that the book could be opened anywhere, and it would synchronistically connect to a personal meaning appropriate for the moment.

So, to begin, understand that this work exists to explain and to do so in a way that lends great value independent of ever using an InnerTalk program. In that sense, it is a genuine motivational self-help book that will inspire you. However, it is also a resource guide for InnerTalk programs. That will not in any way diminish the value of the material that follows, for the Resource Guide is in the back of the book and not something you need to ever look at.

So, whether you are interested in understanding the path of awakening to your true potential or seeking to begin manifesting your best in every endeavor, you will find what follows of great value.

Thank you,

Eldon Taylor

Part One

Why We Need a Self-Improvement Strategy

CHAPTER ONE:

What Everyone Wants to Know

Throughout the many years that I have traveled and shared with people from all walks of life, at all socioeconomic levels, and in many different cultures and countries, there are three questions that are always asked. They essentially go like this:

- What can I do to improve my life?
- How can I discover my purpose?
- How can we make a peaceful, better world?

Interestingly, we improve our quality of life by becoming a better person—a person who we recognize as worthy—a good human being. We do that by taking some intentional steps designed to acknowledge ourselves. We begin by forgiving ourselves for anything and everything we might feel has in some way dishonored us. We deserve forgiveness because we forgive everyone of anything and everything that might have been done in some way that we perceive injured us. In other words, so long as we blame someone, anyone, for something in our life, we invalidate our own forgiveness. Many people miss this important point. It's basically said this way: *"What we sow is what we reap."* When we refuse to find forgiveness in our heart for acts against us, we create a sort of calculus. Using our calculus, we decide: This act is forgivable but this one isn't. That translates to a sliding scale of forgiveness and thereby becomes as applicable to ourselves as it is to others. Another way to think of this is, *"Judge not lest ye be judged."*

Forgive

Further, without forgiveness, we disable our ability to do anything about an issue or event. What is there to do if someone else is to blame—it's their fault, after all. In this victim role we are disempowered from acting in some proactive manner, thereby healing and accepting ourselves. It's not that we necessarily deserve everything that comes to us, it's more a case of what we do with the stimuli that matters. We may not be in charge of everything we will encounter in life, but we are absolutely in charge of how we will respond and integrate these events. So, the first step to improving your life is forgiveness.

Now, there are two very practical matters that I suggest as well. Set aside twenty minutes four or five days a week to meditate. Research shows us that regular meditation can enhance cognitive abilities, reduce stress and anxiety, strengthen the immune system and even increase the amount of gray matter in your brain. When you meditate you slow brainwave activity and enter conscious states akin to dream sleep that you can guide, and thereby obtain answers as well as stillness. This regular practice will assist you in becoming mindful. If you would prefer, use self-hypnosis and actively train your mind while conditioning deeper and deeper levels of inner awareness.

Be Mindful

The third direction I would suggest is that you actively seek to be mindful of everything in your life. You can do this while you go about your daily life. Just pay attention to your thoughts. When you have an aberrant thought, cancel it, but also make a note to yourself to later explore where it may have originated. As you become more and more aware of your stream of consciousness, your inner talk, you can actively become involved in consciously engineering the kind of thoughts you would like to have. Indeed, I developed the patented technology known as InnerTalk to prime self-talk, introducing a positive stream of reinforcing thoughts directly into the subconscious as a means to empower this technique. By attending to your thoughts, little by little you replace those ants (automatic negative thoughts) with positive self-supporting beliefs and the GIGO (garbage in–garbage out) scenario becomes AIAO (awesome in–awesome out).

Now, interestingly, as we answer question one, we actually begin to answer questions two and three. I am absolutely convinced that the way you find your purpose is through service. You may be a plumber, a nurse, a truck driver, an attorney, a doctor or whatever—but when you recognize that what you do is not about you but rather about what you are doing for others, everything changes! In the instant that you think of your work as providing a genuine service to others, rather than being about money, etc., not only will you find your services being sought after, but many other opportunities will open up. In fact, experience shows that when you change your attitude, and dedicate your life to service, then that big shoehorn in the sky will help you right into where you're supposed to be. And you'll know it because you'll love it!

Be the Change You Are Seeking

As for question three, the world changes one person at a time. It may have become somewhat trite, but it is still nevertheless profoundly true: "Be the change you are seeking." By practicing the steps offered above for the first two questions, you are doing just that—making the world a better place one person at a time! In the words often attributed to Mother Teresa, "I alone cannot change the world, but I can cast a stone across the waters to create many ripples."

So, the three answers to our three questions boil down to this:

- Forgiveness
- Service
- Be the change (responsibility)

We'll discuss all of this in more detail later, but remember, it takes only one person, one kind act, one smile, and so forth to change your life and the world around you.

Chapter Two:

Behaviors to Change

Most people have behaviors they would like to change. The more sensitive a person becomes to the purpose of life, the more likely they are to see and feel characteristics about themselves that they know could be better. Personal growth is truly about being the best we can be. There are two difficulties that are almost always encountered before growth is possible. The first is recognition. Denial plays a big role here. All too often the individual, who could remarkably improve the quality of their life, refuses to recognize their role in creating the life they currently live. The bad in their life is due to someone or something else. Their actions are always justified, if not by society such as with notions like, "It's okay to get even," then by their rationalizations.

Now whether people like or love you should not be either the question or the criteria for change. Indeed, the pure fact that these statements may be included in your questioning suggests that there may be some meaningful self-disclosure here. Cognitive scientists inform us that associations are not accidental. The association between acceptance and overt behavior is well documented in the behavioral literature. In fact, almost all behavior is patterned during our formative years, seeking first acceptance and second other forms of gratification. The problem is that most of our individual behaviors are the result of an attention/avoidance calculus that is initially seeded in the subconscious mind. There the seed, analogously speaking, takes root in strategies that accomplish our aim, albeit unconsciously so.

Subconscious Strategies

Very often strategies, that were initially designed to assist us in avoiding rejection and attracting love and attention, are truly self-defeating in our adult lives. For example, a perceived threat of rejection, such as that experienced by an older child when a new sibling enters the family, generally leads to actions designed to bring attention (love) back to the older child. If this action by the child is acceptable, such as caressing the baby and helping Mom, then it is considered adaptive (socially acceptable behavior). It can also, in the above example, actually be beneficial to the child. However, more often than not, the adaptive behavior is defiant, belligerent, and outrageous to the extent that it cannot be ignored by parents. Sometimes the behavior actually chooses illness as its attention-seeking mechanism.

There are, of course, many different scenarios and possible adaptation schemes. The bottom line is that one often acquires a behavior as a compensatory mechanism.

When behaviors are rooted in subconscious strategies, those roots (early fears, traumas, hurts, and so forth) by definition become hidden from conscious awareness. One is able to recognize the behavior but is unable to see its cause. This situation is commonly exacerbated when the behavior is overtly challenged, for deep down in the subconscious mind exists a link to the original root network. Over a lifetime these self-defeating strategies get built up in such a way that it is not uncommon for a person to begin to feel somehow defective, and that, too, worsens the state of affairs.

Magic Bullets

We all have a need to be loved, liked, and accepted. We all have been injured by words and deeds that somehow threatened our security. We all have developed strategies. To uproot a self-defeating strategy, we all must begin to overtly and consciously seek out our fear feelings while holding our behavior in check. There are two *magic bullets* that I have learned from all of my work, which can immediately begin the healing/growing process: Forgiveness and Gratitude.

In a real sense, there is nothing to forgive. Still, the paradox here is that we must forgive in order to realize, truly know, there is nothing to forgive.

It's sort of like the age-old middle pillar or middle path; we need thesis, antithesis, and synthesis in order to advance beyond mere ideas.

We live in a world of duality. The world may call us into action (hopefully right action action—action based on the highest best of all concerned) but our action should not come from fear. That said, fear is a natural aspect of being an animal, alive in this world. It's simply built in. The opposite to fear is gratitude. Fear feeds blame, guilt, shame, anger, and rage. Indeed, in my opinion, as an acronym, FEAR simply means: **F**or **E**very **A**nger **R**esponse there is a fear. It is therefore obvious that fear and anger are circular.

One can choose to forgive any and all actions from everyone, including themselves while accepting everything that comes their way with a gratitude attitude, a sort of, "Wow, I can't wait to see what good comes from this" approach. Taking this overt step and insisting that self be still and feel any threat or fear before responding, gives rise to a form of cognitive behavioral modification of the self-care type. However, expecting that the fear may be increased as you seek it out may cause the initial impulse to temporarily appear to worsen.

We live in a marvelous age of technology. Stilling the mind, rooting out fears, taking control of one's life, and so forth, used to be the path of the guru. Who and what each of us might be if only we had been raised in a monastery or high on a mountain with enlightened teachers, or anywhere or anyplace that would have been free of fear stimuli, is an academic question with little merit. Who we *are* is not what we may become!

CHAPTER THREE:

Free Will?

One of the most important questions of our time is that of free will. It's not generally a subject discussed broadly so it may come as some surprise to many that most serious researchers question the very existence of free will. Recently, a new study shed some light on the subject. Researchers at the University of Berlin, following the work of Benjamin Libet, who showed that conscious decisions were initiated by unconscious brain processes, sought to determine whether or not one could consciously override this unconscious process. In the words of researcher Professor John-Dylan Haynes, "The aim of our research was to find out whether the presence of early brainwaves means that further decision-making is automatic and not under conscious control, or whether the person can still cancel the decision." He continued, "Our study now shows that the freedom is much less limited than previously thought. However, there is a 'point of no return' in the decision-making process, after which cancellation is no longer possible."[1]

Determinism

Those of you who follow my writings know that I have railed against the deterministic perspective often implied by studies such as Libet's, or the fMRI work showing decisions can be known by an MRI technician watching your brain make a decision six seconds before you know your own decision. It's not that there is anything wrong with these studies; it's more a matter of interpretation. Let me unpack that some.

The cortical-evoked potential Libet found allows only a few milliseconds to pass between the P300 wave, the activity in the unconscious, and the conscious action. Given this understanding, it would seem nearly impossible to alter the outcome of an unconscious process dictating a conscious action. However, using fMRI we come to understand more clearly the process and we learn that there is more time than the interval of milliseconds. Still, the likelihood of consciously making the change is not high unless it is made almost instantaneously. This simply means that the nature of free will we experience is seriously limited unless we consciously and carefully choose and sort out the information our mind will use to make its decision.

Please allow me to parse that out a little more. (I have fleshed this out fully in my book *Gotcha! The Subordination of Free Will*, but for our purposes here, this short description will work). Think of your mind analogously to that bio-computer about which so much science fiction has been written. Or for that matter, years ago a great self-help book by Maxwell Maltz titled *Psycho-Cybernetics*, which addressed the mind as a computer that made computations based on its content. If you asked the computer to calculate the sum of one plus one, it would first need a program to do so and then the programmer would have to enter the data necessary to make the calculation possible. In other words, we must learn basic programs, say like physics, or chemistry, or mathematics before we can understand or work with them.

Bio-Computer

Now this bio-computer of ours contains all of the information it has been programmed with, all the no's, don'ts, can'ts—the negative input as well as all of those experiences that produce doubts and fears. Of course, we also hold all of the positive information, but most behavioral scientists acknowledge that the balance between the two is way out of whack, meaning that the negative outweighs the positive by several times.

So here we are when it comes to free will. If the data in your unconscious is not of your choosing, then when you make a choice, a fair question might be, "Whose choice is it?"

The next time you think about free will versus determinism, think instead about programming. To be free we must first acknowledge and then limit the influence of the programming. Today, there are literally thousands of little tricks that can and are used on all of us every day to guide our decisions and actions in accordance with someone else's motive. Whether to win us over to a plank in a political platform or to sell us a product or ideology, our great information age often leads us by the nose. Our only escape is to become fully aware of the means and the methods, as well as the content, and then consciously and carefully select what we choose to put into our minds. We need to use self-affirming positive input instead of reinforcing by repetition all of the no-don't, can't negative content that may have accumulated over the years. Words do matter!

Resources

1. Charité – Universitätsmedizin Berlin. 2016., January 4). "The Brain-Computer Duel: Do We Have Free Will?" Researchers test mechanisms involved in decision-making. *ScienceDaily*. January 4, 2016.

CHAPTER FOUR:

Hurtful Words Damage the Brain

Let's turn now to the power of words and their influence on our brains. We all remember the old adage, "Sticks and stones may break my bones, but words will never hurt me." Well, the fact is, this old stale saying is not only false, but research has shown that words can indeed physically alter your brain.

Words That Change

Neuroscientists Andrew Newberg and Mark Robert Waldman have observed changes in the brain due to the words we use, including those that arise in our thoughts. Think of that for a minute. Words like 'peace' and 'love' can strengthen areas in the frontal lobe, giving rise to increased cognitive function and even arguably influencing the expression of our genes.

Conversely, negative hostile words like 'hate' can influence the production of neurochemicals, increasing the production of stress-producing hormones. Additionally, angry words have been shown to interrupt the optimal operation of our logic-reason centers in the frontal lobe.

In their book *Words Can Change Your Brain*, Newberg and Waldman report their findings this way:

> By holding a positive and optimistic [word] in
> your mind, you stimulate frontal lobe activity. This area
> includes specific language centers that connect directly
> to the motor cortex responsible for moving you into

action. And as our research has shown, the longer you concentrate on positive words, the more you begin to affect other areas of the brain. Functions in the parietal lobe start to change, which changes your perception of yourself and the people you interact with. A positive view of yourself will bias you toward seeing the good in others, whereas a negative self-image will tend you toward suspicion and doubt. Over time the structure of your thalamus will also change in response to your conscious words, thoughts, and feelings, and we believe that the thalamic changes affect the way in which you perceive reality.

Verbal Abuse

In a paper published in the *American Journal of Psychiatry*, Martin Teicher and colleagues at Harvard Medical School shared the results of a new study that revealed:

> ". . . those individuals who reported experiencing verbal abuse from their peers during middle school years had underdeveloped connections between the left and right sides of their brain through the massive bundle of connecting fibers called the corpus callosum. Psychological tests given to all subjects in the study showed that this same group of individuals had higher levels of anxiety, depression, anger, hostility, dissociation, and drug abuse than others in the study."

Bottom line, what you think, how you talk to yourself, your stream of consciousness, the way you verbalize your feelings—all of this has a very real influence on your brain and therefore your body/mind being. Not only that, but the way you express yourself to others may have a lasting effect on both of you!

Mind as Healer or Mind as Slayer

For years I have taught the importance of the thoughts we hold, our self-talk, that inner dialogue that goes on almost incessantly, because these thoughts can and often do become things. Our thoughts, our mind, can be seen as our best friend or our worst enemy, and we have the ability to develop it either way. Mind as healer or mind as slayer—it's really up to you.

My advice is this: tend to the thoughts you have. Cancel those you do not wish to claim. Replace them with a positive set of self-affirming, life-affirming words. Look for beauty, awe, love, and joy in everything, and when you catch a glimpse of it, hold it in your thoughts, dwell on it, enjoy it, and accept the miracle that life is.

Now one more thing, the research clearly shows that it is our subconscious that makes our decisions, so remember to work on actively changing the self-destructive programming that may exist there. It's never too late to change! You can begin creating a new you—designing your character anew, today! InnerTalk was created to help you do just that.

CHAPTER FIVE:

Hope

(Please note: This chapter refers to experiments
that both authors find abhorrent.)

Let's now think about the subject of character. What character traits are indicative of wellbeing? In 2004 Martin Seligman and Christopher Peterson published their findings regarding character in the book *Character Strengths and Virtues*. They studied twenty-four character strengths. In a recent study, Scott Barry Kaufman together with Spencer Greenberg, Susan Cain, and the Quiet Revolution collected data on 517 people looking for a correlation between character as described by Seligman and Petersen, and well-being. They found hope to be the top trait correlated with wellbeing.

Helplessness/Hopelessness

I reported on Seligman's work with helpless-hopeless dogs in my book *Choices and Illusions*. When Seligman delivered electrical shock to dogs who could not escape the pad that carried the shock, he found that even when they were provided with a safe area, an escape, they just lay there hopelessly and took the shock. In other words, the dogs had learned they were helpless; indeed, they had learned it so well that they no longer tried to escape. Further, Seligman found that the conditioned animals' immune systems weakened, and their will to live diminished. Now that should come as no surprise to the student familiar with the earlier work of Curt Paul Richter for he drowned rats to measure learned helplessness.

Energy of Hope

Richter used both domestic and wild rats and discovered that recently trapped wild rats drowned very quickly. Some simply swam to the bottom of the bucket, rammed a few times against the walls, and never came up again. They apparently accepted their situation as hopeless and drowned very quickly. Domestic rats did somewhat better, but they, too, drowned in no more than fifteen minutes. However, when Richter rescued the rat and held it in his hand for a few moments, dried it off, and gave it a rest before returning it to the water, the rats could swim for up to sixty hours before drowning. The hand of hope held out an apparent promise of rescue and that provided the energy of hope.

Hope is a powerful force. Repeated studies with animals, as gross as many of them are, have demonstrated that learned helplessness is a death sentence. This death sentence may well explain the many human deaths that follow when a person believes their life is without hope.

Hopelessness and helplessness often follow tragic events like the Twin Towers or natural catastrophes like tsunamis and hurricanes. Some people have been known to just lie down and die for no medical reason.

Gratitude

The second highest character trait correlated with wellbeing is gratitude. The gratitude attitude is all-important when it comes to engendering a strong immune and endocrine system. I have suggested on many occasions to my audiences, begin your day with a smile and a thank you and you will notice the difference very quickly. Smiling fools the brain and it releases those good feeling neurochemicals, endorphins, and the thank you turns your focus toward the positive aspects of life, encouraging wellbeing.

Love

The third highest character strength positively correlated with wellbeing is love. Love of life! Gratitude encourages love. Hope feeds on love. A real connection with others and with nature spawns the sort of love that finds us loving every moment of our lives. Love excites joy! Unconditional love prospers in an environment where hope, gratitude, and love abide.

The bottom-line message is, of course—wellbeing can arise as much from cognitive events as it can from the physical side of things. I have taught this for years, and indeed, every InnerTalk program includes hope, love, and gratitude messages of one sort or another. What's more, we feel this is so important that we offer our InnerTalk *Freedom from Feelings of Helplessness and Hopelessness* free upon request to anyone who needs it but cannot afford it.

So, the next time you are thinking about changing anything, think about your character strengths. You can change these as well. You can change your personality if you so choose. The fact is, as you change character traits you do alter personality—one small nudge at a time. This, in turn, can have very positive effects on the body. It all begins in the mind. Change your self-talk and you can change your life!

Remember, it takes no more energy to be positive and optimistic than negative and pessimistic—but the rewards or outcome differ immensely!

CHAPTER SIX:

Power of Optimism

It's time to address the idea of optimism. We have all heard about the power of intention and positive thinking. Optimism necessitates both, but for it to have any real value it must also maintain a realistic perspective; it must be reasonable. Reasonable optimism is anchored by hope!

Hopeless/Helpless

The opposite of optimism is, of course, pessimism. In the affairs of the mind, pessimism can lead to helpless/hopeless feelings that literally decimate our own self-healing faculties, something discussed in the last chapter. Optimism is an expression of hope.

Realistic Optimism

So, the challenge deepens: What is a healthy, realistic form of optimism? It certainly isn't one that quits on life, but it is one that takes into consideration the projected reality we live in.

Let me flesh that out a bit with an example I live with. Years ago, my wife was diagnosed with rheumatoid arthritis. Now my pretty bride ignored her doctors when it came to the prognosis, or projection, of where she was headed, but she did not ignore all medical advice or scientific research. She committed herself to beating the disease and, using science and medicine, she did just that.

Now the contrast. A family member was recently diagnosed with RA as well. My wife reached out to them with help from her experience.

Unfortunately, they rejected this by informing Ravinder that the doctor disapproved of any alternative approaches and they would just have to live with the progression of the disease.

In the first example, that of my pretty bride, there was a reasonable optimism that maintained hope, while in the second example, that of a family member, there is a pessimistic acceptance of what they consider to be the inevitable—no hope.

Hope

Allow me to remind you of the power of hope again. In the last chapter we discussed Curt Richter's work, specifically what has been called the horrible experiment. If you recall, Richter placed rats in a glass cylinder filled with water. The rats could not escape and during the first trial, they died quickly. However, given a little hope, they could swim for up to three days. That is the power of hope!

Reasonable Optimism

Never give up your hope! Reasonable optimism refuses to surrender because it is firmly anchored by hope!

It is my hope that you will all remember this and hold onto hope right to the very last breath, and as a *Star Trek* fan, let me add, "May you live long and prosper!"

CHAPTER SEVEN:

Self-Sabotage

Okay, let's look at self-sabotage just a little more deeply than we have up until now. Most people are totally unaware that they are sometimes controlled by internal mechanisms that are designed to protect, but that actually function to sabotage certain goals in their lives. The fact is, all of us possess self-destructive elements that can manifest at any time and in a variety of ways. This not-so-silent enemy within usually remains in stealth mode despite its repeated pattern of interference with our own self-declared desires.

Definitions

Psychologists define self-destructive patterns this way. "Behavior is said to be self-sabotaging when it creates problems and interferes with long-standing goals. The most common self-sabotaging behaviors are procrastination, self-medication with drugs or alcohol, comfort eating in the face of weight concerns, and self-injury such as cutting. These acts may seem helpful in the moment, but ultimately undermine us, especially when we engage in them repeatedly."

Why would we all have these automatic internal self-destructive mechanisms that betray our best intentions? Technically, most of them arise as a result of a defense strategy. They can be as simple as something we do in order to avoid rejection that is the result of an embarrassing childhood episode. For example, take the fellow who simply couldn't laugh; we'll call him John. Indeed, John was unable to even fully smile.

His wife and friends thought of him as stoic and that was fine with John until he discovered that he was often not invited to events because of his lack of humor. When he made enquiries regarding this, he discovered that others found him to be a bore who could wilt the humor in any party. This saddened John so he set about discovering why he behaved this way. What John learned was that a childhood event led to his inability to relax and laugh. He actually found many things humorous, but he withheld his expression of the same because when he was young other children had mocked him for the way he laughed and for his *twisted* smile.

Hidden Away

Now John did not consciously say to himself something like, "Build a defense mechanism that prevents me from being ridiculed in the future because of my laugh." Albeit, that's exactly what his ego managed for him. It is, after all, the job of a healthy ego to protect us. So, John's automatic mechanism simply arrested his expression of humor to protect him from ridicule. And this unconscious, automatic mechanism remained in place until John made his uncovering and set about to consciously change this behavior.

Okay, this is a simple example of how a mechanism can work to destroy our lives, but there are also some very compound and complicated mechanisms that can arise for many reasons including compensation. It is our nature, as the herd animals that we are, to seek acceptance and avoid rejection. It is also our nature to compete for attention or in the alternative, to adopt low to non-competitive strategies as a pattern of avoidance. For some, both of these patterns can actually be operational and activated at different times under differing circumstances.

The bottom line is this; we all have self-sabotaging mechanisms of some sort that raise their ugly heads from time to time, and that is why certain goals can remain unattainable despite our very best effort.

Eliminating self-sabotage then becomes a primary step in getting our own houses in order. In at least one sense, ending self-destructive patterns is the weeding out of ideas and behaviors that prevent us from achieving all that we are otherwise capable of enjoying. As such, the path to success requires the elimination of self-destructive behavior patterns.

Recognizing Patterns

The objective of ending self-sabotage begins by recognizing that we all possess this potential. Pursuing its possibilities, we begin to recognize patterns of behavior that have common antecedents. Diligently attending to your thoughts often reveals inner beliefs, biases, and the like that you really do not wish to continue to own. Strengthening your resolve for deliberation you gain more control over self-regulation. Each time you are successful at halting an automatic mechanism, you begin to break the pattern and thereby end the habit.

Come every New Year most of us make resolutions, and those who don't typically have made so many failed ones in the past that they gave up on the idea. If you're going to be successful changing your life, then remember this: In order to fulfill your dreams and ambitions, you must take the time to retrain your mind. If it was properly supporting you today, your life would be full of what most call magic! That said, perhaps we should all begin to end self-destructive patterns by asking ourselves, *"What do I get out of self-sabotage?"* There is much more to this question than might be obvious, so let's take that question on in the next chapter.

CHAPTER EIGHT:

The Gains in Self-Sabotage?

How do our choices fit into the scheme of self-sabotage? We all make choices every day, and for the most part, we generally think we are certain of why we make the choices we do—but are we? I have discussed the fact that functional MRI scans show that our decisions are largely made in the subconscious followed then by our conscious mind actively constructing the rational basis for our choices. I have also pointed out how our various defense mechanisms develop strategies designed to protect us from everything from embarrassment to physical abuse. The child who is beaten by a parent often internalizes the beating as something they must have deserved and adapts accordingly. The young person who is ridiculed over the way they laugh unconsciously chooses not to laugh, and again adapts accordingly. In all, these defense mechanisms lay at the root of many of our decisions, and obviously, they can be self-sabotaging.

In my book *Choices and Illusions*, the how and why behind this form of self-destructive behavior is fleshed out in detail. That said, I often hear this question, "Why do people habitually do such stupid, self-destructive things?" Think about this for a minute. Do you know anyone who regularly participates in a behavior that is self-destructive or counterproductive?

The Gains in Self-Sabotage

The answer to why always involves what they get out of it. Somewhere in their mindset is a perceived advantage, even if that advantage is no longer valid and disguised or hidden deep in the subconscious. Let me provide an example that is both based on research and easy to understand.

Years ago, I did a fair amount of research on something referred to as psychoneuroimmunology, or PNI for short. This was at a time when the mechanical view of the human body was so dominant that many health care professionals so totally rejected the idea of mind-body wellness that to suggest such a thing was a certain way to find yourself rebuked and even ostracized. Now my research spanned a very large area ranging from cancer remission to the common cold. Here is something the numbers pulled up very fast. The singer who suffered from performance anxiety could easily find themselves on the day of their performance with a sore throat while the skater would suffer from a sprained ankle. Is it coincidence that their affliction prevented the very thing that they feared? —I think not.

What Do You Get Out of This Behavior?

It is for this reason that whenever I am working with someone, the first question I ask is, "What do you get out of this behavior? How do you benefit from it?"

I have found that regardless of the nature of the behavior, there is usually some benefit believed to be gained, albeit often unconsciously. I once worked with the parents of a young man who had been diagnosed as suffering from multiple conditions including MS. He was in a wheelchair and failed to respond favorably to any and all treatments. His father owned a medical company and was therefore well connected with the best physicians available. When I reviewed his history, I discovered that his health began to suffer when a sibling was born, and the more attention this sibling received, the worse his health became. (You can read the full story in my book *Wellness: Just a State of Mind?*). I theorized that the boy's gain from his illness might have its source in his need for attention, for he had been the center of attention prior to the birth of a sibling. With the onset of his illness, he again became the focus of attention. Together with his health care team, we employed an InnerTalk program to alter the subconscious need for attention and thereby hopefully put this boy back on the road to health. The program worked. Within a year his father sent me pictures of the boy, at sixteen years of age, standing alongside his car holding up his newly earned driver's license.

So, the next time you find yourself indulging in some behavior that is not in your best interest, ask yourself, "What do I gain from this?" I think you'll discover something new about yourself when you do. In our next section we'll examine some of the tactics and strategies for manifesting your best life. This section has been all about the mechanisms that can hold us back. If you've recognized any in yourself, then you're already ahead of most. Knowledge is power, and to that end, we wish you the very best you that you have to offer.

PART TWO

A Few Ideas to Consider

CHAPTER NINE:

Your Personal Master Plan

One of the things we see happen with local government is the creation of a master plan, which lays out where development is to take place and what kind. It anticipates the growth of the community, and therefore the nature of services that will be required. Zoning provisions will follow the master plan, and eventually so will easements. If the plan requires the condemnation of personal property in order to satisfy the greater needs of the community, that is handled too. The goal is a prosperous, safe, and healthy city.

Master Plan

Developers and real estate investors will first consult the master plan before considering investing or building. Often money is made in real estate by converting the zoning on a piece of, say, rural property destined to become commercial according to the master plan. In short, the master plan is more than a plan per se; it also represents great opportunity for those who pay attention to their community and its needs.

Do you have a master plan? I have often wondered why so many people stop making plans once they finish their schooling. Their master plan takes them through the level of education they seek, and typically ends with, "Then I will get a job as a _______________ and go to work or begin my career."

Imagine a city with a plan like this. The plan would suggest the basics, water, sewer, sanitation, police, fire, etc. But once these things were in place, the plan ended. In fact, there are examples of this in the world. Cities have often sprung up without a plan. Trailer parks, auto sales, porn shops, tattoo parlors, residences, and the like fill the same general area without a designation for zoning differences, and then a school may be built on the same street as well. The result is a mess and finally a costly redrawing of the city through a master plan is undertaken. Knowing this, why is it that we may fail as individuals to create our own personal master plans?

Your Personal Master Plan

A personal master plan should include the joy side of life. What makes you happy? What provides that warm, fuzzy feeling that informs you your life makes a difference? What activity or action or set of actions can be employed to assist in your personal inner growth? The master plan also must anticipate such things as changes in earning opportunities, re-education or continuing education, potential career changes, alternative goals, and so forth. Then, instead of waiting for something to upset the apple cart, like a layoff at work, you are preparing for these contingencies as you proceed through life. You do that by staying apace of technology, keeping up with trends and training yourself to be flexible, acquiring additional skills, or having a hobby that may be turned into a vocation. Of course, your master plan should also call for saving for that rainy day, educating your children, and various unpleasant "what if" scenarios.

Flexibility and Frequent Assessments

As you can see, a personal master plan is much more than investment counseling or life insurance. It anticipates success rather than loss and plans for continued growth—growth in skills necessary for prosperity and growth in realizing your own full potential. The overall purpose of your personal master plan is to ensure that you remain balanced and at peace with yourself while pursuing your ambitions and realizing your true potential. Your plan should be flexible enough that you can take advantage of opportunities, and should include frequent assessment—are you staying on track or is your current path leading you off on a tangent?

You see, while your current plan may include losing weight or strengthening your self-esteem, once these goals have been achieved you need to know what to work on next—what other areas of your life do you need/ choose to work on? There is always some area of our lives that we can improve, some skill that we can refine, some opportunity we can take advantage of. "How high is up?" is the constant motto in my family, for we all know that there is always more that can be achieved! Why not make it your motto too?

If you do not yet have a personal master plan, I urge you take some time and develop one. It's never too late. Begin today so that all of your tomorrows hold the potential of filling your life with dreams come true.

CHAPTER TEN:

The Rehearsal That Makes a Lifetime Difference

Within every human being exists a propensity for greatness. The gifts may vary, and the greatness may live out in a vast array of alternatives—say from carpentry to rocket science—but the gift that gives one true self-respect, lifts the spirit from "same old, same old," resides within. It is our ability to do our very best with our talents in everything we do. This potential resides within each one of us—but if so, then why is it so often denied?

Every individual essentially has a self-representation that is rehearsed and eventually actualized. The process begins by fantasizing at a very early age. We fantasize a script, perhaps one of those from some Hollywood production. We begin rehearsing it, and we either abandon it to take up a new one or practice it until we role-play that script as who we are. Practicing the script sooner or later automates the behavior. Our imprinting environment plays a significant role in the alternative scripts available to us. If the parents are uncaring and abusive, so are the children and so forth. If warmth and friendliness lead to embarrassment, then cold and aloof compensate. If honesty gets us into trouble, then deception becomes a defense strategy and so forth.

Four Selves

It is much more complicated than expressed here, but simply, it is also just this way. In fact, every one of us divides ourselves among four essential views of ourselves. These four faces include the following:

- Our actual self.
- Our ideal self.
- Our ought-to-be self.
- Our desired self.

These categories were originally developed by P.A.D. Singer to show how the different selves conflict with each other, but I will use it a little differently.

Most of us are aware of a so-called actual self. This is the self that has failed in ways we often will not share with others. This is the private self. This self holds the thoughts we wish we did not have, the acts we wish we had not done, our beliefs about our worth, our sense of our own attractiveness, and so forth. It is the self of our secrets and our ambitions. It is the self that most of us try to change in some way or another at some time in our life—perhaps even perpetually.

The actual self pales by comparison to our ideal self. The ideal self is often a construct built by our culture. This self would live a perfect life—without error and therefore without room for growth.

Then there is our ought-to-be self. This self is full of all our learned *shoulds* and *oughts*. This self differs from our ideal self in the sense that many of the *oughts* are not ours—they are the *oughts* of our culture, our society—but deep down inside they are not ours. Sometimes these *oughts* are the result of rules that make little or no sense to us; sometimes the *oughts* are of codependent negotiations such as those implied when Mom said things like, "If you loved me, you would not behave that way," or "If you loved me, you would do what I said," and so forth. Still, even when one recognizes the source and the nature of the ought relationship from which the *oughts* themselves arise; they often persist.

Finally, there is the desired self. Somewhere among all of our other selves is a self that we believe we could be. This is the self we long for, especially when we are young and planning our future. It is also the source of much discontent in our later life if the desires have not been fulfilled—and they rarely, if ever, are.

Psychic Tension

The ought-to-be self, desired self, and ideal self share certain commonalities, but they also differ remarkably. This creates psychic tension between them and in their totality, and substantial tension with our actual self.

Now, there's one more thing I wish to add before continuing. The actual self is seldom the true actual self. The actual self is the self of self-perception, and therefore is complete with every believed limitation that accompanies one's private self-perception together with every defense adjustment our mechanisms have created to protect our self-image or ego.

Okay, all of this is accomplished while we are still very young. In time we gain the wisdom and insight to become familiar with this maturation process and a myriad of other operations that function in our culture, our homes, etc. to produce socially acceptable membership and behavior. Using one of Shakespeare's metaphors, life is a stage where we play our various parts; perhaps it's time for a new rehearsal. Indeed, change, improvement, true self-actualization, and so forth all require that we create a new character. Using our power of imagination and consciously choosing the role-playing model we will rehearse will greatly assist and facilitate any change.

Therefore, it literally behooves all of us to watch those conversational exchanges that take place in our head as well as every other aspect of our *rehearsing* behavior. To experience our best, we must practice/rehearse our best at all levels of our being, and that includes how we talk to ourselves. This works—but it can also be much easier said than done. Still, life's cornucopia of joy awaits those willing to make the effort.

CHAPTER ELEVEN:

The Impostor Syndrome

Let's now discuss something called the impostor syndrome, or the idea that if others knew what you know about yourself, that somehow this would diminish or even discredit you. This complex, or syndrome, (also known as impostor phenomenon, fraud syndrome, or the impostor experience) is a psychological pattern in which people doubt their accomplishments and have a persistent, often internalized fear of being exposed as a *fraud*.

Many people hold themselves back from success because they fail to believe that they deserve it. As a result, they can develop methods to avoid attention and allow those feelings to govern their behavior.

Compensation

This complex often leads to compensation strategies designed to protect us from being exposed, and these compensation strategies can literally be so self-sabotaging in the long run as to destroy our lives. For example, it may seem somewhat harmless to tell stories, or lie a little, to cover ourselves. However, these lies accumulate and can become dangerously entangled until one day, when exposed, the world sees that we have become what we feared—a liar and a fraud.

Other defensive strategies may include such behaviors as avoidance, as in staying away from situations or people who might jeopardize our perceived exposure, minimizing our role in actions that may bring about praise and so forth.

Undeserved

Of course, not everyone who suffers from impostor syndrome really has anything to hide—they just feel like impostors. I know a successful defense attorney who feels like a fraud because he found law school too easy. As a result, he handles many cases no one else wants that are not high-profile—small-time drug dealers and the like. According to Erica Moss, writing for Trello, "First observed in a clinical setting by Dr. Pauline Clance in 1985, Impostor Syndrome triggers in people 'intense feelings that their achievements are undeserved and worry that they are likely to be exposed as a fraud.' They often feel that any success in their lives can be attributed to pure luck or to the manipulation of other people's impressions."

To some extent and in certain circumstances, we may all at times feel a bit like impostors. Whenever we are called upon to do something we consider outside our so-called wheelhouse, the discomfort becomes obvious. So perhaps we're asked to speak at a PTA meeting about our success as a parent, since our child is doing so well in school. However, we really feel that we don't deserve that much credit for their success and thus we feel the twinges of the impostor syndrome. Or maybe you have climbed the ladder of success well, but you wonder if it is due to your charm rather than your abilities, or some quota within the company, that has really been the reason for your success.

Guilt

What are we to do about this feeling of guilt—this nagging sense described as the impostor syndrome? Well, first, be honest. Be honest about yourself and your achievements. Avoid exaggeration and do not attempt to defend attacks that strike at your so-called weaknesses. If, for example, you obtained a college degree without finishing high school first, recognize that so have many other people. There is no reason to become defensive over this. Second, normalize the feeling. Understand that it is a state and not a trait. It's a bit akin to that feeling of anxiety one might get before a public address, just something very normal that many people feel.

The bottom line is this: Understand that fear and self-doubt haunt everyone from time to time. This does not make you a fraud. Your contribution to others is not in any way minimized by your feelings of doubt. As long as you're honest about who you are—you have nothing to hide. So, unleash your potential and be all that you can be!

CHAPTER TWELVE:

Using Different Forms of Mindfulness

Mindfulness is generally understood as meditation—meditation with the intent of relinquishing the capital I, the sense of self, and entering a state of oneness. One is therefore taught to let their thoughts go by and not follow them like some puppy on the sidewalk following every set of legs that passes by. Instead, the teaching emphasizes the need to let thought just go by and focus on your breathing.

Mindfulness to Reframe

There is another form of mindfulness meditation that is very useful, and one I often suggest to those interested in knowing themselves. This form of mindfulness is also meditation, and focusing on your breath is good place to begin. However, instead of ignoring your thoughts, you accept them in a nonjudgmental way. The thought comes in and you both acknowledge and note the sort of thought it is. Perhaps you wait for a moment to see what thought next comes and is therefore somehow connected to the last thought. If it is a thought you would prefer to place in a different context, say a thought about something you hate, then take a moment to think of how you might reframe the thought. For example, if the thought is about some crazy driver who upset you on your way to work, just the reminder of this situation creates some emotional content, so you take a moment and imagine the driver was in a real hurry because she needed to get to the hospital.

Clearly, this reframing idea will not only remit your thoughts but ameliorate your emotions when placed in this context. It has the additional benefit of predisposing how you respond the next time something like this happens.

Mindfulness for Associations

Now there is another aspect to mindfulness that I like to encourage. This technique looks inward toward those secret, unconscious associations and beliefs—many of which intrude and even govern our conscious activity. To illustrate this, please allow me to share some fiction from the HBO show *In Therapy*.

The therapist in the show, one Dr. Paul Weston, experiences an erotic transference with a patient who is a medical doctor he has been treating for a year. Although it is difficult for him to admit, he has experienced a genuine countertransference. His patient, Lara, is a very attractive woman who is very outspoken, so without mincing words she makes it clear that she is in love with him and wants him sexually. He properly informs her that he is not an option, but his real feelings are not so easily extinguished.

Meantime his wife is having an affair. When she informs Paul of the affair, she explains that it is, in part, because he seems so removed and so indifferent to her. Paul fails to see that his obsession with Lara has dominated his thoughts for months. Like a dieter facing a tabooed confection, he has held it a few inches from his lips for a long time and can't quite get his mind off of it. (Lara is the confection in this analogy). As a result, Paul fails to see his complicity in his wife's extramarital affair.

Looking into the Subconscious

When we connect thoughts together, we often discover links that we consciously fail to observe. When Paul seeks his own therapy, he slips in a conversation about sexuality and uses Lara's name in place of his wife. What does this tell us?

Listening to our own thoughts in a nonjudgmental way, allowing them to flow and connect as they will, but remaining alert to the connections while questioning why they might connect can provide some genuinely helpful insights to our inner feelings and mental processes. It is for this reason that I believe this form of mindfulness can be so very helpful in sorting out the sources of unidentified anxieties, worries, fears, and the like.

CHAPTER THIRTEEN:

Change Your Mental Group

It was Jim Rohn, entrepreneur, author, and motivational speaker, who famously said that "We are the average of the five people we spend the most time with." But what exactly does this mean, and what can we do about it?

Evidence Around Us

As a general rule, Jim Rohn's quote is used in the context of business or career success. However, I believe this also applies to every aspect of our lives, ranging from relationships to body image, from our educational achievements to our fitness goals, from our parenting abilities to our spiritual aspirations, and everything in between.

Whatever goal you would like to achieve, just take a look at the people who are closest to you. If you would like a wonderful personal relationship, you will be more successful if those around you are in good relationships. If you (subconsciously) wish to be a victim, then chances are there will be victims in your immediate circles. You will increase your odds of success with your weight loss goals if your closest circle includes those who are already slim or those who have the same goal as you.

The fact is we frequently set our success bar according to the success of those around us. It is all too easy to make excuses based on what we think is the norm. So, in the aging process, we tend to slow down at the same rate as our peers, *for isn't that the normal thing to do?* Or in relationships, *doesn't everyone get tired of their partner at some time or another?* In our careers, *doesn't everyone take a sick day when they just need some time off . . . or to recover from a hangover?*

In Eldon's New York Times best-selling book *Choices and Illusions*, he talks about *bad luck cookie collectors*. These are groups of people who get together to complain about the same things and compete to see who has it worse. It doesn't matter what the subject matter is, everyone competes for the group sympathy by expressing how they have it worse. And all of this kind of thinking will hold you back from achieving, or even creating, goals that will make a real difference in your life.

Oftentimes, though, we cannot, or choose not to, change the people we associate with. So, is there anything else that we can do to keep from limiting our success?

Change Your Mental Group

I took up running a few years ago. When I started, I had problems even running for the one- and two-minute intervals, but last year I managed my first half marathon. This year I am training for a full marathon and I was feeling pretty good about it. I am fifty-five years young and am more active than the vast majority of my peer group. That sounds like success, right? Simply completing a marathon is the only goal I need to think about, especially for my first attempt . . . isn't it? (After Note: I did complete my first as planned.)

Recently I was online, researching the different marathons and trying to decide which one(s) to register for. In the process, I found the page on the times for everyone who had participated in the Spokane marathon last year. Included in this information were the ages of the participants and the times they achieved. I found a number of participants in my age group and older, for whom this was their first race—and many of them had significantly better times than the goal I had already set for myself. I immediately started to think in a different order.

The next time I went running, I no longer had the headset of being 'top of my group.' My mental circle of friends had changed, and I no longer felt as though I should hold myself back, take it slow, be super careful, etc. Now of course, this did not mean that I stopped listening to my body and being smart about what I did. It only meant that I stopped putting a cap on my success. As a result, my speed increased, as did the joy I felt running. I came home and told Eldon what a great run it was and how I felt like I was flying. I also stopped choosing the easier routes that avoided the harder hills, and instead I became the woman who hunts hills! I did not change the people I associated with in the real world, but I changed my mental group.

The Personal Empowerment Group

Now, if you are reading this, you are obviously already interested in self-improvement and personal empowerment, but which sub-group are you in? Did you come to InnerTalk searching for help with one particular goal, and now find yourself sitting happy with your achievements? Have you achieved success in one area and are now toying with what other areas you care about? Or are you in the elite group who constantly looks at ways to improve their lives and fly higher and higher? Are you part of the crowd or are you your own *Jonathon Livingston Seagull?*[1] How much more can you really achieve—in your personal life, with your personal relationships, in your spiritual aspirations, in your career, etc.? The fact is you can only fly as high as you dare . . . so I dare you to fly higher. Change your mental group and soar free!

Resources

Bach, R. 1973. *Jonathan Livingston Seagull.* Avon: NY

Chapter Fourteen:

Thoughts That Manipulate Matter

For as long as I can remember, I have innately known that thoughts can have the power of manifesting in matter. When I was only five or six, I used my mind to guide me to lost items like some sort of compass. I would close my eyes and follow the unspoken voice within as it guided my footsteps. At about the age of eleven or twelve, I well remember thinking that I needed glasses. My father unsympathetically referred to men who wore glasses as four-eyes, and I feared disappointing him. As such, I just imagined passing the school eye test over and over again. My eyes didn't improve, but when it came my turn to take the eye test the doctor looked at me and said, "You can you see the 20-20 line can't you?" I answered, "Sure." That was the test, so it was a few more years before I would put glasses on.

When I was fourteen or so, I imagined becoming six feet tall. That was taller than anyone in my family. I would go to sleep at night imaging myself as six feet tall, and I did this repeatedly over the summer of the year between eighth and ninth grades. When I returned to school, I was six feet tall, and at that time six feet was tall! I towered over almost everyone in my school. (Today we think of this sort of thing as possible through epigenetics, the influence of our minds on genes). It was at about this time that I began imagining myself as a successful author, and again I would fall asleep at night visualizing myself signing books, lecturing, and the like. Today I have more than 400 titles published in print form or audio and video media, and many of these titles have been translated in more than a dozen languages.

Mind Over Matter

Now all of this visualization that I have just discussed, together with much more, took place over fifty years ago, long before *The Secret* or the law of attraction were published. How I knew this about the power of thought is not what this piece is about. No—what I really want to address today is how well documented the idea that "thoughts are things" has become in scientific circles.

In December of this last year, the *American Physiological Society* reporting in an article titled, "Mind over matter: Can you think your way to strength?" suggested that indeed you could do just that. *Science News* explained it this way:

> "Now researchers at the Ohio Musculoskeletal and Neurological Institute (OMNI) at Ohio University have found that the mind is critical in maintaining muscle strength following a prolonged period of immobilization and that mental imagery may be key in reducing the associated muscle loss."

The article continued with an explanation of the study which involved wrist-hand immobilization:

> At the end of the four-week experiment, both groups who wore casts had lost strength in their immobilized limbs when compared to the control group. But the group that performed mental imagery exercises lost 50% less strength than the non-imaginative group (24 percent vs. 45 percent, respectively). The nervous system's ability to fully activate the muscle (called "voluntary activation" or VA) also rebounded more quickly in the imagery group compared to the non-imagery group.
>
> "These findings suggest neurological mechanisms, most likely at the cortical level, contribute significantly to disuse-induced weakness, and that regular activation of the cortical regions via imagery attenuates weakness and VA by maintaining normal levels of inhibition," the research team wrote. "Thus, our findings that imagery

attenuated the loss of muscle strength provide proof-of-concept for it as a therapeutic intervention for muscle weakness and voluntary neural activation."[1]

Visual Imaging

Years ago, research demonstrated the idea of neuromuscular training. The idea began by using visual imaging techniques or proprioception to improve physical performance. In one study, subjects were split into three groups and each group was tested on how many free throws they could make. The first group practiced free throws every day for an hour. The second group visualized themselves making free throws but did not actually practice. The third group did nothing. Thirty days later the groups were tested again. The first group who actually practiced shooting free throws improved by 24%. The second group who visualized shooting free throws improved by 23% without touching a basketball. There was no change in the third group.

Today neuromuscular training is often recommended as a preventive care modality to eliminate injuries such as Anterior Cruciate Ligament (ACL) tears as well as a modality for performance improvement. So, we can visualize ourselves stronger, we can improve our coordination and athletic performance, we should be able to even tighten muscles as around our abdominal area, and more by just regularly visualizing. Indeed, mindfulness research has demonstrated that boosting brain activity through meditation and/or visualization can reduce even addictive behavior patterns, such as those resulting from pain management medications. In one study carried out at the University of Utah, this intervention was found to reduce opioid misuse among a sample of chronic pain patients compared to another sample of chronic pain patients participating in a conventional support group.[2]

The fact is, most of this, if not all, can also be accomplished without the conscious mind's active attention. Indeed, much of it can be cued by subliminal priming. This technique has been repeatedly demonstrated to be effective, and I have had personal experience with this—having had the honor to work with elite athletes as well as entire teams. I have witnessed many go from so-called losers to win gold medals and team championships as a result. But again, it's not just me reporting; the data has accumulated where it is now commonplace to see science articles detail this information such as the one published in *Science News* on December 1, 2014. The title says it all, "Athletes perform better when exposed to subliminal visual cues."[3]

Your mind is truly magical! One of my favorite activities is reading your notes and letters telling of your successes after unbridling your imagination and turning your mind lose to create all the good things in life. That's one of the grand rewards I so much enjoy as a result of creating InnerTalk. So, I guess my challenge to you is: Dare to turn your mind's creative power loose!

Resources

1. American Physiological Society (APS). 2014. "Mind Over Matter: Can You Think Your Way to Strength?" ScienceDaily. December 312014

2. Garland, E. et al. 2017. "Pain, hedonic regulation, and opioid misuse: Modulation of momentary experience by Mindfulness-Oriented Recovery Enhancement in opioid-treated chronic pain patients." *APA PsychNet.*

3. University of Kent. 2014. Athletes perform better when exposed to subliminal visual cues. *ScienceDaily.* December 1, 2014.

CHAPTER FIFTEEN:

Pollyanna and Pragmatics

It seems that everywhere one turns today there are problems—problems in the world such as global warming, terrorism, inflation, crime, and so forth with so many etc., etc., etceteras that one is reminded of the classic movie *The King and I*. The list is long and to many, very depressing. It may surprise you--it has me--but one of the most popular new search terms emerging recently is *anxiety*. There is an unspoken but deep feeling of anxiousness among many today, and there is no end to the so-called cures offered in the marketplace for this guttural discomfort that can nag at one, waking them from sleep and disturbing their daytime activities with just some indefinite but uncomfortable feeling.

Why the anxiety? One could easily suggest a myriad of reasons. However, the most important feature of anxiety is the sense of or lack of control and the perceived need to somehow take a hold of the stimulus or stimuli and direct the potential outcome. Alas, the anxiety persists chiefly when one is unable to affect the stimuli in any real way. So, global warming, terrorism, inflation and other economic concerns, shortages, and other doom-and-gloom forecasts, thoughts, etc. are not the "stuff" that the average individual can directly affect.

Perspectives

Like the ocean, anxious feelings tend to have crests and troughs and come in waves that propagate each other. Escaping this pattern requires a new perspective. There are many alternatives, but essentially, they come down to just two. The first is somehow finding something that one can do that minimizes the power of the stimuli. So, if you're powerful enough to persuade the world to eliminate the causes of global warming, then you can minimize the power of this stimulus if not destroy its grip altogether. The second option is to simply attend to that which we can control and let go of that which is beyond our control. This so-called, "Let go and let God," has been referred to by some as a Pollyanna perspective that is solipsist.

The term Pollyanna comes from the heroine of a novel by the same name by Eleanor Porter. In general terms it is used to describe an irrepressible optimism and a tendency to find good in everything. A solipsist in its strict sense is a person who maintains that the self can know nothing but its own modifications. To some thinkers this translates into egocentrism, a sort of self as the only existent thing. However, if the notion of self-modification is viewed from the perspective that each of us knows ourselves, our history, our changes, our fears, our limitations, and so forth, then from this perspective one can easily admit that they are not in control of the future, or any other stimuli that is otherwise out of their control. For many, the old question, "If a tree falls in the forest and there is no one there to hear, does it make a sound?" is answered by the quantum physics perspective that suggests without consciousness there is nothing. In other words, remove the *someone to hear* and there is no sound for there is no tree. In this sense, our reality is one that is created by each of us in many more ways than most might have thought. This, too, can be taken as rather solipsist.

Pragmatics

The great philosopher psychologist William James had a better term, and that is "pragmatic." The word originates from the Greek, meaning officious and pertaining to matters of fact and practical affairs. James used this word to set apart the practical from the idealistic. In good old country talk, the meaning goes like this: "If it ain't broke, don't fix it." The pragmatic view is one of what works. The fact of the matter is, letting go and letting God works! Now saying this and doing it are not necessarily the same thing so let's look at a couple of quick, painless, and easy ways by which we can all let go—including let go of anxiety.

First, begin your day with a simple thank you. Acknowledge but for a moment that all that you have, all that you are, is a gift. The new day is a gift. Accept the gift with gratitude. Take that gratitude attitude like a sincere Pollyanna into your day, knowing that all that comes to you does so for some higher good. So-called problems are really opportunities in disguise. These opportunities assist us in our personal growth. From them we become better people.

Second, forgive—forgive yourself, forgive all others and accept the worthiness to be forgiven. When some fearful or angry thought enters your mind, bless it. Give it love—all the love you can. You'll probably find that a smile strangely wanders onto your face—the whole idea of blessing those that we blame is so counterintuitive to the way most are raised that I cannot overstate the power of this simple practice. While you're smiling, realize that the simple act of smiling turns certain neurochemicals on in the brain. In other words, the act of smiling tells the brain life is good, and the brain says in neurochemical language, "Great—it's feel-good time!" and pumps some good old feel-good chemicals through our bodies. So, if you don't naturally smile when you do your blessing then "fake it till you make it."

Third, let go. Let go and let God. Do what you can do and let God do the rest. When I have suggested this in the past I have been asked, how? How do I know what I can do? There is a sense that there is nothing that I can do, and you have pointed this out, so what is it that I am to do? Here is the answer. Short and sweet—do a good deed for someone else. Go to the aid of another. Help someone in some small way. Help someone that may never expect you to give them aid of any kind. Give someone a smile, a compliment; add some give-good-feelings-to-others' repertoire to your acumen of abilities and watch the world around you change. Helping others is our ultimate mission in some manner or another. The purpose-driven life could be summed up without sermons as one aiding others to the best of our abilities.

Strengths from Struggles

Now perhaps you say to yourself something like, "Ya' sure, sounds good but...." and go on filling in the blanks behind the buts with all of your own real and imagined experiences. Like the bumper sticker, for many "Life sucks and then you die." However, there is another perspective; from struggles we grow stronger. There is a marvelous story that illustrates this. The story is one of my favorites for it teaches at many levels like most good stories of this type. It seems that there once was a scientist that beheld the glory of an emperor moth and was so totally taken by the creature that he decided to study it. So, for over a year he monitored the activities of the giant moth. One day he came upon a caterpillar ready to spin its cocoon, so he seized this opportunity to study the moth more closely. He gently captured the caterpillar and took it back to his lab. Here within a glass container he watched the caterpillar build its cocoon and enter that state of deep sleep while it underwent the chrysalis-changing form from crawling on the ground to floating in the sky.

Then the day came that the moth was ready to leave the cocoon. The scientist watched anxiously as the tiny head chewed its way into the light of the laboratory. The moth struggled and struggled, seemingly getting nowhere. Its body was simply too large to fit through the tiny hole in the cocoon. The moth tired and laid its head to rest on the shell of the cocoon when the scientist took it upon himself to help the tiny creature. "How could I stand here for so many hours watching this beautiful moth go through such agony and pain?" he questioned. "Where is my mercy?" he continued as he took his tweezers and cut away the cocoon. Unfortunately, the moth died.

Later the scientist discovered that it was precisely the struggle that forced the fluids down into the body of the emperor moth and gave rise to its aerodynamic ability. The cocoon forced the fluids back into the body perfectly proportioning the moth as it forced its way out. Cutting away the cocoon in an effort to help had only killed the moth.

From our conflicts and our struggles strength is gained, learning takes place, personal empowerment can happen, and wisdom can be attained.

Find the Good

Why the proverbial "bad things" happen to all of us is something that is not easy to understand, albeit we eventually often discover the reason. However, the reason a driver cutting me off in traffic is upsetting is due to how I choose to view the world. Expectation often is negative because we can tend to project our fears, insecurities, and so forth on everything.

The look given us by our employer or loved one that causes uneasiness whilst one works in their mind to figure out what's behind the look is another example of our projection mechanism. If we were to learn that the employer was disguising a surprise birthday party in our honor, or the person in traffic was actually attempting to rush their small child to the hospital, we would think differently and that would produce a different psychophysical response.

It is on behalf of our psychophysical response that dictates selfishly why we should choose to take a higher ground and find the positive in everything. As I pointed out repeatedly in my book *Wellness: Just a State of Mind,* the stress response inhibits just those little things in our body that we like to work optimally—like our endocrine and immune system or our autonomic nervous system. We all want these "little things" to work optimally if for no other reason than to improve the quality of our lives, relationships, health, longevity, etc. The lesson: Find the good and focus on the positive, even if it is only to have that Pollyanna expectation that simply says, "I can't wait to see what good comes from this!"

CHAPTER SIXTEEN:

Control

Let's flesh out a little more of the difference between what we can control and what we can't. We all know people who are, what is commonly referred to as, control freaks. Generally speaking, a control freak is a person who feels an obsessive need to exercise control over themselves and others, and to take command of any situation. To some extent, we are all somewhat inclined to be a bit of a control freak, especially in light of the idea that we should be in control of ourselves—but just how much control do we ever truly have?

Subconscious Control

Researchers have demonstrated that most, if not all, of our thoughts originate from the subconscious. We do something, say something, and perhaps we wonder why. This, too, is something we have all experienced. Where is control at times like these?

Most of us fuss over little things involving ourselves as well. How much we weigh, how good our clothes look, the shine on our shoes to the makeup we wear, these things we also like to think we have some control over. However, as one ages, they quickly discover that something outside their volition is really in control of much of their appearance. So again, what are we controlling?

Personal Improvement

We talk a lot about personal improvement today, and that generally means everything from making more money to becoming a better person—but are we really in control of these things? Just how much negative self-talk do we hear coming from the inside out? Research has repeatedly demonstrated connections between our environment and genetics that can lead to everything from criminality to genius. Are we truly in control of this maturation matrix, the so-called nature/nurture aspect of who we are? Further, can we really expect to totally control its influence in our adult lives?

If we listen to many experts today ranging from the philosopher to the neuroscientist, the answer at best is "Maybe—depending—conditionally, etc." My own research along these lines suggests the only long-term way you can gain control is by reprogramming your subconscious mind. That said, there are many things in life that we simply can't control with our minds.

From time to time the world throws us curve balls that alter our course of direction and sometimes change our lives. We can't control the obvious things like the weather, and we can't control many other outside factors as well. So, the question arises again, "What exactly are we in control of?"

The Paradox

One of the tactics deployed by behavioral scientists often illustrates how little we are in control of, while creating a sort of paradox at the same time. The paradox proceeds along a dichotomous line this way—on one side rests the understanding that we are not in control while on the other side is the encouragement to improve ourselves by gaining more self-control. This sort of self-composure accepts what cannot be changed and is challenged by that which is believed to be within the grips of change possibilities.

So, we can be better people, we can be more caring and sharing, we can find more happiness and experience, more quality in our lives, but paradoxically so, often only because we quit trying to control everything—and that often includes ourselves. Indeed, the whole notion of self-forgiveness is anchored by the realization that what's done is done and crying over the proverbial spilt milk is only counterproductive.

Self-Realization

Change your InnerTalk and thereby change your thinking, and you will change your life—this has long been a motto my company has flown. Recognizing that some things are beyond our ability to control or change is a giant leap forward in the process of self-realization.

Chapter Seventeen:

Our Identities

In this chapter we will address the notion of self and unpack just some of the ideas discussed earlier, such as the four selves. We all have a self-portrait of sorts—that is, we all know ourselves by some common measures like our name, marital status, home, occupation, etc., and we also all know ourselves in interior ways such as our likes, dislikes, proclivities, attitudes, ambitions, secrets, and so forth. As such, our identity is who we have come to know ourselves as.

Constant Self

Now imagine that you lost your senses altogether—would that change who you know yourself to be? Probably not. So, what if you suddenly became an acquired savant like Jason Padgett? For Jason, one day he is okay with math and the next day he is a mathematical wizard.

What if a head blow turned you into a synesthete like Dr. Joel Salinas, author of *Mirror Touch*, and like him, you actually felt the pain of others? Would taking on another's pain change you enough that your self-identity would become foreign to your former self?

Now what if you lost all of your memories like Debra Sanders, author of *A Matter of Panache*. Suddenly, you wake from a horrible accident and know not who you are, where you are, or anything else about yourself. Clearly now your self-identity is different. Perhaps it is limited to your body—but that's not who you are, or is it?

Aging teaches all of us that who we are is not our self-image as photographed when we're babies, or small children, or teenagers, or young adults. No—this body thing is an ever-changing event, and I would suggest that so is your self-representation or identity. As Heraclitus once put it, "You can never step into the same stream twice."

Dynamic Beings

We are all dynamic beings in constant flux, just as all of nature. Our personalities are malleable, our attitudes frequently change, our likes and dislikes can vary from time to time, but most importantly, so can our view of our role in the world.

The world changes one person at a time. A friend of mine recently reminded me of a quote by George Bernard Shaw, "We have no more right to consume happiness without producing it than to consume wealth without producing it."

Think about that for a moment. How much happiness are you producing today and how could you increase it? Life isn't about your past—it's always about the present. What can you do in this moment to increase the happiness in your world? As you produce happiness, you gain happiness. Isn't that what we all want and isn't that what we always want to be? For me, it seems the rest is only details.

CHAPTER EIGHTEEN:

Relationships

Let's pause for a moment and reflect on the importance of relationships. In a recent newsletter Ravinder reminded me of something I wrote many years ago as a result of a dream. The next morning, I wrote the dream down and ultimately it became *The Little Black Book*. The bottom line, something I have referred to as the three R's—and not for reading, writing, and arithmetic. No—my three R's can be said this way, *Reality is Relative to Relationships!*

Lasting

Think about it this way, when we leave this corporal life, we will not take our trophies, diplomas, possessions, and so forth. What we will take is our experiences and especially those with other beings. In other words, our relationships are the one thing that will survive, assuming we survive at all—and I do!

I remember watching Tom Hanks as Chuck the UPS driver struggle over the loss of his soccer ball in the film *Cast Away*. Stranded on an island, no companionship, no one to talk to, not another human being to even watch, authentically portrayed what life alone could be like. The screenwriter, "William Broyles, Jr., spent several days alone in Mexico's Sea of Cortez trying to fend for himself. He speared and ate stingrays, learned how to open a coconut, befriended a washed-up Wilson-brand volleyball, and tried to make fire, which ended up in the movie. His experiences led to an epiphany regarding the Chuck character: 'That's when I realized it wasn't just a physical challenge,' Broyles told *The Austin Chronicle* in 2000, 'It was going to be an emotional, spiritual one as well.'"

Alone

Just try to imagine your life without another human being. What would your world be like? What would you desire most in your life? Just asking yourself a few questions of this nature quickly leads to the appreciation we have for others.

Life is full of challenges, and often these challenges come down to other people. Difficult people with antagonistic ideas are not hard to find in today's world. Sometimes they are our relatives, our neighbors, someone in the workplace, or in our schools; and sometimes they are relatively unknown characters that we friend on social media platforms or watch in some television broadcast—but wherever we find them there doesn't seem to be shortage nowadays.

Or could it be—just maybe, that we have lost sight of how important others are. I read a definition of humility last week that impressed me. In the words of Rick Warren, "Humility is not thinking less of yourself, it's thinking of yourself less." That reminded me of something said by James Faust, "A grateful heart is a beginning of greatness. It is an expression of humility. It is a foundation for the development of such virtues as prayer, faith, courage, contentment, happiness, love, and wellbeing."

Three R's

I would encourage you to think back to that great film *Cast Away* and how grateful Chuck was to have other people. Think about my three R's——and then set your own intention for positive interactions with all. Add the gratitude for others into your life with the humility that comes from recognizing that it is only your relationships that will leave this earth plane when you do, and only your relationships that will therefore define your success in this life.

A gentle, forgiving heart with a mindful sense of humility will reward you, not just in the here and now, but on the other side as well. The peace, balance, and harmony we all seek in this world begin with a single act, a single person, a single intention to be what we want the world to be.

CHAPTER NINETEEN:

Cookie Keepers

One important element in the notion of personal freedom is self-responsibility. It may go unnoticed today, but so long as one remains dependent upon blaming another for their misfortunes, they effectively have tied themselves up. This is something we discussed earlier. As such, there is nothing they can do about it but get even. Thus, the bumper sticker, "I don't get even, I get evener."

The fact is, blame is a bind that wraps us from one end to another as though we had been literally tied up. Blame says, "There's nothing I could do—it was done to me." Blame informs us that we're just pawns in the matter, like billiard balls bouncing off the cue ball to the rails.

I'm not saying that bad things don't happen to some people. We are not in charge of all the stimuli that may come our way in life, but we are always in charge of our response. So long as we blame, there is nothing we can do about the matter—we are just victims. You know, "Life just sucks—and then you die." How can you think of yourself as being free when you're just a pawn in the game of life?

Fortune Cookies

There are those who cling tenaciously to their *right* to blame. I have a friend in South Africa who is a lie detection examiner. He has a model I like. He calls it something else, but we'll call it the "bad-luck fortune cookies" game. So, this is the story of these special cookie collectors. They go through life collecting all the cookies they can. Riding on the escalator of life, they will even jump high in the air to catch one, just so they can put it in their backpack of life experience and share it later. And share they do. Each evening, whether at home or in the pub, on the telephone or on email, they tell their friends all about the cookies of the day. These sharings go like this:

First Person: "Do you know what happened to me today? The clerk in the gas and grocery would not take my credit card because I left my purse at work with my identification in it, and she knows me. Heck, she sees me nearly every day—but she is a real grouch anyway."

Second Person: "That sucks, but do you know what my boss said to me today? He informed me that I was always late from lunch and told me in no uncertain terms that I would either be on time or lose my job. He knows that the traffic is horrible at lunch, and he's always gone more than an hour. I should just tell him to stuff it!"

Third Person: "Your day was nearly as bad as mine. I had a damn cop stop me for nearly nothing. Everyone in traffic was changing lanes, and just because I cut in front of him, he gave me a ticket. That's my third one this year, and my insurance costs are going to go through the roof as a result. These damn cops should be out catching criminals, not honest tax-paying citizens."

First Person: "Life sucks. Is your husband still being a jerk? Oh, but you know, speaking of insurance rates, my insurance company canceled my insurance just because I was late with their payment. Then that blankety-blank that ran into me led to a fine for my not having insurance. And on top of that, they blamed me for the accident, and it wasn't my fault!"

The Blame Game

By now you get the idea. These people gather to share their cookie stories, and that is largely what their social life is all about. If you want to have some fun, step up to the cookie keepers and point out how wonderful life is. You might even explain the blame game and cookie keeper philosophy, but make sure you have a plan for a quick retreat.

Cookie keepers choose, whether or not they want to admit it, to hold tightly to the blame game. An otherwise productive and joyful life is thrown away in exchange for the "Don't you feel sorry for me?" exchanges. That is another part of the cookie keeper game. To belong to their group, you must be willing to be understanding and sympathetic. It's okay to top the cookie of another with a more unpleasant cookie of your own but not if you fail to recognize the poor, picked-on nature of the other cookie keeper.

Codependence

A dear friend of mine grew up in a codependent family relationship, one of those Melody Beattie so aptly defines in her book *Codependent No More*. It's the relationship most of us know something about, for we have heard many of those conditional statements growing up. They are the ones that go like this: "If you loved me, you would ____. If you had any respect for me, you would not ______. I did this for you. Is it too much to expect _________ from you? I think if you cared about me, you would______." And so forth. You fill in the blanks. Beattie sets out several criteria for recognizing codependence. In her words:

> "Codependents are the people who consistently, and with a great deal of effort and energy, try to force things to happen ... We control in the name of love. We do it because we're 'only trying to help.' We do it because we know best how things should go and how people should behave. We do it because we're right and they're wrong. We control because we're afraid not to do it. We do it because we don't know what else to do. We do it to stop the pain. We control because we think we have to. We control because we don't think. We control because controlling is all we can think about. Ultimately, we may control because that's the way we've always done things. Tyrannical and dominating, some rule with an

iron hand ... Others do their duty behind a costume of sweetness and niceties, secretly going about their business—other people's business."

Two of the keystone elements in all of this codependency is, according to Beattie, "Suffering people's consequences for them," and "Solving people's problems for them." In other words, there is a real quid pro quo in cookie sharing, and it, too, is at least somewhat based on codependent patterns.

Self-Power

My friend gave up her codependent behavior and threw all of her cookies away. She chose to become self-empowered and has made wonderful strides in the process. If you asked her, she would say that life is a miracle, and she is very happy today. Still, her sister, with whom she has always been very close, has not budged. Her sister carries all the cookies she can and spends nearly every moment sharing them. Despite soft approaches at trying to turn on a light in the sister's head, my friend now finds herself in that place where she has difficulty in understanding why her family members fail to see the game they're playing.

It is hard to change when those you love the most are fixed in ways that steal your power. My friend has decided that the next time her sister plays the blame game, she will say something to end this behavior. You see, when you stop saving your cookies and get on with taking responsibility for everything in your life, your life improves. When that happens, you lose any and all desire to be a cookie keeper.

Chapter Twenty:

True Self-Responsibility

True self-responsibility means taking responsibility for *everything* in your life, even those events or people that do not in any way seem to be your problem or responsibility. Often the people who most antagonize us are the ones we need most to teach us what we want to learn. My mother used to say, "Birds of a feather flock together." Call it that, or call it simple attraction, anger attracts anger, hostility attracts hostility, love attracts love, and so forth. When we see something in someone we do not like, we need to be careful, for often they are mirrors of ourselves. What we dislike in them is likely to be a behavior of our own. When we are alert to this, it's quite easy to do something remarkable, something that truly changes your own reality. Genuine freedom does not exist in blaming anyone or anything for who we are or what we have become. Once we accept responsibility for the situation, whatever it might be, we are empowered to act. It is our action that brings about change. It is our actions and reactions that we are responsible for. Next time, instead of thinking, "So-and-so is to blame for this," think instead, "What can I do to improve this matter or situation?" It is with this attitude of self-responsibility that our true potential can finally be realized.

Equality

One of my early lessons in life came as the result of a question I asked of a minister. In all teenage pomp and wisdom, I interrupted the man and suggested that his statement, "All men are equal," was obviously unmitigated rubbish—a bald-face lie!

Unlike most who might have simply dismissed my arrogant query with words such as, "In the eyes of God—all men are created equal in the eyes of God," he quite calmly asked me to imagine two men—the first, a rocket scientist who after much work launches an interstellar voyager. Imagine the pride he feels in the accomplishment. Now imagine a so-called menial laborer, a janitor. On his hands and knees for endless hours, he scrubs and polishes a floor. He has worked so hard and with so much pride that he has scrubbed his knuckles raw. Now he stands back and beholds his labors. The floor absolutely glistens—every square inch of it. It never looked this good even when it was new. Now, I was further then instructed, which man senses the most pride, the rocket scientist or the floor scrubber?

This minister turned the entire question around to the talents we are all given. They may be different, but it is what we do with our talents and abilities that tell the real story.

The Habit of Excellence

Over the years I have had the great opportunity to work with some truly wonderful people ranging from elite athletes and entrepreneurs to farmers, truck drivers, salespeople, and more. I am certain that I have seen a good cross-section of people from many countries, and the successful folks all have one thing in common: They do their best.

Best is a habit. Indeed, Aristotle is credited with pointing out that excellence is not an act, but a habit! Now, I have spoken with many people who say they do their best—they try their hardest—and I believe them. But trying is not doing. There's an old trick used by hypnotists to demonstrate trying, and it goes like this. Take a pencil and hold it between your thumb and forefinger. Grip it tight. Do not let go until I tell you to. Now do exactly as I say. Follow my instructions literally. Now, hold it tightly, tighter and tighter. Grip it with all of your finger strength. Now try to drop—you can't. Try again, you can't. Now drop it.

Now what's going on here? First, understand that if you did drop the pencil initially, you failed to follow my instructions. If you did follow the instructions, then you found yourself unable to drop the pencil when told to try but perfectly able to release it when I told you to drop it. There is a significant difference in our mental processes between trying, an act in progress that has not succeeded, and actually doing. So how does this relate to success?

Skill Set

Everything we undertake in life requires a skill set. We learn to walk only after learning to maintain balance, to stand on one foot, and so forth. We build upon earlier skill sets in acquiring advanced abilities, so we crawl before we walk. I can try and try to walk, try my very hardest, and yet fall again and again until I finally acquire the necessary skill set. But to acquire the skill, instead of literally trying, I must stand and do.

There are many tools and tactics that make up the skill set for success, but there are definite common denominators. There are many books that offer to share and even teach various skills, whether they are the skills necessary to enjoy a lifelong loving relationship or those necessary to build a fortune. I personally like Steven Covey's *Seven Habits of Highly Effective People* as a starting place. Covey outlines seven habits that can help you in most areas of life. They're simple and for many, rather obvious. Here they are:

1. Be proactive.
2. Begin with the end in mind.
3. Put first things first.
4. Think win-win.
5. Seek first to understand and then to be understood.
6. Synergy—think teamwork.
7. Live a balanced life.

Now these seven tactical approaches, when converted to habits, will take you a long way, but in my opinion, the most important set is missing. Of course, we could add still more tactics and there are plenty of authors who have done just that. But the most important strategy one can employ to become and remain successful is to build a strong character.

Character

The tools and the tactics are not the strategy. Some might insist the strategy is to be successful. I think the strategy is different, although it leads to the same end. I believe the strategy should be one of building a strong character.

What are the elements of a strong character? In my view, they come down to this.

1. The first is truthfulness—plain old honesty.
2. The second is courage—courage to do and be your very best in everything you undertake. Assume that your personal signature is on the line for every effort you make.
3. The third is persistence—the tenacity to improve in every way every day.
4. The fourth is service—the realization that life is most worth living when you are helping others.
5. The fifth is forgiveness—forgiveness of all including yourself. Forgiveness and kindness are opposite sides of the same coin. After all, we all make mistakes. As Lorii Myers puts it: The power behind taking responsibility for your actions lies in putting an end to negative thought patterns. You no longer dwell on what went wrong or focus on whom you are going to blame. You don't waste time building roadblocks to your success. Instead, you are set free and can now focus on succeeding.
6. The sixth is gratitude—the conviction that everything that comes to you, does so for some good.
7. The seventh, be self-responsible! You may not be in charge of everything that will come your way, but you definitely can be in charge of your responses. In the words of the author of *The Working Mom Manifesto*, Heather Schuck, "Taking personal accountability is a beautiful thing because it gives us complete control of our destinies."

So, I would suggest that creating and reinforcing a strong character until it is natural, until it is your habit, this is the foundation upon which prosperity in all walks of life exists. We are fortunate in that we are free people, but with that comes a responsibility. In the words of Jean-Paul Sartre, "Man is condemned to be free; because once thrown into the world, he is responsible for everything he does. It is up to you to give [life] a meaning."

CHAPTER TWENTY-ONE:

What Is an Authentic Life?

I am often asked two questions, "What is an authentic life?" and "How does one know whether or not they are living authentically?"

Sometimes the best way to answer a question is to provide a clear understanding of its opposite, so what would an inauthentic life look like? After all, we are living, breathing, eating animals, doing natural things, so just what is meant by living inauthentically?

The quick answer is probably less than satisfying. The quick answer is living a life untrue to ourselves, but then, what exactly does that mean? Does it mean that I wanted to be singer when I was young, and now I'm a scientist instead? Does it mean that I make a meager wage and therefore I can't live the style I'm entitled to live in order to discover my authentic self? Or does it mean something more like my life is simply not satisfying, so how could it be authentic?

Self-Deprecation

The Native American philosopher Lame Deer suggests that an authentic life would not include self-deprecation. Lame Deer believes that we can't stand our natural animal selves, so we hide from who we are. We use deodorants and perfumes to hide our smell, we disfigure our faces with cosmetic procedures in desperate attempts to hold aging at bay, and we enslave ourselves to a system that reduces us to cogs in the economic machinery. In fact, we spend our lives focused on money and define ourselves according to our role in the machination of humanity, and thus become not much more than work robots contributing to the never-ending cycle of production and consumption, lost from our true being and from nature itself.

Gandhi believed that modernity was inherently evil and that liberalism—promoting the freedom to do as you please, to make your own consumption decisions—actually made slaves of some in order to benefit others. For Gandhi, the capitalistic industrial complex carried with it the promise of inequitable distribution and that means the subversion of democracy and the growth of consumerism.

So, what's wrong with consumerism? After all, the hunt, the chase, the capture—all of this is a part of our primitive makeup, and isn't shopping just our modern sublimation for the good old tribal hunt?

Perspectives

Tolstoy tells us in his work *The Death of Ivan Ilych* that for life to be truly meaningful we need to have a connection both with nature and with human relationships. The artificial life, for Tolstoy, is one led in a secular world disconnected from the natural; while devoted to the artificial forms of society that give rise to losing any meaning other than our role in the herd, that leaves us hopeless when the certainty of death draws nigh.

Nietzsche informs us in his *Twilight of the Idols* that above all, we should always retain our authenticity and take full responsibility for doing so. In his words, "If we possess our why of life, we can put up with any how." He further adds, "The will to a system is a lack of integrity." What he means by that is quite clear. Nietzsche asks us to consider who we are, and he begs us to evaluate our lives from the maxim of whether we live for ourselves, or as some cog in a machine pursuing the goals and purposes of other people? Nietzsche believes that it is our nature to pursue our freedom to rise above and not just be an equal member of the herd.

One of my favorite authors, Og Mandino, compared our modern world and the people that inhabit it to a Nabisco factory. He put it this way: We are no more individual "than any of the millions of saltine crackers that emerge daily."

Lame Deer speaks of the Little Big Horn and General Custer. He narrates a story of how the soldiers under Custer had just been paid and they carried all this paper money—what the Sioux children called "green frog skins." They died for their money, their green frog skins. Those that sent them into battle were doing so for gold in the Black Hills. The Sioux children used the green frog skins to make toy buffalo and the like. According to Lame Deer, white folks dedicate their lives to green frog skins, and that's why when you ask them who they are, they answer defining their position as a cog in the great machinery: I'm a lawyer, a carpenter, a plumber, a doctor, a truck driver, a waitress, or what have you.

Definition

Now, I don't mean to suggest that money is evil. I have a small business, and the people who work for me depend upon their jobs for income, just as my family depends upon me. I hope my employees and associates find their work helping people as rewarding as I do. Still, there are bills to be paid and we all face that fact every day. So, the real issue is not about those green frog skins so much as it is about their utility and how much of our lives they define.

How do you define your life? I choose to think that we are spiritual beings inhabiting a human body for a special experience, and it's not the one acting as a pawn controlled by all of those who would own our every thought. No—it is the mindful life, aware and engaged in our inner most self-discovery, alert to the fact that as we live, we literally live into who we are—or we don't, and that is our only real choice!

I hope you recognize not only all that you are and all that you can become, but all that you still have to live into.

CHAPTER TWENTY-TWO:

Blessing Success and Money

Money is more than little green frog skins. Money is a subject everyone tends to think about. Altogether too many people want it and yet push it away because they believe that money and profit are evil. Is profit evil in your mind? Should entrepreneurs and businesses in general seek to do business at a loss, or even at some break-even point, in the name of social good? Would creativity be kindled if we but shared and shared alike—I mean what if the Bill Gates', Steve Jobs, Mark Zuckerbergs of the world shared equally with the folks sitting at home watching TV who are unwilling to take a job that pays no more than what they can collect on welfare and/or unemployment? Do you really believe that these economic drivers would have worked as hard, taken the risks, been as creative, contributed as much to production in our economy as they have under those circumstances? If you do, I think you should rethink the matter from your own private perspective.

Share and Share Alike

Think of it this way. Most of you work hard for your pay, so the next time you see some panhandler on the street with a camouflaged bottle of wine in his pack, stop and give him half of what you have earned. If you prefer to be really fair, gather all of the homeless in your area together, and divide your earnings between them equally. Most will actually have a gut reaction to this idea that goes something like, "But I am barely getting by. This is the job of those rich people who don't know what work is."

Recently a friend of mine on Facebook brought an interesting article to my attention titled "We Are Wealthy. And Why It Matters". The article begins by pointing out three significant facts:

1. It is currently estimated that by the year 2016, the richest 1% will control more than half of the world's wealth.

2. Even more shocking, the combined wealth of the eighty richest people in the world is the same as that of the bottom 50% of the Earth's population—totaling 3.5 billion people.

3. In America, the wealth inequality gap continues to grow as America's middle class shrinks. The share of American households in the middle class fell from 56.5 percent in 1979 to only 45.1 percent in 2012. And there is no indication this trend will reverse itself.

The Mind Gap

The author Joshua Becker is quick to acknowledge that the fix for this problem is not easy, but then he recognizes yet another and perhaps more important problem. In his words, "But recently, I have begun noticing another unhealthy trend. One that may be related to the widening gap, but more likely, finds its root in the human spirit. It, too, requires a solution, albeit a much easier one to define. This equally negative trend is the wealth gap we focus on in our mind and the resulting division we artificially create because of it."

Think about that for a moment. What sort of gap in the mind might he be addressing? Could he be addressing the notion of the other 1%, the jealousy many have when they see someone in that new Cadillac or Mercedes, or when they hear of someone's incredible monetary success, or the wages paid corporate executives versus the poor working person laboring for the same company, and so forth? It turns out that it is exactly this sort of thinking that betrays our desire for success.

We Are the Rich

Comparatively speaking, people in this country are quite wealthy. Again, quoting Becker,

"Globally, an estimated six billion people live on less than $13,000/ year. And nearly half the world's population, 2.8 billion people, survive on less than $2 a day. According to the non-profit group Giving What We Can, an annual income of $40,000 places you in the richest 2% of the world's population. An income of $25,000/year puts you in the top 3%. Even a minimum wage job ($7.25 an hour, forty hours a week, fifty-two weeks a year) puts you in the top 8% of all people on the planet in terms of income. Adjusting for actual purchasing power makes little difference in the percentages. In other words, we are the rich ones."

Most of us seek to improve our way of life, perhaps to pay for a child's college education, or to take a much-deserved vacation, or to buy that new high-definition giant-screen television, or to purchase the car of our dreams and so on. All the while we are seeking increased monetary success, we can be condemning it—consciously as well as subconsciously.

Blessing Wealth

Here's my suggestion for what it's worth. The next time you see someone who appears to be wealthy, say to yourself with as much conviction as you can muster, "Wow—that's for me!" When you pull up behind that fancy new expensive automobile, bless the owner for in all probability he or she has contributed to the production in this country, and that contributes to everyone's welfare. Blessing them also acknowledges the fact that it's more than okay to have, to realize, the economic prosperity you seek. And then, offer a sincere thank you for everything you do already have.

Remember this, the root of money is exchange. Money represents your stored energy. It is the result of your labors. Money is a tool of exchange and without it we are left to the jungle, rule by force and guns. Money is the tool of the honest. Money is the material manifestation of value in exchange for value. It means most to those who recognize this and least to those who are moochers convinced that somehow, they're entitled to a share of the bounty of another's production without producing anything themselves. Now that's not to suggest that there isn't a real problem with the distribution of wealth, and particularly its application when used to buy political sway, but it makes no sense to sabotage our own success by thinking of money or profit as a vice or the root of all evil.

CHAPTER TWENTY-THREE:

Choosing Perception

We live in a wonderful world, if we choose to see it that way. Let me flesh that out some. I was enjoying myself last evening while contemplating on life and the many experiences it has delivered to me. I reflected on several different occasions where perception defined the experience. For example, one warm summer evening not long ago, my youngest son, wife, and I were cruising in our freshly restored 1969 Impala SS Convertible, when suddenly there was no power! The car just halted in its tracks—shorted out! I smiled, don't ask me why, and almost immediately there appeared another 1969 Impala convertible (for you car buffs, it was a red 427 but not the SS package).

Problems are Often Opportunities

The driver very nicely offered to provide a jumpstart and we tried, but to no avail. We thanked him and decided to call a tow truck. However, we were stuck in the middle of the street at a light—not the safest place to break down. Just then four lovely people, three men and a woman, ran to the car from the sidewalk and offered to help push it out of the street. Again, I smiled and thanked them.

The tow truck arrived in less than five minutes, and the driver, against the rules, very nicely agreed to provide us a ride to my friend's home where the car would be repaired. We had a great conversation and some laughs during the journey with the four of us in the front of the 4x4 rig, my pretty bride on my lap.

Then the taxi home—we expected a long wait, but the taxi actually arrived before I finished business with the driver of the tow rig. The ride home was equally pleasant and perhaps even more rewarding. The driver was a Bible teacher, who had studied the ancient scripts, and we delighted in a terrific exchange of information and ideas.

Perception Makes the Difference

I have often taught that the world is about perception—reality is something we define in our minds. Think of the wonderful lesson my son had that evening while we all laughed and made an adventure of the entire matter. In a different frame of mind, the situation could have been nasty. As it turned out, the adventure led to meeting wonderful people and sharing great conversation—and you know, I'd take that again over just driving under the stars, as pleasant as that is to me.

CHAPTER TWENTY-FOUR:

It Begins With a Story

We have often been asked what we do at InnerTalk. In answering this question, I usually begin by saying something like, "Well, that begins with a story." So please allow me to share that story with you now.

In the mid-1980s I owned a private agency specializing in intelligence and counterintelligence. The practice of lie detection testing and forensic hypnosis were among my specialties. I had developed a form of dichotic masking that we used to play subliminal messages such as "the truth shall set you free" during detection of deception interviews and examinations. The use of this technology substantially increased our confession rate while reducing our inconclusive test results. This, again, was in the 1980s when the field known as subliminal priming was basically in its infancy. There has been a lot of research since then and a great review of the state of the art was recently published in *Behavioral Sciences*.[1]

Utah State Prison

But, back to our story. A friend of mine, Lee Liston from the Utah State Prison, asked me whether or not the technology I had developed could be used to rehabilitate inmates incarcerated in the prison. So together we recruited a statistical expert employed by Utah State and set up a study. Lee recruited a group of volunteers from the Youth Offenders Facility, and our statistics man, Charles McCusker, evaluated the MMPI (Minnesota Multiphasic Personality Inventory) applied through the Fowler Lens (a lens specifically designed for the incarcerated environment). The results were of little use since we already assumed there would be high scores in self and social alienation. However, when we visited with the inmates, we discovered a common denominator—it wasn't their fault. Society had made them this way. An exaggerated story might lay the blame at the feet of others with explanations such as, "All but for the grace of God, there go you. My mommy was a prostitute, my daddy an alcoholic, and the neighbor hung drugs on me when I was only fourteen years old."

The three of us decided that in order to get the inmates to truly take responsibility for their actions, we needed to end the blame game. To that end we built positive self-image messages together with what, for over 30 years now, I have now called the Forgiveness Set: *I forgive myself, I forgive all others, I am forgiven.*

We had developed a tight double-blind study, and the results were impressive enough that the prison system installed voluntary libraries throughout all facilities, from minimum to maximum security. Eventually a number of other prisons copied the Utah model. However, we had discovered earlier that most inmates were not motivated toward a forgiving program, but they were interested in issues such as bodybuilding, weight gain or loss, athletic performance, and so forth. As such we began to expand our title list while always including the Forgiveness Set and a healthy dose of positive self-image messages.

Today we have over 300 titles designed to facilitate everyone with the issues they find most pressing in life. Bottom line—the fact is we all experience self-defeating and self-sabotaging thoughts and actions during our lives. This self-sabotage originates in our thinking despite the fact that much of it may go consciously unrecognized and/or rationalized away. All but for this self-doubt we would all be able to achieve the bulk of our goals in life with ease. If it weren't for those self-limiting thoughts, what might you achieve? If it weren't for those sabotaging thoughts, would any of those issues such as weight loss, smoking cessation, confidence, self-esteem, etc. ever be an issue?

InnerTalk, the patented dichotic masking technology I developed and used in the Utah State Prison, has since been independently verified in multiple double-blind and clinical studies carried out in prestigious institutions such as Stanford. It has been studied in foreign languages, such as Spanish and German, and has always been demonstrated effective at priming that stream of consciousness we think of as our self-talk. When you change the way you talk to yourself, you change your inner beliefs about yourself and abilities. Doubt and fear seem to just disappear, and you are free to achieve the success that has previously eluded you. That's why we say, *InnerTalk: When Believing in Yourself Matters!* If you think about it—when does believing in yourself **not** matter?

Now you know what we do and why we have been doing it for more than thirty-five years. Indeed, we feel blessed to have been able to help millions during that time with the tools necessary to empower each and every one of them, and we plan to continue doing just that for millions more. We think of our customers as part of our family, and many of them have been with us since the beginning—ever seeking to answer the question: How high is up? For once you achieve one goal, the next rung in the ladder is easier, and up and up you go.

We welcome you to join our InnerTalk family and begin attaining your ambitions and goals today.

Resources

Elgendi, M. et. al. 2018. "Subliminal Priming—State of the Art and Future Perspectives." *NCBI.*

CHAPTER TWENTY-FIVE:

Why Self-Help

Choosing to find every day an opportunity is only a slight shift in perspective from those who would choose, "Same old— same old," but what an empowering difference it is. I like to think of the famous Vince Lombardi quote through a different lens than winning. Rather I like to think of it this way, "Attitude is not everything—it's the only thing!"

More and more research supports the simple fact that from health to wealth, from relationships to sports, from agitation to bliss—the difference is attitude. Attitude is the mind's method of injecting either good or bad chemicals into our physical systems. Good chemicals make us smile, they make us feel good, they promote health and longevity. Bad chemicals tend to suppress the immune, endocrine, and autonomic nervous system, often leading to breakdowns in our physical system or disease and discomfort. Attitude—that old stream of consciousness, our inner talk, what a difference it makes!

Attitude is not everything—it's the only thing!

Since 1984, we have been honored every day to be doing something that enables others to enjoy the amazing and beautiful cornucopia of life. Your letters, emails, phone calls, and personal feedback continue to inspire and motivate us to do as much as we can.

At Progressive Awareness, we all wish you the very best in everything, every day of the year! We welcome your input and feedback. Our resource guide is full of opportunities to maximize your self-actualization.

The InnerTalk Effect

InnerTalk programs tap into our natural human ability to absorb information even when we're not thinking about it. On the surface, the programs may seem to sound like any other easy-listening music or nature programs you may have heard . . . but there is a powerful difference. Carefully blended in the background are dynamic affirmations such as *"I feel good," "I am successful,"* etc., that make long-lasting, positive impressions. While the conscious mind enjoys the pleasant music or nature sounds, the subconscious mind recognizes and receives the powerful, life-changing affirmations.

**The powerful results may seem like magic,
but the programs are pure science.**

Results can often be noticed in as little as a few days to a few weeks. InnerTalk technology is so powerful it is patented with the U.S. government, backed by independent studies at leading universities, and proven effective by the hundreds of thousands of satisfied users around the world.

All programs come with a list of the recorded affirmations. We recommend you review this list once a week or so to monitor your progress.

CHAPTER TWENTY-SIX:

The Foundation Stone for All Forms of Self-Help

There are many different forms of self-help: books, audio and video programs, training courses, philosophies, seminars, motivational speakers, and on and on. Inspiration can be found in a large number of different arenas. However, most of us have had the experience where we have encountered *something* that is absolutely marvelous, something that rings that little bell inside of us that says, "The truth can be found here." We have all vowed to follow this new "path" only to find that vow impossible to keep. Why is it that failure is so much more common than success? Why is it that an inspirational book only "inspires" us for so long? Why is it that an exit poll from some motivational seminar will show that the majority of attendees were inspired to make certain changes to their lives—but a follow-up poll just a month later will show that a very small number, maybe just 5%, will still be following the tenets presented in the seminar. The answer really can be found within ourselves and are twofold. Firstly, for some reason or other, we simply talk ourselves out of taking the steps to "improve" ourselves. This inner talk can be that of:

- Procrastination (e.g. "I am too busy today; I will start the changes tomorrow.")
- Self-destructive (e.g. "I don't have the right personality for that so why should I even try?")
- Poor esteem or self-confidence (e.g. "I could never do that!")
- Fear (e.g. "I'm too afraid.")
- and on and on!

Secondly, while a new philosophy can be very inspirational, we all need some help in intaking this new message at a much deeper level. How can we make these new ideas and concepts a part and parcel of who we are?

Success

Whatever form of self-help you enjoy, the patented and proven effective InnerTalk technologies can add that extra boost that turns the failures into success. InnerTalk works from the inside out, changing the self-talk that causes the failures and reinforcing the values that are being taught in the book, seminar, or whatever. InnerTalk is the foundation stone that will assist in taking these new learning tools to the very core of your being. By using InnerTalk to reinforce all the new things you wish to learn, you will achieve successes that go beyond anything you have achieved before.

CHAPTER TWENTY-SEVEN:

What's in a Subliminal Program?

Now let's address the question, *What's in a Subliminal Program?* I was recently asked if all subliminal products are basically the same. The quick answer is absolutely not! Just because a product is labeled as subliminal does not equate to sameness in any way whatsoever. Let me flesh that out some.

Silent or Subliminal?

Years ago, I was asked to assist a company in trouble with an attorney general's office for making claims that the AG wanted substantiated. The threat appeared to exist in the evidence demonstrating efficacy from the use of subliminal programs, and since I had done more research at the time than probably anyone else in the field, I agreed to help this company. To that end, I requested a statement from the audio engineer informing me of his method for mixing the subliminal content.

The engineer obliged and informed me in writing that he mixed the verbal messages 50db beneath the primary carrier (music or water sounds). Now think about that for a minute. The theoretical limit to most home stereos is around 30 to 40db. Anything beneath that is simply non-existent in terms of reproducing the so-called subliminal content through some playback device. I think of this sort of mixing as invisible, and many companies still simply bury the messages so well that they are gone for all intent and purposes.

Technology

So, the first issue when comparing subliminal programs is the technology or method used to accomplish this without losing all or part of the message. You see another thing that can happen as a result of partially burying messages is that the words can become disengaged from their original meaning. For example, we might process the con in confidence or the sin in sincerely, missing the entire word meaning simply because of the method used to hide the messages. Once again, the first concern is technology.

Next, we shift to the subliminal content. Now some companies tell you that the messages are a secret and that if you know what they are then they will not work, and this is pure, unsupported hogwash! There is no real basis for this argument. As far as I'm concerned, I want to know what messages I'm being programmed to accept—and you should want to know!

Messages

That said, there are those messages that no matter how well-intentioned can defeat your goal or objective from the get-go. Take, for example, messages that are delivered in the second person, such as "You are good." When you process subliminal messages, they enter your stream of consciousness, thereby priming your self-talk, your expectation—indeed, your belief. So, let's say you want to build your esteem because you feel inferior and inadequate, and you play the message "You are good." Obviously when this message enters my self-talk, it validates the fact that you—some other person, is good and that in no way helps me with my feelings of inadequacy or inferiority. As such, the message must be in first person— "I am good!"

Here is another example of poor messaging. Let's say that you are a heavy smoker and you want to cut down. Perhaps you currently smoke two packs or forty cigarettes a day. So, you create your subliminal affirmation, "I find twenty cigarettes a day more than enough for me." The problem with an affirmation of this nature comes in how the mind tumbles words, a process known as subconscious cerebration. Think of a lottery drawing on TV with the balls rumbling before one is drawn—now think of your mind playing with sentences in this same way. Alas, when we tumble this seemingly positive affirmation, we discover that it can easily become, "I find more than twenty cigarettes a day enough for me." The design behind the meaning of this affirmation has not just been lost—it's been reversed.

Not all alike

Now there are still a number of other matters that should be considered before choosing the subliminal program that you're going to work with, but the answer to today's question should be obvious. No—not all subliminals are alike! I have contributed journal articles and written entire books on this subject, but this should give you enough information to consider before plugging your mind into some unknown subliminal product.

CHAPTER TWENTY-EIGHT:

A Beginner's Guide

We receive many calls from customers anxious to try out our program but unsure as to where they should start. We are often asked if there is a certain order in which they should be working with the programs. After being in the business for over twenty years, our product line has become very extensive, and while this is a good thing, for some people the choice can be a little overwhelming. Especially when some of the titles, e.g. Weight Loss, come in a number of different formats, such as OZO™, Echo-Tech™, Power Imaging™, and Power Sets™.

The beauty of InnerTalk is that there is no set course. You may start with whichever program you wish. Most people come to us looking for a solution to one specific problem. They choose a program, find it successful, and then start thinking about whatever other areas they could work on. When you are new to our technology, it is reassuring to see/feel the results so quickly.

Choose a Title

If you are just starting with our programs then, our suggestion is that you choose a title that is very significant to you. You should think carefully about exactly what it is that you are trying to achieve and what would be involved in achieving it. Comparing the sample affirmations can be very helpful. Which set of affirmations most fit the goal you are trying to achieve?

Choose a Technology (where appropriate)

Once you have chosen a title, you then need to decide how you will be working with the programs. Do you want a program that you can simply play in the background, or would you prefer a program whereby you put on headphones and take a *trip?* The key to your success is to play the programs regularly. InnerTalk can simply be played in the background twenty-four hours a day if you wish, whereas OZO, Echo-Tech, Power Imaging, and Platinum Plus all require headphones and focused attention. OZO is very forceful and is perfect for the highly competitive personality such as athletes or high-performance business people, whereas Echo-Tech is very gentle and soothing and is enjoyed by everyone. If your personality type is such that you do not like being told what to do, then we strongly advise against the OZO programs. Power Imaging utilizes a guided imagery scenario and assumes there is a reason you have not achieved your goal. Power Imaging helps you discover this reason and helps you to deal with it. Platinum Plus incorporates the leading edge of sound technologies, sound patterns, tones, frequencies, and on and on! Platinum Plus does not have an audible voice component to it. All of our programs utilize the patented and proven Whole Brain InnerTalk technology.

Although the headphone programs will make you feel different immediately, it is not possible to say that this makes them more powerful than the InnerTalk programs. InnerTalk can be played twenty-four hours a day whereas the headphone programs can only be played once or twice a day. While the effects of the headphone programs can be felt for some time after using them, the difference in effect is nonexistent after thirty days of use and therefore it really is a matter of how one prefers to use our programs. The fastest results are sometimes obtained by using a combination of headphone and InnerTalk programs. For this reason, we do offer a number of Power Sets, which provide both a headphone program and an InnerTalk program. We have also put together some collections bringing together similar titles across several different technologies. There can be times that having a number of different approaches to one goal can be beneficial. Our four program sets generally bring together Inner-Talk, OZO, Power Imaging, and Echo-Tech. Here the idea is to play the

InnerTalk program as much as possible and then play a headphone program once or twice a day, choosing whichever headphone program feels the most appropriate for the moment. The key is simply to decide how much time you wish to dedicate to achieving your goal and which approach suits your life style the best. Do not buy a program if you do not have time to use it.

Choose a Format

Simply decide if you would like the programs on CD/MP3 or video/MP4, and if selecting an InnerTalk program, decide if you would prefer the music or the nature soundtracks. Remember, the nature format is not only for night-time use, it can also be played during the day while you watch television, play your own music, or any other time that music would be too intrusive. Also remember, that you do not need to turn the volume up on our InnerTalk programs for them to be effective. No concentrated effort is required. Simply play them in the background as you go about your day or all night long while you sleep. Most InnerTalk subliminal titles can be purchased as double sets, incorporating both the music and nature formats.

Chapter Twenty-Nine:

Different Ways to Use
Your InnerTalk Programs

One of the most common questions we get asked about InnerTalk has to do with the best way to use the programs. While we do have our official recommendations on this, I am not really one for following rules. As such, I have played with it and have tested out some different techniques on myself. Today then, I want to share with you some of my experiences and how they have worked for me.

Officially

The official recommendation is to play the InnerTalk subliminal programs once a day for thirty days. While this is very effective and is based on research that was done at Colorado State University, I have found that for myself, I get better results when I play the programs more extensively. In fact, whenever I try out a program for the first time, I will play it just as much as I can—all day long in the background as I go about my day and all night long while I sleep. Played this way, I can tell within the twenty-four-hour period what kind of effect that particular program is having on me.

This is also a great technique to use if you have a number of issues you want to work with. While theoretically you could play twenty-four different InnerTalk subliminal programs over the course of one day, it would be impossible for you to know which program was having what effect. Once you know the kind of effect each program is having, then you can decide on a day-to-day basis whether you want to focus on a specific program, or if you want to combine a few.

Many Issues

Most of us have a wide range of issues that we wish to deal with, ranging from Prosperity and Abundance to finding the Right Love Relationship, Accelerated Learning to Positive Parenting, Opening Up to a Higher Power to Networking for Sales, etc. However, it is important not to get bogged down by the enormity of the list of things we want to fix or improve. I always advise people to start with just a few issues. Many times, self-improvement in one area has a cross-over effect to several others. You fix one area and you discover that you feel better about some of the other issues without even trying.

Collections

I am a strong believer in approaching the one issue from different angles. In the last couple of years, my own self-improvement work has resulted in us creating several new albums:

I decided I wanted to make sure my cognitive abilities did not start slipping, and I certainly did not want to accept the idea that a decline in brain power was just a part of growing older, so we created the Brain Power collection.

I decided to dive in and deal with a bunch of traumatic issues related to my childhood, and so we created the Reclaiming Your Inner Power collection.

I wanted to maximize my ability to turn off stress and truly relax—knowing that real rest would simply help me be more productive when I needed to work. As such, we created the Eliminating Stress: Experiencing Joy.

As you can see with each of these albums, I combined several Inner-Talk subliminal programs that I could play throughout the day, with a few headphone programs that I could use once or twice a day for that more immediate boost. When I work with the programs this way, I generally see the changes happening very quickly. In fact, when I used the Reclaiming Your Inner Power album, it was less than two days before I started connecting together dots from my childhood, experiences I thought I had left way behind me, in fact, experiences I had totally forgotten about. I was amazed at some of this recall, but as I acknowledged the pain from yesterday, it totally lost its power over me today.

Mixing It Up

But what happens when I don't have something specific I am working on? Well, those are the times I find ways to boost my positivity in several areas — areas I know to be important in the big picture, but which are not causing me actual problems right now.

For the past month, my playlist, which runs on continual play all day long while I am at the office, consists of:

- Cognitive Enhancement
- De-Cluttering
- Creative Writing
- Blood Pressure
- Weight Loss

I really don't know how much I get to hear of each of the programs. I am in the office about eight hours, but I often visit other offices or going out to the warehouse. I think I get to hear each of the programs about once a day, but sometimes I could well miss a program on a particular day. Even so, I am finding the results very interesting.

De-Cluttering

When we first created this program, it only took playing it a few times for both Eldon and I to get into deep-cleaning mode—we sorted out parts of the office and our home that we had not looked at in years. However, with the more relaxed way I have been playing this program, it is not the deep cleaning I am doing, but rather those little odds and ends are just getting sorted out without me even noticing. My workload no longer has so many uncompleted tasks; the piles on my desk are decidedly smaller; clear spaces are opening up in my home, and I am generally feeling more relaxed.

Cognitive Enhancement

Using the Brain Power album last year really highlighted to me how a lot of cognitive issues really are a case of stress (too tired to think through problems) and simply bad thinking (some cognitive loss is just part of ag-ing). I reversed many of the issues I felt I was having then, and now, just playing the program a little every day, I am watching my mental abilities actually becoming sharper every day. My own self-talk has changed, and

I frequently tell myself I can remember — and that is exactly what I do. It is as though I feel memories turn around and come back towards me.

Creative Writing

This year I finally finished the first draft of a book I have been working on for about eight years. The second draft was completed in about a month, which absolutely amazed me, and I am expecting to have my third and final round of edits done very soon—so that I can turn and write the non-fiction book that has been rattling around in my head for the last couple of years.

Blood Pressure

I have this program in my play list more for my husband's sake, as my own blood pressure is excellent (Eldon has speakers in his office, so he also listens to the same list of programs that I have chosen). However, maybe my blood pressure is so good simply because we simply play this program a lot. We both find it very relaxing and just enjoy the music. Also, although Eldon had triple bypass surgery in 2007, his doctors are always very impressed with how well he is doing. He has even been told that he now has the heart of a twenty-eight-year-old!

Weight Loss

I have never had a real weight issue, but for the past few years I have been aware that there are a couple of vanity pounds that I would really like to take off. However, I must confess that I added this title to my playlist simply because it is one of my all-time favorite pieces of music. The piece is by Emmy award-winning musician, Jim Oliver, and it always transports me to a very calm, inspirational place. It is simply an added benefit to me that I have now dropped those few pounds and feel stronger and healthier than ever.

Summing It Up

So, as you can see, there are a variety of ways in which you can work with InnerTalk. The only thing that I cannot stress enough is to always strive to be better—small changes accumulate, and in time, your world can look very different. So, what InnerTalk programs will you put in your player today?

CHAPTER THIRTY:

Your Personal Coach

The patented InnerTalk subliminal technology has repeatedly been demonstrated effective as a training method for self-talk. Each of us has a stream of inner talk or self-talk which can either enhance our abilities and help us perform to our highest capability or drastically limit our abilities to the degree that it can sabotage our own efforts. InnerTalk affirmations are presented in such a way that they offer optimal training of both halves of the brain simultaneously. Soon you will find that your own inner talk reflects the affirmations on the program and the effects become obvious. Think about it for a moment. If your self-talk is full of negativity such as, *"I am no good. I can't do it. I am fed up. I hate my life,"* and so on, then you must be having a pretty bad day. If that self-talk was replaced with, *"I am good. I know I can do it. I am happy. I love life,"* then it is easy to see how much better your day would be.

At Progressive Awareness, we offer an extensive line of products so that you can design your own inner talk training course. While InnerTalk programs are relatively easy to use as you can simply play them in the background as you go about your day, they do not do the *doing* for you. All InnerTalk can do is provide you with a powerful training mechanism to assist you in revealing the *real* you. Since 1984, Progressive Awareness has specialized in providing leading-edge personal coaching tools. We have hundreds of thousands of satisfied customers worldwide, who believe that the InnerTalk personal coaching method has helped them to significantly improve the quality of their lives. Their personal achievements range from improved relationships to the alleviation of sicknesses, from weight loss to parenting skills. While we would love to be able to take credit for transforming their lives, we have to say that the real credit belongs to each and every one of them and the amazing power of their minds.

Create a New You

Wouldn't you like to find out the true powers of your own mind? How far can you go? How high is "up" for you? What could you do if you only but believed? Take a look at the science behind our technology, see how independent researchers tested our technology and demonstrated its efficacy, read the samples of testimonials and then ask yourself if you wish to take responsibility for your own mind. If the answer is yes, then InnerTalk is for you. Decide the area you would like to focus on first, find the title that fits your goals, take a look at the sample affirmations on the program, and ask yourself if this kind of inner talk would help you achieve your goal.

Be specific about what it is you are trying to achieve. For example, most people find that our *Weight Loss Now* program is extremely effective at retraining their self-talk and helping form habits that are more conducive to the goals of losing weight. However, if you already do all the right things, eat properly, drink lots of water, and so on, and still find it hard to lose weight, then maybe you want to focus more specifically on using the powers of your mind to access the mind/body connection, get active, exercise, and speed up your metabolism instead. *Using Metabolism to Melt Fat Away* may therefore be a more appropriate program for you.

The point is—you must take responsibility for what it is you wish to change in yourself and choose your InnerTalk programs accordingly. If you do not have a self-esteem problem, then you will not feel any different when using our *Soaring Self-Esteem* program. If on the other hand, you have a poor self-image and you speak negatively about yourself to yourself, then you should be very happy with the way *Soaring Self-Esteem* works for you. Remember, it is the power of your own mind that does the *doing* for you. InnerTalk simply helps you train your mind to perform at peak efficiency.

The Spiritual Connection

You should also be aware that, due to the large body of scientific evidence in this field, the philosophy of Progressive Awareness promotes the belief in a higher power. We do not make any judgments about your spiritual path and offer no guidance in that area at all. However, a belief in a higher power, whatever you choose to call that higher power, has been shown to help in increasing longevity, health, happiness, and contentment. Many of our programs do therefore refer to a higher power. While the word "God" may be used, it is used in a very general way and in no way tries to promote a specific religious path. It is simply the term well known in the Western world. The subconscious mind is very smart, and it is the belief in a higher power, not the specific name used that gives our programs that extra edge. If you are atheistic, you may prefer not to use our programs. Most other religious groups should have no problem with our programs. However, if there is any question, then simply seek the guidance of your own spiritual leader.

In the same vein, while we offer a number of programs like Weight Loss or Stop Smoking, again, this is not to say that we are promoting these lifestyles. Our goal is very simply to help our customers achieve their own, very personal goals, and if losing weight is important to you, then we have the tools to help you achieve that goal. We should probably make it clear as well that although we have a number of programs that are health-related, our programs do not actually "do" anything, they simply train your own self-talk. It is your mind and its connection with the body that does the "doing." Our programs are in no way a replacement for professional health care and are not a medical device or modality.

So, if you are ready to take responsibility for your own personal growth, if you believe in the power of the mind, if you wish to experience yourself at your own personal best, then InnerTalk is for you.

CHAPTER THIRTY-ONE:

The Missing Element

Why do we even need this InnerTalk technology? There are so many other self-help methods out there, ranging from lectures, seminars, and training courses to music and exercise. None of them, however, deal with the real *you*. The *you* inside that somehow doubts your own ability to do something, or questions your right to be successful, maybe believes that prosperity is a bad thing and on and on. We have all read wonderfully inspirational books, or attended some amazing seminar, or learned some wonderful new technique. At the end of the seminar, or book or whatever, we vow that we will make some changes and thereby be able to hold onto this new *me* who is capable of achieving so much more. And some of us do put these things into practice, at least for a while. But somehow, the old habits come back into play for the best of reasons. We don't have the time to do it, it is not our fault, and there are too many other competing demands on our time. But the best excuses in the world will not help us achieve our real goals.

Self-Sabotage

Unfortunately, there is an aspect within each of us that seems to like sabotaging our best efforts, some element deep within that really believes that there is nothing we can do to improve our lives anyway, so why bother? Maybe somewhere deep within we also believe that we deserve all the problems we have. This is the very inner talk that our InnerTalk technology addresses. The very inner talk that is born from our upbringing, our histories, our successes and failures, the beliefs of our friends and family, and very often from our own misconceptions about why we are treated in certain ways, or why certain things happen to us.

For some of us, this inner talk really can be an expression of our worst opinion about ourselves and the world around us. For most of us, it is not quite that bad, but surely anything that gets in the way of us expressing our greatest potential should be dealt with. Simply telling yourself that you are good, brilliant, capable, a genius, etc. simply does not do it. Think about it. What was your inner talk saying to you as you read that statement? A common response often says, *"Yeah, yeah, who are you trying to kid? I am just little old me. I cannot do great things."* That is not to say that there is not a time and place for verbal affirmations, only that there is a component missing. The very same component that is missing from the very best of self-help books and techniques—the element known as true self-belief.

Real Change

InnerTalk has been created as a personal coaching method for you to practice positive self-talk in such a way that the aspect of you that sabotages your best efforts cannot argue against it. The affirmations appear to be coming from within you; they become a natural part of your own self-talk. InnerTalk programs are relatively easy to use. In most instances, you simply put them on and play them in the background as you go about your day. You may be aware of soft speech in the background, but most of the time you will not hear the actual affirmations, although occasionally some of them may sound more obvious.

InnerTalk is perfect for use on its own or as a complement to any other self-help technique. Simply decide what it is you wish to achieve and find the title with the appropriate affirmations to help you achieve your goal. If you have read a book such as *Think and Grow Rich* and want to put the principles into practice, then work with the InnerTalk program, *Millionaire Orbit.* You will be amazed at how much easier it is to stick to your new resolutions. Regardless of which self-help approach you like to use, using complementary InnerTalk programs will make it exponentially more powerful.

How High Is Up?

But back to the original question: Will InnerTalk make us *perfect?* The answer to that can best be answered by the question, *How high is up?* Most people on the path for self-improvement find that while they begin with one specific goal, when that goal has been achieved, there is yet another goal to achieve. We have customers who have been with us ever since we started producing the patented Whole Brain InnerTalk programs. They all say that InnerTalk has improved the quality of their lives, improved it immensely, but that just makes the whole journey of self-actualization even more fun!

CHAPTER THIRTY-TWO:

The Science Behind InnerTalk®

Research and research contributions regarding the patented "Taylor method," (also known as Whole Brain® InnerTalk® subliminal technology.)

Freedom from Dental Anxiety

Under the direction of Dr. Jose Salvador Hernandez Gonzalez and on behalf of the Department of Social Security for Mexico, twenty-five patients were exposed to both video and audio *Freedom from Dental Anxiety* programs for thirty minutes prior to treatment and thirty minutes during treatment. The conclusion: ". . . the use of InnerTalk before an integral odontological treatment is 100% effective, reducing patients' anxiety and the noise made by the high-speed hand piece used in this type of work, and furthermore, reducing the pain suffered by comparison to previous experience." The report goes on to recommend InnerTalk: "Therefore it is convenient to promote, among dental surgeons, the use of InnerTalk to improve their patients' comfort and achieve a better collaboration to treatments. In the same way, use will change the Estomologist image (feared for so many years)."

Weight Loss

Combining Whole Brain InnerTalk Weight Loss audio and video with Echo-Talk audio and a special nutritional program developed and marketed by Oxyfresh International, Dr. Harbans S. Sraon, a biochemical geneticist) of the University of California at Irvine conducted a ninety-day weight loss study. Dr. Sraon coached each subject to visualize their clear goal in terms of body fitness and reviewed progress weekly. Sraon reported that 90% of the subjects (ten men and fifteen women) lost significant weight.

Stop Smoking

Research carried out under the supervision of Dr. Diaz Lopez at the Instituto Mexicano Del Seguro Social. 75% of the participants stopped smoking.

Joy of School: End Dropout

Under the direction of Maurice P. Shuman, Jr., General Director Special Programs of Instruction, a pilot study was conducted by Duval County Public School System at the Pre-trial Detention Center in Jacksonville, Florida. Twenty-two incarcerated juveniles participated in a study program using Progressive Awareness Research programs designed to assist in preparation for the GED examination. "The GED final test results show that eighteen students passed the full GED examination."

Test Anxiety

Thomas Plant, faculty member of Stanford University and director of the mental health services for the Children's Health Council, together with Michael DiGregorio and Gerdenio Manuel of Santa Clara University, evaluated the effect of Whole Brain on test anxiety in a double-blind experiment. The statistical data indicated significance supporting the hypothesis that Whole Brain subliminal technology could be an effective tool in lowering test anxiety.

ADHD

Kim Roche of Phoenix University studied the effect of Whole Brain with children diagnosed as having attention deficit hyperactive disorder in a double-blind experiment. Her findings indicated a significantly positive effect.

Accelerated Learning

Diana Ashley at the University of Southern California studied the effect of subliminally presented reinforced stimuli on factual material using the Taylor's Mirrored Imaging Processing (MIP) model in a double-blind experiment. Her conclusion found a significant increase in learning among students in the experimental group.

Weight Loss

A study carried out by Professor Pelka of Munich University in Germany on a Whole Brain InnerTalk program for weight loss, showed average weight losses of thirteen pounds in subjects who used the program.

Spiritual Healing for Cancer Remission

The findings from a longitudinal study on the Whole Brain Inner-Talk program for Cancer showed that 43% of the patients who used the program went into remission. For the patients who had passed away, the average life span beyond the original prognosis was significantly extended.

Procrastination, Time Management, Confidence, Stress, Relationships, Assertive, and Esteem

Experimental psychologist Julian Isaacs investigated the effects of the following Whole Brain InnerTalk programs *No More Procrastination, Time Management, Confidence Power, Freedom from Stress, Positive Relationships, I Am Assertive,* and *High Self-Esteem.* After three studies, it was concluded that the programs produced significant positive results that were verifiable.

Decision Making

A double-blind study conducted by Professor Peter Kruse at Bremen University in Germany, using a specially created Whole Brain program, strongly demonstrated the influence of the program on decision making. Kruse said, *"The Taylor Method"* works!

Freedom from Stress

A double-blind study was carried out at Weber State University on the effects of the Whole Brain program *Freedom from Stress.* The psychological test results showed a significant decrease in stress.

Freedom from Depression

In a double-blind study carried out at Colorado State University, it was found that using the Whole Brain InnerTalk program *Freedom from Depression* for more than seventeen hours led to a significant decrease on the Beck Depression scale. This study not only shows the effectiveness of the Whole Brain program, but also indicated that the effectiveness of the programs was dosage-related.

Pre and Post-Operative

Cosmetic surgeon R. Youngblood and surgical staff tested the effect of the Whole Brain program *Pre- and Post-Operative,* on 360 patients. They reported a decrease in anesthetic requirements of 32% by volume as compared to a historical control group.

Self-Esteem

In a double-blind study at the Utah State Prison, which was performed by McCusker, Liston and Taylor, the Whole Brain technology was deemed effective in altering self-esteem among inmates. As a result, the Utah State Prison installed and maintains a voluntary audio library for inmates.

Numerous clinical studies with single and multiple subjects have also found effectiveness with Whole Brain in areas as diverse as anorexia to dyslexia. Additionally, Whole Brain has been credited by professional coaches for significantly contributing to winning sports events ranging from football championships to National and Olympic judo medals.

Listing of Research Papers

Ashley, D. 1993. "The Effect of Subliminally Presented Reinforcing Stimuli on Factual Material." *University of Southern California.*

Galbraith, P. & Barton, B. 1990. "Subliminal Relaxation: Myth or Method." *Weber State University.*

Gonzalez, J.S.H. 1998. Unpublished Report.

Isaacs, J. Unpublished report, 1991.

Kruse, P. et. al. 1991. "Suggestion and Perceptual Instability: Auditory Subliminal Influences." *Bremen University*, Germany.

Pelka, R. "Application of Subliminal Therapy to Overweight Subjects." *Armed Forces University*. Munich, Germany. 1993.

Plante, T.G. at al. 1993. "The Influence of Aerobic Exercise and Relaxation Training on Coping with Test-Taking Anxiety." *Stanford University* and *Santa Clara University*.

Reid, J. 1990. "Free of Depression, Subliminal Tape Study." *Colorado State University*.

Roche, K. 1993. "The Effect of a Whole Brain Subliminal Program on Children Diagnosed with Attention Deficit Hyperactive Disorder." *Phoenix University*.

Sraon, H.S. 1997. "Weight Loss Study Produces Early Success." *Oxygram*, Vol 13, Issue II. Dec. 1997.

Taylor, E. 1990. "The Effect of Subliminal Auditory Stimuli in a Surgical Setting Involving Anesthetic Requirements." *St. John's University.*

Taylor, E., McCusker, C. and Liston, L. 1990. "A Study of the Effects of Subliminal Communication on Inmates at the Utah State Prison." *Subliminal Communication*, 2nd ed. R.K. Books: Medical Lake, WA.

Taylor, E., & McCusker, C. 1995. "The Use of Subliminal Auditory Stimuli in Terminally Ill Oncology Patients." *International Journal of Alternative and Complimentary Medicine*. Feb. 1995.

CHAPTER THIRTY-THREE:

What You Can Expect

When I was in my teens, I decided that I wanted to find a career where I could really help people. I never had any idea that I would end up doing something quite so inspiring. Hearing customer feedback can be so heartwarming and is a large part of the reason why I answer the office phone myself just as much as I can.

How High Is Up?

Sometimes the customers I speak to are brand new to InnerTalk; they come in looking for a solution to a specific problem and then, when I hear back from them, they are so thrilled with the results that they have decided to explore more titles. We have a number of customers like this who have now placed well over twenty orders (some have placed thirty to sixty orders) in just the last year or so. They often tell me that they are so happy with the results that they have to get some programs for their friends and loved ones.

Freedom from Pornography

Most recently I heard from a customer who told me that our *Freedom from Pornography* program saved his life . . . and his marriage. He had been aware that the addiction was wreaking havoc in his life, but until he used the InnerTalk program, he was unable to do anything about it. Now he is just thrilled to be back in control of his life.

Sales Power

Another customer works in sales but had a real fear of rejection. Of course, this severely hampered his sales abilities. He worked with both *Fear of Rejection* and *Powerful Selling and Closing* and was happy to report a significant increase in sales . . . and in his own comfort level.

Some of our customers take the time to write to us and tell us their success stories. Here is just a small sample:

Prosperity and Abundance

For years now, I have been stuck in a rut and getting nothing accomplished in my life. So, I began listening to your *Prosperity and Abundance* subliminal program all day and at night while I was sleeping. The third week into listening I started marketing again and working on my business—working daily and having a routine down, which I felt was difficult to do before and I credit your subliminal for it. Thank you for helping me get my motivation back.

~ J.B.

Survivors of Abuse

I just wanted to let you know that I purchased the *Survivors of Abuse*. I played it, and after maybe three times, I felt somehow different, stronger. I was able to finally verbalize what I expected from the person I was attached to and being mistreated by, and without crying or sinking into depression. It's been transformational for me. I've now gone on to your Accelerated Learning program and found myself having the courage to succeed in believing I could achieve *something* in my life.

I was born naturally gifted in intelligence (skipped several grades till H.S. and graduated early), but growing up in an abusive and unhappy home, somehow my gift diminished, and I lived in poverty with my kids for too many years. God has gifted me with million-dollar creative ideas, but fear of failure kept me bound.

I'm sending you tremendous bear hugs, you and Ravinder both.

Thank you so much for helping me climb back up from a death battle with cancer, memory loss from a concussion, child abuse and domestic violence, and low self-esteem. I will continue to do all that I can to be healed and continue to play your music.

Somehow Ravinder seems to feel what may help me. God bless and keep you both for all the good you are doing.

~ Z

Procrastination

The last two years or so, I have been using some of your programs. I have lost forty pounds and have kept it off for well over a year. I no longer procrastinate, especially with small projects.

Even if I am watching TV and my wife asks me to do something, I get up and do it right then. She will sometimes say, "I didn't expect you to stop watching your program."

I am very happy with the results from these programs because it's easy to see the results. I am seventy-three and sleep most nights with some program playing all night.

~B.B.

Ultra-Success Power

I listen to *Ultra Success Power* on my daily hikes. I noticed immediately I had the energy to move faster and go for longer hikes. I started craving more fruits and vegetables. I also noticed I feel happier. There is a huge difference in my attitude. I listen every day and started to notice a difference within two weeks.

T.T.

Accelerated Healing and Wellbeing

I just listened to *Accelerated Healing* in music while getting acupuncture today. It brought me to such a wonderful place! I love your products!! Thanks again!

~J.

Especially for Actors

I've been using the *Remembering Lines: Especially for Actors* for a couple of weeks now and love it! I was on set last week for a scene and it was so easy and natural! The words just flowed. Thank you!!!

~ Wanda Morgenstern

Freedom from Alcohol

I felt it was only right to send you a positive message. I thank God for Eldon Taylor and what he has done for me. I own several of his InnerTalk mp3s. I usually listen to the subliminal ones because I can listen to them passively during the day. I really appreciate someone like Eldon creating an alternative product like he has. I have spent many years believing in hypnosis and the power of the mind. I bought one of his *Freedom from Alcohol* programs. I have cut down my drinking by more than half. My drinking now is about once a week and not as much consumption. I have also had much better success with my anxiety level after listening to another of his programs. Lastly, I have been listening to his *I Have High Energy* level the past few days and can already tell a difference.

~B.L.

Magic Happens

I will never be able to praise you and Dr. Taylor enough. He has created and continues to create fantastic programs, and the way you describe them, one easily learns from the descriptions what one can do and how a program can easily help one to fine tune themselves. I consider myself fortunate to have learned about Progressive Awareness Research. It has helped me very much!

Every time you make a suggestion to me to get a particular title to overcome something or improve on something, Magic Happens!

~ S.M.

Forever Thin, Fit, and Healthy

I just wanted to thank you for your amazing product! Your *Forever Thin* mp3 immediately changed my terrible eating habits, something I've tried for many, many years to fix.

~ R.E.

Prosperity/Sabotage/Cancer

I just wanted to tell you how much these CDs have helped me and my family over the past three years. I was brought up in a very violent home: mother a sociopath, father an alcoholic. Despite years of therapy, and being drug-, sugar-, carbohydrate-, and alcohol-free, my self-esteem and subsequent depression was still an issue, and it greatly affected my work as a professional artist as well as my health.

I started by getting individual CDs for *Prosperity and Abundance* and noticed a steady improvement in the quality of my art commissions (I am a historical reproduction fine artist); I started getting a few jobs from movie companies and museums as well as from high-end clients. Money started coming in unexpectedly as a direct result of my doing the action to allow it. But best of all, by using your *Eliminating Self-Sabotage* album, my self-esteem improved enough so that I, together with a brother from whom I had been estranged for many years, was able to do an intervention and rescue my special needs sister from my elderly sociopath mother who was using her as her assisted living plan, and get them both placed into appropriate housing.

This same brother was so impressed by the change in me (he is an M.D. BTW) that he and his family have started using your CDs as well, with great success. My husband, who is a cancer survivor with very similar self-esteem issues as I have, has been using them as well, and I have noticed a huge difference in him. There are no words to thank you enough. I have just ordered your *Resolution Solutions* and OZO *Fitness* and am looking forward to using them. I also very much enjoy receiving your inspirational newsletters as well as reading your blog.

Please feel free to publicize this, but kindly withhold my name. Thanks!

~ J.P.

Happy

Been a customer since 1993, and I just can't get enough! ~A.M.

Your Story

As I said, this is just a small sampling of the feedback that we get, and nothing is better than the warm fuzzy feelings we get we hear these stories. We would love to hear your stories too. Please email them to us at innertalk@innertalk.com. Better still, make a video and send that. We'll post it on our site. You can also visit this link for more testimonials: www.innertalk.com/testimonials1.html

PART FOUR

Resource Guide

How to Use This Resource Guide

InnerTalk programs are available in a variety of formats. Decide if you really want to tackle an issue from every perspective and really home in on improving that part of your life and use one of our complete libraries or albums, or if there is a variety of different issues you wish to address.

InnerTalk subliminal affirmations are used it the background of all of our programs, but some people want a more experiential kind of approach. It is for this reason that we created our special use programs, such as OZO, Echo-Tech, Power Imaging, Platinum Plus, and Video Entrainment.

Whatever your goal, choose a format that suits your lifestyle the best.

Complete Packages

Libraries

Our InnerTalk libraries provide a complete course, addressing the many aspects of an issue. When you are determined to succeed in a particular area, find the most appropriate library and immerse yourself in mastering all levels of that issue!

Albums

A small variety of complementary titles to assist you in achieving your goals. Albums generally consist of a number of InnerTalk programs and a few headphone programs.

Collections

Approach the same issue using a variety of technologies: InnerTalk programs to play in the background and headphone programs for whenever you need that additional boost.

Power Sets

Our two-program Power Sets include one headphone-only program (program 1) using tones and frequencies together with fully audible verbal coaching (as with OZO and Echo-Tech) and one InnerTalk program (program 2) using a nature soundtrack. Power Sets get you started with that right now *"I feel it"* response from using program 1 and back it up with our patented and proven thought modification technology to reinforce and sustain the change. Power Sets were created as a result of the vast amount of customer feedback reporting faster results when a headphone program was combined with an InnerTalk subliminal program.

Single Programs

InnerTalk Subliminal Programs

InnerTalk Technology is a patented technology that has been researched by numerous independent universities and institutions and been demonstrated effective at priming how you speak to yourself. InnerTalk is designed in such a way that the change you desire begins from within as a result of changing the way you talk to yourself. As you change that internal chatter from self-doubt and worry to assured confidence and self-composure, you find that your expectations, attitude, and perception also change.

InnerTalk audio programs feature pleasant, easy-listening music or nature sounds that are specially mixed with positive background affirmations on the chosen self-help topic.

InnerTalk programs are extremely easy to use. You simply play them in the background on any regular stereo player while you are working, driving, relaxing, reading, playing sports—even sleeping or watching TV. They can also be used with a personal audio player while jogging, bike riding or any other activity.* No conscious thought or effort is required to produce dramatic—and automatic—results.

InnerTalk programs may work like magic, but they're based on new

---

*Please note: There are some obvious contraindications. You would not play a program such as High Energy while sleeping, or a program such as Sleep Soundly while driving.

scientific discoveries about how we learn and process information—and how this affects our everyday life.

InnerTalk programs tap into our natural human ability to absorb information even when we're not thinking about it. On the surface, the programs sound like any other easy-listening music or nature programs you may have heard . . . but there is a powerful difference. Carefully blended in the background are dynamic affirmations such as *"I feel good," "I am successful,"* etc., that make long-lasting, positive impressions.

While the conscious mind enjoys the pleasant music or nature sounds, the subconscious mind recognizes and receives the powerful, life-changing affirmations.

Results can often be noticed in as little as a few days to a few weeks. InnerTalk technology is so powerful it's patented with the U.S. government, backed by independent studies at leading universities, and proven effective by the hundreds of thousands of satisfied users around the world.

All programs come with a list of the recorded affirmations. We believe you have the right to choose which thoughts to put into your mind.

OZO and Echo-Tech

While the InnerTalk programs are played in the background during regular daily activities, the Echo-Tech and OZO programs are designed for use once a day when there is time to just sit and relax, usually at the end of each day.

Echo-Tech and OZO programs are designed for headphone use only. The programs combine a number of leading-edge sound and music technologies, along with audible verbal coaching, to promote full acceptance of the new you.

As with InnerTalk programs, you'll enjoy the pleasant music or nature sounds while your subconscious mind hears and accepts the positive background/subliminal affirmations.

But the Echo-Tech/OZO experience goes much further. Added are a special mix of three-dimensional sounds, tones, and echo-effects that stimulate positive and highly receptive brain states. We refer to this as *subliminal hypnosis*.

Also featured is an audible narrator who provides powerful verbal coaching. OZO and Echo-Tech differ in that the audible coaching in Echo-Tech is supportive, whereas in OZO it is authoritative. For example, in Echo-Tech the supportive coaching includes suggestions such as *"You can do it. You do have the ability."* Many users report using Echo-Tech for its sense of warmth and love. (If you are just beginning your self-actualization journey, we recommend Echo-Tech for a more supportive and permissive experience.) With OZO, the audible coaching uses positive, directive commands such as, *"Do it now!"* OZO has been called the *afterburner* of self-help programs.

Users report faster results when both of these technologies are combined on the same subject.

The echoing effects and other soothing sounds and tones, along with the three-dimensional sound patterns, help synchronize the left and right hemispheres of the brain, allowing the program to create powerful, long-lasting impressions that will make a big difference in your life!

Use your InnerTalk programs throughout the day, then play your Echo-Tech or OZO programs once a day in the evenings. By combining the methods, you'll receive the maximum benefits of this proven and patented technology!

Power Imaging

This technology combines the InnerTalk subliminal affirmations with a complex, audible, guided imagery program.

For those of you interested in the technical details, Power Imaging does not simply create a scene where you picture yourself succeeding; it assumes an underlying reason for your previous inability to succeed and works at both uncovering the source of the problem and in discovering the solution. This is definitely a voyage of self-discovery.

Power Imaging audio hypnosis programs require forty-five minutes of *eyes-closed* imagery sessions. They are a method of conditioning the mind away from the negative experiences while reinforcing positive experiences. Power Imaging is the best of the tried and tested methods all in one easy-to-use program. All you have to do is sit back, make yourself comfortable, and be guided through simple scenarios that can change your life! Excellent for sleep learning.

Platinum Plus

Our Platinum Plus compact discs are designed for headphone-only use. They have been called a shortcut to the years and years of training normally required in order to obtain states associated with advanced meditation. Platinum Plus provides an experience that will take you to new insights and adventures within. Platinum Plus includes the best of the best of cutting-edge tools. As a quick overview, this series incorporates the following:

- The proven Whole Brain InnerTalk patented subliminal method to insure the best results;
- New PHI ratio generated sound signature to facilitate coherent emotional and brain states. (Recursive Golden Mean geometry);
- Patterned mantra intonations to assist in producing a peaceful state of relaxation and balance. (Ayurvedic addition);
- Neuro matrix sound patterns to entrain brainwave activity bringing it within the optimal learning range. (Alpha brainwave pattern); and
- Direct pathway commands: "I can," "I am," "I will," "I choose," "I have," "I love," "I create," "I enjoy."

Video Entrainment

Our Video Entrainment programs have been described as *"an experience that is indescribable."* They have also been referred to as *"a technology so advanced that its power may not be comprehended even by those that use and love them."* Eldon Taylor simply describes the video series as *"a right use of light and sound.* "What you will see on your television screen is an ever-changing kaleidoscope of colors. Embedded in this color show are visual subliminal messages to support your goals. In the accompanying soundtrack are the InnerTalk subliminal affirmations along with tones and frequencies to get you even more relaxed and open to the positive affirmations. This technology will simply mesmerize you while filling you with a strong sense of wellbeing. You will not only enter an altered state of brainwave activity, but will find yourself so relaxed, at ease and comfortable, that it may be how you both start and end every day. Special note: The video titled *Cardiac Care* was developed by Eldon for patients who were recovering from open-heart surgery.

Please note: Our DVDs come in the NTSC format (the standard used in North America and most of South America). Most other regions require the PAL format. Please check your ability to play the NTSC videos before ordering.

Libraries

Introduction

Our most complete packages for creating deep changes in your life. Approach the issue from every angle and utilize the numerous technologies. When you are committed to change, then success will be yours.

Happiness (The Master Secret: Happiness is Success) ~ Library

~ Uncover the seven fundamentals of the master secret and bring real joy to your life!

There are seven fundamentals to what has been called The Master Secret. This is the secret to happiness; some call it the peace that passeth understanding. Others refer to it as an ecstatic state of joy. It is also known as the doctrine of non-resistance. Whatever the tradition, the state of true happiness is recognized as a state of inner and outer balance, in harmony with ones' self and others around them. Intuitively, most of us are driven, at some point in our lives, to find and express true happiness. However, most believe that success at things brings them happiness when indeed happiness brings success at things.

This library consists of 20 programs, which utilizing four different technologies, and three lectures.

TITLES INCLUDE:

InnerTalk: Confidence Power, Optimism Plus, Forgiving and Letting Go, Powerful Self Esteem, Acceptance is Mastery, Freedom from Co-dependence, Do It Now, and Success is Happiness.

Lectures: Seven Fundamentals of the Master Secret, Owning Your Own Controls, Living in Love with Life, and The Co-Dependent Ego.

Power Imaging: Personal Peace, and Well-Being and Esteem.

Echo-Tech: Have It All, Self Esteem, Without Codependence, and Shed Stress. *OZO:* Joy, Self-Peace, Confidence, and Motivated Now.

innertalk-store.com/products/master_secret_library

Health and Wellness ~ Library
~ Youth, Vigor, Health and Wellness: treasures to be nourished & protected

There is an undeniable connection between the mind and body. Now, you can learn how to empower your mind to directly influence your body. Whether it's a matter of staying youthful, fit and healthy, or recovering from a so-called terminal "dis-ease," the mind is, without a doubt, an important player in the ultimate outcome. Learn how much control you have over your own state of health and how to care for and improve your wellness with proven techniques.

This library is easy to use and to understand. It's much more than ideas and research findings—it's a practical experience with many actual exercises. You get 6 audio programs, one video, one presentation, and a booklet, all designed to train your mind to create your healthiest you! We guarantee you'll find this library more than worth the small investment.

TITLES INCLUDE:
Lectures: Health and Wellness.
OZO: Health and Healing.
Echo-Tech: High Self Esteem.
Power Imaging: Health and Pain Relief.
InnerTalk: Accelerated Healing and Well-Being, Powerful Immune System and Forgiving and Letting Go.
Video Entrainment: Psychoneuroimmunology.

innertalk-store.com/products/health_wellness_library

Mystical Mind: A Path to Mastership ~ Library
~ Hours of exercises and meditations designed to explore and fully awaken mind, body and spirit.

It is said that *"to be a success, you should emulate the successful."* Would it surprise you to know that many of the world's greatest thinkers have followed a path developed from inner knowing or noetic knowledge. Their genius has often been attributed to this knowing followed by a search for the proof. Einstein himself asserted that he dreamed the curvature of space, and then spent the next twenty years trying to prove it. The path of the awakened mind fused with body/spirit intuitiveness simply sees the world differently. The openness to universal life force enables them to access abilities that many believe to be pure fiction.

The path of the awakened mind fused with body/spirit intuitiveness simply sees the world differently. The openness to universal life force enables them to access abilities that many believe to be pure fiction.

Mystical Mind consists of 21 programs, two books, and a workbook—hours of exercises and meditations designed to explore and fully awaken mind, body and spirit—five years in the making and a lifetime of study.

TITLES INCLUDE:

Lectures: Six Talks With Eldon, incorporating numerous meditations and exercises;

Meditations: Wonder and Joy, Golden Orb, Past Lives and Other Dimensions, Out Of Body

Journeys, Visit With A Master, Past Life Meditation, Healing Dream, Astral FQ, Personal Peace, and Bedtime Meditation.

InnerTalk: Aura Awareness, Lucid Dreaming, Spiritual Quotient, Miracle Mindedness, and Serenity.

Bonus CD: Conscious Expansion (Platinum Plus + audible meditation).

TITLES INCLUDE:

Books: Exclusively Fabricated Illusions and Just BE

Workbook: Workbook with exercises

innertalk-store.com/products/mystical_mind_library

---

*"I think that the **Path to Mastership** is the crown
jewel in the InnerTalk line. This should definitely be in
everyone's library. It is the most powerful program and
works so well for the busy lives we all now live."*
—Cristian Enescu, M.D.

Prosperity (Your Personal Best: Prosperity Power) ~ Library — OUR BEST!

~ Rid yourself of self-limiting beliefs with these 28 amazing programs.

Success is planned. To be successful, one must engage their very best skills and abilities. Many say they wish to be successful, but they never act. The tools for success come from inner strengths more than any other thing. Fortunes have been built from nothing more than personal best!

Do your best in every endeavor and success will be yours. This is the perfect tool for those involved in sales, marketing, entrepreneurship and leadership. This greatly enhances your ability to prosper in all that you do. Athletes to millionaires have praised this *Prosperity Power* library. When you're ready, it's the next step.

You get 28 programs with four different technologies to facilitate rapid learning and two lecture programs to instill motivation and success thinking patterns. Learn how the best of the best and do it, day in and day out. Feel the energy as you are guided to become your very best at everything you do! Sense the power of ideas flowing through you as your creative juices are turned on with confidence and a real *"do it now"* attitude.

TITLES INCLUDE:

Lectures: The Inner Game.

Echo-Tech: Self-Esteem and Have It All.

OZO: Soaring Self-Confidence, Motivated Now, Success, Joy and Self-Peace.

Power Imaging: Well Being and Esteem, Creativity, Relax Now and Power Learning and Memory.

InnerTalk: Successful Networking, Confidence, Motivated Now, Unlimited Personal Power, Optimism Plus, I Visualize Successfully, I Am Creative, Freedom from Stress, Prosperity and Abundance, Millionaire Orbit, Money Manager, Time Manager, Goal Power, Have It All and Organized and Efficient.

"I ordered the Prosperity Power program, and in a short time, I found myself able to see a clearer path to the future I will have. Prosperity Power is the most well-rounded set, dealing with all issues from esteem to ultimate prosperity and gently opens those doors that for most people remain forever locked. Also, the staff at PAR are the most knowledgeable, kind, and patient people I've ever dealt with. Eldon Taylor, "God Bless You!"
~ L.A., CA

innertalk-store.com/products/prosperity_power_library

Weight Loss (Turbo Charged Weight Loss) ~ Library

~ Boost your metabolism using the power of your mind, kick up your activity level, learn to enjoy exercise and feel good about your body.

We all know what we are supposed to do to lose weight—eat healthy, exercise, diet, reduce sugar intake, drink more water, etc. But sometimes this is just too hard.

There are many reasons why you may be eating incorrectly—perhaps you were taught to always finish everything on your plate, or you eat when you are tired and stressed, you simply just love the wrong kinds of food, etc. Long-term unhealthy habits can also play their part in making it hard to lose your weight and can bind you to weight gain forever.

This library addresses all the areas related to weight loss including the foods you like to eat, how much activity you enjoy each day, and the mind/body connection. Release your desire for junk food, salt and sugar and learn to enjoy the natural flavors of all the foods that are good for you. Boost your metabolism using the power of your mind, kick up your activity level, learn to enjoy exercise and feel good about your body. This program makes losing weight simple and effortless.

TITLES INCLUDE

Power Imaging: Optimal Weight Loss.

Echo-Tech: Weight Loss, and Stress Free.

OZO: Optimum Weight Loss, and Optimum Fitness

Video Entrainment: Weight Loss

InnerTalk: Weight Loss Now, Using Metabolism to Melt Fat Away, Freedom from Junk Food, Freedom from Sugar, Freedom from Salt, I Like Water, Joy of Exercise, Walking for Health, Firm Body, Forever Thin, Fit and Healthy.

innertalk-store.com/products/turbo-charged-weight-loss-library

Albums

Introduction

A focused way for really homing in on the issue at hand. Approach various facets of the issue and use the different technologies to create the most important changes in your life.

Abuse (Healing from Abuse) ~ Album
~ Set yourself free!

Abuse comes in many forms. Sometimes it's physical and sometimes it's verbal; sometimes it's inflicted upon us and sometimes we inflict it upon ourselves. The long-term damage sometimes caused by abuse can be unspeakable. The feelings of guilt, shame, and/or anger can lead to serious self-destructive behavior. We can lose our ability to trust, to share, to create close relationships, and so much more, to say nothing of delimiting our own worth.

As you use *Healing from Abuse*, you will begin to sense a new expression of freedom—for in letting the abuse and all those associated feelings go, that's exactly what happens—you set yourself free! Free to be yourself, to achieve your highest best and to live life to its fullest.

TITLES INCLUDE

Power Imaging: Personal Peace,

Echo-Tech: Powerful Self Esteem,

OZO: Inner Peace,

InnerTalk: Survivors of Abuse, Healing from Invalidation, Healing the Past, Healing from Grief and Trauma, Healing Emotional Pain, and Releasing Anger.

innertalk-store.com/products/healing_from_abuse_album

Brain Power (Maximizing Brain Power)
~ Reverse cognitive decline, and then move into positive territory and become mentally sharper than ever before!

There are many reasons cognitive abilities can often decline as we age. Stress and ill-health are obvious factors, but there are two other factors that are easy to rectify.

One is of course the belief that we are no longer as smart and sharp as we used to be, and this can quickly become a self-fulfilling prophecy. We think we are incapable of performing a task, so we don't try (or we don't try our hardest) and the next thing we know, we really are not capable anymore!

The second factor can be found in the adage, *"Use it or lose it."* The more ways we can find to use our different cognitive abilities, the sharper our cognitive abilities will become.

Are you ready to, not only reverse some of the cognitive decline that you are aware of, but to also move into positive territory and actually become mentally sharper than before? If so, *Maximizing Brain Power* is the perfect tool. Believe in yourself and start exercising those brain cells!

TITLES INCLUDE

Power Imaging: Creativity is Natural

Echo-Tech: Stress Free

OZO: Inner Peace

InnerTalk (in nature): Genius Power, Accelerated Learning and Study, Powerful Memory, Concentration is Easy, Creative Writing, and Cognitive Enhancement.

innertalk-store.com/products/maximizing-brain-power-album

Child (Gifted Child) ~ Album
~ Give your children the head start they deserve!

Today's children represent tomorrow's future. Bob Keeshan once stated a fact of life, *"Parents are the ultimate role models for children. Every word, movement, and action has an effect. No other person or outside force has a greater influence on a child than the parent."* In the role of parent, you decide what's important to your child. Do you want them to practice good manners, be confident, stress free, have a positive mental attitude, show respect in their relationships, become leaders, learn easily, cooperate with others, and realize their maximum potential?

Children today face many challenges, from family dynamics and peer pressure, to the entertainment industry. All of these things and more can have a negative impact on our children. Use this album as an antidote to today›s pressures and give your child the head-start they deserve.

TITLES INCLUDE

InnerTalk (in nature): Successful Child, I Can: Building a Child's Esteem, Positive Interactions for Young People, Respect and Good Manners, Leadership for Young People, Stress in School, I am Cooperative, Gratitude Attitude, and Positive Mental Attitude.

innertalk-store.com/products/gifted-child-album

Childbirth (Miracle of Childbirth) ~ Album
~ Enhance the wonder of bringing a new life into the world!

Childbirth is a very special event. It begins when you discover your pregnancy. Whether it's your first pregnancy or your tenth, how you deal with your pregnancy largely depends on your state of mind. Pregnancy can be full of worries and concerns or can be a special time in your life when you savor near every moment of it. Bottom line, our mental attitude can make a huge difference in how comfortable your pregnancy is. You're entitled to remember this special event as the truly special lifetime defining event that it is.

You do deserve a happy pregnancy and an incredibly awesome childbirth experience followed by an ever-improving love for life. Give yourself the gift today!

TITLES INCLUDE

Echo-Tech: Stress Free

OZO: Inner Peace

InnerTalk (in nature): Comfortable Pregnancy, Wonder of Childbirth, Releasing Anxiety, Positive Relationships, Natural Pain Relief, Just for Newborns, and Freedom from Maternal Depression.

innertalk-store.com/products/miracle-of-childbirth-album

Esteem (Reclaiming Your Inner Power: Ultimate Self-Esteem) ~ Album

~ Heal those inner wounds today!

How much are old fears, insecurities and feelings of inadequacy holding you back today? Oftentimes, it can seem as though we have been successful at putting a band-aid over old problems and emotional hurts, as we simply get on with life. However, a little trigger here and a minor confrontation there can be all it takes for those feelings of inadequacy to come roaring back.

Now it is time to finally heal those inner wounds and reclaim your inner power.

TITLES INCLUDE

Echo-Tech: Have It All!

OZO: Inner Peace

Power Imaging: Well-Being and Self-Esteem

InnerTalk: Eradicating Inadequacy, Releasing Anxiety, Healing Emotional Pain, Healing from Invalidation, Healing the Past, and Freedom from Worry.

innertalk-store.com/products/ultimate_self_esteem_album

Fit and Healthy ~ Album

~ Release a healthy, fitter you!

It's never too late to change unhealthy habits. With the proper attitude we can find exercise fun and rewarding. With a healthy outlook on life, we can enjoy good nutrition and pass on the fast foods and fattening sweets. With an optimistic attitude we have every right to expect a long healthy life full of smiles and laughter. With an attitude of respect and love toward ourselves, we find our body remains young, fit and healthy! Using this special InnerTalk album, achieving your fitness goals can be both fun and easy!

TITLES INCLUDE

Power Imaging: Weight Loss.

Echo-Tech: Weight Loss.

OZO: Fitness.

InnerTalk: Joy of Exercise, Walking for Health, Posture, Firm Body, Quantum Younging.
Self-Talk: Sports (audible affirmations).

innertalk-store.com/products/fit_and_healthy_album

Fitness (Sports Fitness) ~ Album
~ Unleash the joy of sports to create the fittest you ever!

Athletic activity is a healthy outlet for stress and a great way to keep your body and mind fit. Whether you compete with yourself or others, obtaining the mental edge together with the appropriate attitude can provide advantages both in competition and in the joy one finds in the practice of their sport. Tune up your mind so that you are psychologically ready to practice and perform at your best.

TITLES INCLUDE

Power Imaging: Sports
OZO: Optimum Fitness *and* Excel at Sports
Echo-Tech: Stress Free
InnerTalk: Joy of Exercise, Winning Sports Performance, Self Confidence and Body Building
Self-Talk: Sports (audible affirmations).

innertalk-store.com/products/sports-fitness-album

Income (Maximizing Income Potential) ~ Album
~ Stop waiting for the solutions to your problems—Go out and BE the solution!

What does it take to stand out from the crowd? How can you make sure that you are the one who gets the next promotion, who doesn't get laid off, or gets hired from the huge pool of applicants? Or, if you are self-employed, how can you make sure your business succeeds where many others are failing? For most people maximizing their income potential is challenging when the economic environment is tough. However, if you bring the right mind-set to the game, it can not only be easy, it can be fun!

TITLES INCLUDE:

Power Imaging: Creativity.

Echo-Tech: Stress Free.

OZO: Success.

InnerTalk (in nature): Have It All, Communicator, Finding Employment, Joy of Work, Ending Self-Destructive Patterns, and Leadership.

innertalk-store.com/products/max_income_potential_album

Luck (Becoming Lucky: Attracting and Enhancing Good Luck) ~ Album
~ Luck is preparedness meeting opportunity

Luck can be defined as preparedness meeting opportunity. Good luck seems to be a force that operates in the universe and shapes the destiny of many. Have you ever felt left out when it comes to good luck? Have you ever felt that only bad luck visits your doorstep?

Recognizing luck is something many of us fail to do. As such, we are unable to capitalize on it, or for that matter, simply appreciate it. You deserve luck in everything you do. Expect it—prepare for it—and luck will accompany you throughout your days.

TITLES INCLUDE

Power Imaging: Creativity

Echo-Tech: Have It All!

OZO: Joy

InnerTalk: Have It All, Lucky, Optimism Plus, Miracle Mindedness, Millionaire Orbit and I Believe.

innertalk-store.com/products/becoming-lucky-album

Meditation (Deep Meditation) ~ Album
~ Mediation is the path to unleashing your inner potential!

innertalk-store.com/products/deep-meditation-album

Research has repeated demonstrated the efficacy of meditation for everything from simple relaxation for stress relief to a favored cardiac care practice. Today the meditative arts are used by sports professionals, business people, and lay alike to crystalize their thinking and manifest their goals. Bottom line, whether your objective is health and wellness, enhancing cognitive abilities and increasing memory, spirituality, waking the sixth sense, or the exploration of those hidden powers, meditation is the vehicle of choice. This library will lead you on the path to deeper insights and a more meaningful understanding of yourself and the world around you. As with any journey, you set the destination, but this is your vehicle to the inner exploration that awaits you with this new powerful skill set.

TITLES INCLUDE

Audible Meditations: Answers Through Meditation, Power Meditation, The Healing Dream, and Hyperemperia.

Power Imaging: Personal Peace.

InnerTalk: (in music): The I Am Presence and Contact Meditation.

DVD: Inspirations.

innertalk-store.com/products/deep-meditation-album

Mindfulness (Optimal Mindfulness)
~ Album

~ Quiet the mind and accept yourself!

Mindfulness is strictly a mental state achieved by focusing one's awareness on the present moment, while calmly acknowledging and accepting one's feelings, thoughts, and bodily sensations. Everywhere a person turns today they hear more and more about mindfulness. Your health care professional encourages you to practice mindfulness for blood pressure, cardiac care, stress levels, relaxation, releasing anger, improving relationships, and so forth. This library was created specifically to facilitate you in accessing the many advantages you gain from a mindfulness practice. Mindfulness is a matter of a mental skill set and attitude. Why not begin your daily mindfulness practice today?

TITLES INCLUDE

OZO: Inner Peace, and Boundless Joy.

InnerTalk (in music): Contact Meditation.

InnerTalk (in nature): Cultivating Mindfulness, Living in Now, I Believe, Self-Control, Joyous Day and Positive Mental Attitude.

innertalk-store.com/products/optimal-mindfulness-album

Money (Wealth, Money, and Prosperity) ~ Album

~ Imagine the good you could do if money was not a problem.

This album was created using the knowledge that the ultra-successful have accumulated in their path to riches. Every program in the set contains important elements necessary to achieving the riches you desire and to do so in ways that honor you and everyone you interact with.

Some people believe riches are evil and further, that the rich can never enter the kingdom we know as heaven. This is the language of those too fearful to become rich. Imagine the good you can do if money was not a problem. Think about all the good that men like Bill Gates and Warren Buffet have accomplished.

If you doubt your abilities to succeed, then remember this quote by Bill Gates, *"If you are born poor it's not your mistake, but if you die poor it's your mistake."* Don't wait any longer to begin to create your own destiny.

TITLES INCLUDE

Echo-Tech: Have it All!

OZO: Success.

Power Imaging: Creativity is Natural.

InnerTalk: Prosperity and Abundance, Ultra Prosperity, Millionaire Orbit, Money Management, Manifesting Your Vision, and I Visualize Successfully.

innertalk-store.com/products/wealth-money-and-prosperity-album

Relationships (Positive Relationships) ~ Album

~ Create positive, mutually beneficial relationships wherever you go!

Regardless of the kind of relationship, life is simply a lot more fun when our interactions are honest, open, and respectful. We are all a lot happier when we feel that we are being heard, and when we feel inspired and charismatic as opposed to just plain boring!

If you wish to have ideal relationships, then you need to take responsibility for them. You need to cultivate an attitude that is free of codependence, communicate effectively, listen carefully and release the fear of rejection (as this is one of the surest ways to bring you rejection). You need to bring honesty to relationships if you expect to be treated with honesty, and you need to believe in yourself!

When you become the kind of person you would like to have a relationship with, then you will find that all of your relationships begin to follow the same pattern.

TITLES INCLUDE

Echo-Tech: Ending Codependent Patterns

OZO: Personal Peace

InnerTalk: Listening, Communication, Ending Codependent Patterns, Positive Relationships, Releasing the Fear of Rejection, I am Charismatic, Honesty.

innertalk-store.com/products/positive_relationships_album

Resolution Solutions ~ Album

~ If we are programmed to 'fail,' how can we expect anything else?

Why is it so easy to fail at our resolutions? What happens to that firm resolve we have in the beginning, to finally make the changes we desire in our lives? Do we decide we really do not want the changes after all . . . or is there something else at play here?

The problem lies in our sub-conscious, or rather in the way we allow our subconscious to be programmed. New research shows that approximately 90% of our decisions are made in the subconscious and as much as 10 seconds before we consciously 'make' that decision! So, if we are programmed to 'fail,' how can we expect anything else?

Use this album to replace the negative, self-destructive internal dialog with a new script—one that leads to a shift in self-belief, which in turn, allows for the success that has previously eluded you.

TITLES INCLUDE

OZO: End Procrastination and Self-Confidence.

Echo-Tech: Ending Self-Destructive Patterns.

InnerTalk: End Procrastination, Impulse Control, Enthusiastic and Motivated, Positive Mental Attitude, Goal Power, and Power of Intention.

innertalk-store.com/products/resolution_solution_album

Sales (Super Sales Power) ~ Album
~ Unleash the super salesperson within!

Regardless of the field of work you are in, sales is an important component. Being an effective sales person is a real art and requires sincerity, enthusiasm, knowledge and confidence. Even if you do not sell products of services, there are still plenty of times that you will need to sell yourself or your ideas, even if it is just at a PTA meeting or Home Owners Association!

Learn not only how to enjoy being a sales person, but become the best sales person you can be.

TITLES INCLUDE

OZO: No More Procrastination

Echo-Tech: Esteem

InnerTalk: Just for Closers, Networking for Sales, Telephone Sales, Powerful Selling and Closing, Strategic Planning and Peak Performance, and Doing My Best with Pride.

Video Entrainment: Powerful Salesperson.

innertalk-store.com/products/sales-power-album

Self-Sabotage (Eliminating Self-Sabotage) ~ Album
~ What could you achieve if you finally got out of your own way?

Self-sabotage occurs when our subconscious mind clings to an old defense mechanism that was designed to protect us from some kind of hurt and applies it to a situation where it is no longer appropriate. These patterns of behavior can cause us to fail in our goals despite our very best efforts. Self-sabotage can affect all areas of our lives, including weight loss, relationships, addictions, employment, time management, academics and more.

This album is designed to neutralize that inner saboteur, helping you to align your inner goals of protection and self-preservation, with your outer goals of success! With this album, you can finally re-script your inner child, release anger, heal from feelings of invalidation, discover your inner self-confidence, become joyful, find your inner peace and learn that you really do deserve to have it all!

TITLES INCLUDE

Echo-Tech: Ending Self-Destructive Patterns

OZO: Boundless Joy

Power Imaging: Personal Peace

InnerTalk: Ending Self-Destructive Patterns, Healing from Invalidation, Re-scripting the Child Within, Releasing Anger, Confidence, and Have It All!

innertalk-store.com/products/eliminating_self_sabotage_album

Smart and Sharp ~ Album

~ Make learning both fun and easy!

How would you like to do something that will enable you to live longer, happier, and healthier while boosting your brainpower so that you could learn faster and easier at the same time? While this may sound like two totally different subjects, the two areas are actually very closely inter-twined—the more you exercise your brain, the more you open yourself up to new experiences, the more challenges you take up, the happier and longer you will live.

Learning and education are not things only the young need to be concerned about? Most of us are also aware that we too have learning and memory issues at certain times. Whether this is due to our current stress load or is something we attribute to the aging process, there is no deny-ing the fact that most of us wish we could eliminate these kinds of issues.

Life just is not fun when we find it difficult just to keep up—learning really does appear to be on ongoing process! And with Smart and Sharp, learning can be both fun and easy!

TITLES INCLUDE

Power Imaging: Power Learning and Memory.

Echo-Tech: Learn Easily.

OZO: Accelerated Learning.

InnerTalk: Powerful Memory, Mathematics is Easy, I Am A Great Reader, Word Power: Spelling and Vocabulary, Concentration, Awaken the Genius.

innertalk-store.com/products/smart_and_sharp_album

Spiritual Connectedness ~ Album

~ Experience the awesome power of spiritual connectedness!

Mankind has an innate spiritual intelligence, and the development or awakening of this intelligence has both social consequences and individual health benefits. Affirmations that appeal to a higher sense of being, a supreme purpose to creation, the beauty and miraculous nature of life itself, can produce remarkable outcomes.

Spiritual Connectedness affirmations, regardless of when they are applied, can directly influence the way in which we view a problem. When we view a problem through a connected lens, the problem not only diminishes, but can disappear altogether. By priming our self-talk with connectedness affirmations, we can awaken our spiritual quotient and it will empower our innate spiritual intelligence.

By increasing our innate spiritual intelligence, we can experience greater creativity; develop abstract reasoning abilities; maintain a more stable emotional state; and enjoy healthier and longer lives.

TITLES INCLUDE

InnerTalk (in music): Metaphysical Oneness, Opening Up to a Higher Power, Love, Light and Life, Contact Meditation.

InnerTalk (in nature): Humble and Powerful, Expecting A Miracle, Centering, Power of the Spirit.

innertalk-store.com/products/spiritual_connectedness_album

Stress (Eliminating Stress: Experiencing Joy) ~ Album

~ Make your days joyful, regardless of the pressures you are under.

We all experience stress at some point—and for most of us this can happen all too frequently. Between work pressures and deadlines, personal relationships and family members, and health and time restraints, there are plenty of places to find stress! However, stress does not need to control you. Use the InnerTalk subliminal programs in this collection and watch as the stress just melts away. Play them on auto-repeat in the background while you are at work, while relaxing at home, and even all night while you sleep. Then use the headphone programs whenever you feel you need an extra boost.

Make your days joyful, regardless of the pressures you are under. Your mood will benefit, as will your health and your productivity. And it will even benefit those around you!

TITLES INCLUDE

Power Imaging: Personal Peace.

Echo-Tech: Stress Free.

OZO: Boundless Joy.

InnerTalk: Releasing Anxiety: Discovering Self Peace, Freedom from Fears, Serenity, Optimism Plus, Joyous Day and Freedom from Stress!

innertalk-store.com/products/eliminating-stress-album

Success (Essential Pillars of Success) ~ Album

~ The vital mental strength required to achieve any goal!

There are certain character traits that must be in place if you are to experience success, regardless of the goal. You must believe in yourself, believe that you deserve, be motivated, be physically well, have a sense of optimism, eliminate stress, refine and implement your strategies, have a clear vision and then allow the prosperity to flow to you. For all of this, you need the *Essential Pillars of Success.*

TITLES INCLUDE

Power Imaging: Esteem.

Echo-Tech: Have It All!

OZO: Motivation.

InnerTalk (in nature): Freedom from Stress, Prosperity and Abundance, Be Well Stay Happy, Strategic Planning and Peak Performance, Manifesting Your Vision, and Optimism Plus.

innertalk-store.com/products/pillars_of_success_album

> *"I have bought your **Pillars of Success** and I love it!*
> *It has really helped me to focus in on my dreams and*
> *make them into a reality. I believe GOD brought these*
> *programs to my attention and I use them every day to*
> *further my success. Thank-you!"*

Thinking (Creative Thinking) ~ Album
~ It takes only one idea to change your life!

Creativity—the ability to think outside the box—is a necessary skill, whether you're working on your next artistic masterpiece or diligently searching for a new and exciting marketing approach. This special album was designed with you in mind and were paired for their ability to infuse creativity into every area of your life.

It only takes one idea to change the world; one idea to build a fortune; one idea to end conflict; and one idea to change your life! Creativity spawns everything from harmony to prosperity.

TITLES INCLUDE

Platinum Plus: Creativity, and Hyperemperia.

Power Imaging: Creativity is Natural.

Video Entrainment: Creative Genius.

InnerTalk: Infinitely Creative, Breakthrough Thinking, Creative Writing, and Empowering Intuition.

innertalk-store.com/products/creative_thinking_album

Weight Loss (Active Lifestyle for Weight Loss) ~ Album
~ The simple way to control your weight and tone your body!

According to Marketdata Enterprises, Americans spend more than $60 billion annually on weight loss products such as exercise equipment, gym memberships, joining weight loss programs, special foods and shakes, and supplements. So why is weight loss still such a big issue? It's quite simple really—none of these techniques address the real cause of your weight problem.

Becoming more active is the best way to lose weight and improve your health, but it can be really hard to create the habits necessary. Using this album, you can train your mind to *want* to exercise and eat correctly—the complete program for addressing all the activity aspects of losing weight. Use the power of your mind to help you lose weight. Enjoy eating the correct foods. Fire up your enthusiasm to get active, get fit and lose weight. Exercise does not have to be a chore.

TITLES INCLUDE

Power Imaging: Optimal Weight Loss

Echo-Tech: Weight Loss, and Stress Free

OZO: Optimum Weight Loss, and Optimum Fitness

InnerTalk: Weight Loss Now, Joy of Exercise and Being Fit, Walking for Health, and Firm Body.

innertalk-store.com/products/active-lifestyle-for-weight-loss-album

Weight Loss (Healthy Eating for Weight Loss) ~ Album

~ Release the need for unhealthy eating!

There are many reasons why you may be eating incorrectly—perhaps you were taught to always finish everything on your plate, or you eat when you are tired and stressed, you simply just love the wrong kinds of food, or you use food to assuage anxiety, etc. Long-term unhealthy habits can also play their part in making it hard to lose your weight and can bind you to weight gain forever. Unless you address the thinking/subconscious programming that sabotages your weight loss goals, success will just never happen.

This is the complete program for addressing all the dietary aspects of losing weight. Release your desire for junk food, salt and sugar and learn to enjoy the natural flavors of all the foods that are good for you.

TITLES INCLUDE

Power Imaging: Optimal Weight Loss.

Echo-Tech: Weight Loss.

OZO: Optimum Weight Loss.

InnerTalk: Weight Loss Now, Using Metabolism to Melt Fat Away, Freedom from Junk Food, Freedom from Sugar, Freedom from Salt, and Forever Thin, Fit and Healthy.

innertalk-store.com/products/healthy-eating-for-weight-loss-album

Writing Dreams (Fulfilling My Writing Dreams) ~ Album

**~ "Any writer worth his salt writes to please himself."
– Harper Lee**

Many people today dream about becoming a best-selling author. Many more think about writing their memoir, if for no other reason than to leave their story to their family and loved ones. Still others journal, sometimes recording their dreams, and sometimes putting down the significant aspects of their daily lives. The fact is, research has demonstrated how therapeutic writing can be, both for our psychological wellbeing and our physical health.

Taking a few minutes every day to write is a well-kept secret that can lead to health and joy. It can assist in bringing balance into your life while fueling your creative juices. Writing can be a path for transformation for self and society.

You too can realize the release, the ecstasy, the pure sense of creating, and all the other benefits that come from writing!

TITLES INCLUDE

Echo-Tech: Powerful Esteem.

OZO: End Procrastination.

Power Imaging: Creativity is Natural.

InnerTalk: I am a Writer, Creative Writing, Releasing Mental Blocks, Using Both Halves of the Brain, Unleashing Curiosity, and Word Power: Spelling and Vocabulary.

innertalk-store.com/products/fulfilling-my-writing-dreams-album

Young (Forever Young) ~ Album
~ You really can remain forever young!

Up until relatively recently, most people equated getting older with loss of health, mobility, flexibility, brain power etc. But now we know that most of this is simply influenced by our attitudes. Fact is, if we think that turning 50 (or 60 or 70) means looking and feeling a certain way, then we are more likely to achieve this. If on the other hand, we see the aging process as just another notch on the calendar while we continue living life to the full, then once again that is what we are likely to experience.

TITLES INCLUDE

Platinum Plus: Fountain of Youth, On Fire with a Passion for Life

Video Entrainment: Quantum Younging.

OZO: Health and Healing, Boundless Joy

InnerTalk (in nature format): Quantum Younging, Ultra Success Power: Health, Wealth and the Fountain of Youth, Accepting Change, and Memory.

innertalk-store.com/products/forever_young_album

Collections

Introduction

Approach the same issue using a variety of technologies: InnerTalk programs to play in the background and headphone programs for whenever you need that additional boost. While the use of these additional technologies invariably means that the programs require dedicated time for their use, they also provide a 'right now' result. Each of these collections consists of four different programs, targeting a specific issue.

Titles Available

Cigarettes (Forever Free of Cigarettes) ~ Collection

~ You really can stop smoking and be happy in the process!

If you truly wish to stop smoking, but have found it too difficult, this collection may just hold the key. InnerTalk affirmations change the thinking patterns which have you reaching for the next cigarette; audible coaching both support your efforts and encourage you, while a special guided imagery program helps you discover the real reasons behind your habit.

TITLES INCLUDE:

InnerTalk: Stop Smoking.
OZO: Stop Smoking.
Echo Tech: Stop Smoking.
Power Imaging: Stop Smoking Forever.

innertalk-store.com/products/forever_free_of_cigarettes_collection

Esteem (Soaring Self-Esteem) ~ Collection

~ Life is better when you like yourself!

A strong sense of self-esteem instructs us that we are good, capable and deserving. It is this inner cheerleader that informs us we can succeed, that lifts our confidence and presses the persevere button when needed.

TITLES INCLUDE:

InnerTalk: Esteem.

Power Imaging: Esteem.

OZO: Self Peace.

Echo-Tech: Esteem.

innertalk-store.com/products/esteem_collection

Learning is Fun-damental ~ Collection

~ Learning really can be fun and easy!

Give yourself or someone you love the gift of learning. A good education is the key to so many opportunities, why not maximize all of your abilities. Learn quickly and easily with the tools which have helped many people achieve their goals.

TITLES INCLUDE:

InnerTalk: Accelerated Learning.

Power Imaging: Accelerated Learning.

Echo Tech: Learn Easily.

OZO: Accelerated Learning

innertalk-store.com/products/learning_is_fundamental_collection

Loneliness (Overcoming Loneliness) ~ Collection

~ Connect with yourself and others on a more emotional level.

Feelings of loneliness are not only caused by a lack of social connections, and it is perfectly possible to feel lonely even while you are in a crowd or surrounded by family and friends. The solution to loneliness therefore does not simply entail being with other people but finding ways to connect with yourself and others on a more emotional level.

TITLES INCLUDE:

InnerTalk: Resolving Feelings of Loneliness and Isolation.
Echo Tech: End Co-Dependent Patterns.
OZO: Inner Peace.
Power Imaging: Well-Being and Esteem.

innertalk-store.com/products/overcoming-loneliness-collection

Loving Relationship ~ Collection

Bring the magic spark to your personal relationship.

With the fast pace of today's life-style, finding and maintaining a loving relationship can be difficult. Enhance your relationship, whether you have been with your partner for years or you are just starting out, communicate well with the opposite sex, and believe in yourself so that your relationship can be built on a very strong foundation.

TITLES INCLUDE:

InnerTalk: Enhancing Romance, Intimacy and Love, *and* Confidence with the Opposite Sex.
Echo-Tech: Co-dependent No More.
OZO: Personal Peace.

innertalk-store.com/products/loving_relationships_collection

Pain Management and Relief ~ Collection

~ Relax and release the pain!

When you really need help controlling pain, try this collection. Put the awesome powers of the mind to work for you, not against you! It is well known that the sensation of pain is significantly reduced when fear and tension are gone.

TITLES INCLUDE:

InnerTalk: Natural Pain Relief.
OZO: Health and Healing.
Power Imaging: Pain Relief and Health Imaging *and* Personal Peace.

innertalk-store.com/products/pain_management_and_relief_collection

Relaxation (Deep Relaxation) ~ Collection
~ Release all tension pressure . . . and r e l a x!

The ultimate in relaxation training. Use this collection of technologies and learn to let go of all the tension and pressure from the day and stop things from building up and out of control.

TITLES INCLUDE:

Power Imaging: Relax Now *and* Personal Peace.

Echo-Tech: Stress Free.

InnerTalk: Relaxation.

innertalk-store.com/products/deep_relaxation_collection

Sales (Powerful Sales) ~ Collection
~ Selling is natural and easy!

Selling yourself is a required skill—no matter what your vocation. Selling is natural and easy. Build the confidence and acquire the skills to be the best salesperson—without 'high-pressure' and other tasteless techniques.

TITLES INCLUDE:

OZO: Success *and* Motivated Now.

InnerTalk: Selling and Closing *and* Networking for Sales.

innertalk-store.com/products/sales_collection

Sleep (Peaceful Sleep) ~ Collection
~ Wake up feeling refreshed and ready to go!

Nothing puts a bigger damper on the day when it is preceded by a bad night's sleep. End bad dreams, sleep more soundly and enjoy some serenity with this wonderful collection.

TITLES INCLUDE:

InnerTalk: Peaceful Sleep *and* Ending Bad Dreams.

Power Imaging: Relax *and* Personal Peace.

innertalk-store.com/products/sleep_collection

Speaking (Public Speaking) ~ Collection

~ Public speaking really can be fun!

Clear your mind of the negative feelings you have towards speaking in public. The carefully scripted affirmations will help you speak with confidence, poise, clarity, and enable you to be persuasive and comfortable in your speech.

TITLES INCLUDE:

InnerTalk: I am a Communicator *and* Performance Anxiety.
Echo Tech: Esteem.
OZO: Confidence.

innertalk-store.com/products/public_speaking_collection

Sports (Optimum Sports) ~ Collection

~ Train your mind to win!

The perfect collection of programs to have you more disciplined, regardless of which sport you play. All serious athletes understand that training the mind is as important as training the body.

TITLES INCLUDE:

InnerTalk: Winning Sports Performance.
OZO: Optimum Fitness and Excel at Sports.
Power Imaging: Sports Hypnosis.

innertalk-store.com/products/sports_collection

Stress Management ~ Collection

~ Reinterpret your stressors and experience much less stress and anxiety.

Relieve stress and achieve a state of calm and well-being. Regardless of how much you need to get done, you will achieve more when you tackle the task in a calm, relaxed, stress-free manner.

TITLES INCLUDE:
InnerTalk: Serenity.
Power Imaging: Anxiety and Stress.
OZO: Peace.
Echo Tech: Stress Free.

innertalk-store.com/products/stress_management_collection

Substance Abuse (Overcoming Substance Abuse) ~ Collection

~ Believe you can be free of drugs . . . and you will be!

A huge part of overcoming a chemical addiction is the belief that you can actually do it. Change your thinking and the process will become easier.

TITLES INCLUDE:
InnerTalk: Freedom from Substance Abuse, *and* Impulse Control.
Echo-Tech: End Co-Dependent Patterns.
OZO: Peace.

innertalk-store.com/products/substance_abuse_collection

Success ~ Collection

~ The ultimate in success and motivation management conditioning.

For the elite few who are committed to Success! Manage information overload and stress, increase productivity, enhance creativity, instill soaring confidence, be motivated and prosperous.

TITLES INCLUDE:
InnerTalk: Ultra Success Power.
Echo Tech: Have It All.
OZO: Soaring Self-Confidence *and* Success.

innertalk-store.com/products/success_collection

Weight Loss (Maximum Weight Loss) ~ Collection

~ Make losing weight simple and effortless

innertalk-store.com/products/maximum_weight_loss

Use this powerful combination of programs to reach your weight loss goal even faster.

TITLES INCLUDE:

InnerTalk: Weight Loss.

Echo-Tech: Weight Loss.

OZO: Weight Loss.

Power Imaging: Weight Loss.

innertalk-store.com/products/weight_loss_collection

Sets

Titles Available

Child Guidance Series ~ Audible/Subliminal

~ Learning was never this much fun!

All the programs in this wonderful series use the patented InnerTalk subliminal technology behind audible stories, adventures and fantasies. The affirmations are self-esteem builders and, while the audible stories are tutorial, learning was never this much fun!

TITLES INCLUDE

Audible Stories: Why? Leadership and Wise Choices, and Miracle of Life
InnerTalk (in nature): I Can: Building a Child's Esteem.

innertalk-store.com/products/child_guidance_set

Exams (Learning for Examinations) ~ Subliminal Set

~ Maximize your learning abilities for exams!

Sharpen those skills you need in order to perform your best in exams.

TITLES INCLUDE:

Program One*: InnerTalk* (in nature): Concentration *and* Excel in Exams
Program Two: InnerTalk (in nature): Advanced Memory Skills *and* Accelerated Learning and Study.

innertalk-store.com/products/learning_for_examinations_set

Fighting Power ~ Subliminal Set

~ This program WILL produce the fighting intent within you

This dual InnerTalk subliminal set for Wing Chun was created in collaboration with Master Ron Heimberger. This makes learning the art easier than ever before. Internal Power helps produce a flexible, relaxed strength called "spring energy" within the student listening. Fighting Power is for serious martial artists only!

TITLES INCLUDE:

InnerTalk (in music): Fighting Power I Internal Power

innertalk-store.com/products/fighting_power_set

Love (Attract Your Perfect Partner) ~ Set

~ Allow your perfect love relationship to come in!

Spend a little time changing your own thoughts about yourself and your chances of a relationship and then step out of the way so your perfect love relationship can come in!

TITLES INCLUDE:

InnerTalk (in nature): Attracting the Right Love Relationship, Releasing the Fear of Rejection, I Listen Intently *and* Magnetic Personality.

innertalk-store.com/products/your_perfect_partner_set

Love (Enhancing Your Love Relationship) ~ Set

~ Bring back the magic in your relationship.

Bring back the magic in your relationship. Rekindle those warm feelings of love, respect and companionship. Relight the fire of passion. Listen and be heard. Let your own personality shine.

TITLES INCLUDE

InnerTalk (in nature): Enhancing Romance, Intimacy and Love, Intimacy and Relationships, I Listen Intently *and* I Am Charismatic.

innertalk-store.com/products/enhance_the_romance_set

Psalms 23 and 91 ~ Subliminal Set

~ A special two CD set with both Psalm 23 and Psalm 91.

Taken from the King James version of The Bible.

TITLES INCLUDE:

InnerTalk (in music): Psalm 91

InnerTalk (in nature): Psalm 23

innertalk-store.com/products/psalms_23_and_91_set

Sixth Sense (Developing the Sixth Sense) ~ Subliminal Set

~ Developing Psychic Abilities

innertalk-store.com/products/developing_the_sixth_sense
According to the world's most studied Psychic, Ingo Swann, awakening this latent power is a matter of remembering our senses and changing our beliefs.

TITLES INCLUDE:

InnerTalk (in music): Awakening *and* Using the Force.

InnerTalk (in nature): Developing Psychic Abilities.

innertalk-store.com/products/developing_the_sixth_sense_set

Subliminal

Success

For our most complete success-related packages, please see:

Prosperity (Your Personal Best: Prosperity Power) ~ Library

    innertalk-store.com/products/prosperity_power_library

Income (Maximizing Income Potential) ~ Album

    innertalk-store.com/products/max_income_potential_album

Money (Wealth, Money, and Prosperity) ~ Album

    innertalk-store.com/products/wealth-money-and-prosperity-album

Resolution Solutions ~ Album

    innertalk-store.com/products/resolution_solution_album

Sales (Super Sales Power) ~ Album

    innertalk-store.com/products/sales-power-album

Success (Essential Pillars of Success) ~ Album

    innertalk-store.com/products/pillars_of_success_album

Thinking (Creative Thinking) ~ Album

    innertalk-store.com/products/creative_thinking_album

Writing Dreams (Fulfilling My Writing Dreams) ~ Album

innertalk-store.com/products/fulfilling-my-writing-dreams-album

Sales (Powerful Sales) ~ Collection

innertalk-store.com/products/sales_collection

Speaking (Public Speaking) ~ Collection

innertalk-store.com/products/public_speaking_collection

Success ~ Collection

innertalk-store.com/products/success_collection

Confidence (Strong Confidence) ~ Power Set

innertalk-store.com/products/strong_confidence-ps

Motivated ~ Power Set

innertalk-store.com/products/motivated_ps

Procrastination (End Procrastination) ~ Power Set

innertalk-store.com/products/end_procrastination_ps

Success Power ~ Power Set

innertalk-store.com/products/success_power_ps

Actors (Remembering Lines: Especially for Actors) ~ Subliminal

~ Take the stress out of learning lines!

Remembering lines can sometimes be very challenging. If you have any fears of apprehensions that you will not learn the lines in time, then you have just made the task even harder.

In addition to learning the script, how an actor learns it can directly influence the quality of their performance. When you learn them and how you practice them, the context you place them in, and more all enter into the performance package.

When you know that learning lines is easy and employ all your strategies to commit the lines to memory, then the task can become easy and fun!

"I read my script over and over again. I practice my lines. I get into my character. I find my lines are natural to my character. My lines become what I would have said as the character. I imagine every scene vividly. I practice my lines with emotion. I feel myself as my character in every scene. I embody the character in my mind and emotions. My lines come effortlessly to me. I move when practicing my lines. I am animated when practicing lines. I use space as though I was in every scene when practicing my lines," etc.

innertalk-store.com/products/remembering-lines

Assertive (I Am Assertive) ~ Subliminal

~ You really can express yourself and set comfortable boundaries—without coming off as aggressive!

Do you have difficulty getting others to take your opinions seriously? Do you ever doubt the validity of your own perspective? Do you have problems setting boundaries? The ability to be straight forward, upfront, and convincing is a skill. It is a skill that includes the appropriate level of assertiveness, sometimes referred to as the iron hand in the velvet glove. You have the right to expect to be able to express yourself and to set comfortable boundaries and you can do this without coming off as aggressive. When you are appropriately assertive, you will also find it easier to obtain all that you deserve.

"I am confident. I am whole. I am enough. I make my own choices. I choose wisely. I trust myself. I have self-esteem. I like myself. I am good. I am capable. I am powerful. I am eternal. I am loved. I am truthful. I am assertive. I have positive relationships. I am positive. I choose. I choose confidently. I assert myself. I am loving. I am honest. I am assertive. Assertiveness is natural. I am pleasantly assertive," etc.

innertalk-store.com/products/assertive

Best (My Best with Pride) ~ Subliminal

~If a job is worth doing, it is worth doing well!

The fact is, we all tend to let down from time to time, but as Edward Albert put it, *"Let us begin by doing our best to do our best, every single time, no matter what, forever."* Doing your best is taking the effort to add that extra little something, even just 1% more, to what you have done in the past. As such, doing your best is all about doing better and better. Leaving the ruts behind, committed to ever improving—that is doing your best!

It matters not whether you're a student, a plumber, an attorney, doing your best always yields rewards. Not just the praise and influence it builds with others, but honestly earned self-esteem.

"If a job is worth doing, it is worth doing well" is a saying most of us are familiar with. Bring your best to all of your efforts and see for yourself how much easier it is to achieve your goals. You may be surprised at how good this makes you feel about yourself.

"I am good. I am a gift from the Creator of all. I am blessed. All that I am is a gift. All that I do with what I am is my gift back to the Creator. I do my best. I take pride in all that I do. In all that I do, I do my best. I am grateful for all. I demonstrate my gratitude by doing my very best. Waste not—want not. I use my talents wisely. I use my best abilities in all that I do. I know that if it is worth doing, it is worth doing right. My best improves. Every day in every way I improve. I am patient with myself and others. I practice my talents when appropriate. I improve daily," etc.

innertalk-store.com/products/my_best_with_pride

Burnout (Freedom from Burnout) ~ Subliminal

~ Bring joy and passion back to your work!

Life is simply too busy. We all have so much to do! Oftentimes, our responsibilities can involve lots of repetitive work, and it is easy to just feel burned out. Unfortunately, suffering burnout does not relieve you from your responsibilities. You still have to face the fact that tasks need to be completed, whether you *want* to do them or not. But there is a solution. You really can bring joy and passion back to your task. Make your responsibilities fun and feel rewarded at the end of each day. Rekindle your excitement for your job and learn to have fun again while you work. Change the thinking that has you dreading your work into thinking that makes your work joyful. As a result, you will find work easier and quicker to do.

"I enjoy myself. I enjoy my profession. I am in control of myself. I enjoy challenges. I do what I can do. I am accepting. I enjoy humor. I love life. I love living. I am okay. I am good. I treat myself well. I respect myself. I remain balanced. I am happy. I enjoy my activities. I am successful. I am detached from pressure. I am detached from outcome. I am detached from stress. I experience positive. I focus on the positive. I image positive. I treat others with respect. I am balanced," etc.

innertalk-store.com/products/freedom_from_burnout

Closing Sales (Just for Closers) ~ Subliminal

~ Remove the pressure and make closing sales easy!

Closing a sale takes a special kind of ability. Many sales people are great at presenting the product, but they just don't have the confidence to finish the job. This program was created for those professional closers and salespeople who wish to be the best closers in their organization. A good closer can pick up from a poor presentation made by another salesperson and lead the customer quickly to a close. Is this the kind of salesperson you want to be? If it is, this program was designed for you.

When you believe in yourself, when you know you have done a good job, when the customer's like you, then closing sales become easy!

"I sell easily. I close sales easily. I close sales effortlessly. I am confident at selling. I genuinely help my customers. My customers find me genuine. I am a natural salesperson. I am natural at selling. I am natural at closing sales. I achieve my sales target easily. I am charismatic. Customers are attracted to me. I am passionate about selling. I love selling. I am good at selling. I attract success. I am successful. I attract wealth. Selling is fun. Selling is natural. I am comfortable at closing sales. I am good at selling. I am natural at selling. I attract customers easily. My customer base grows every day. I find it very easy to close sales," etc.

innertalk-store.com/products/just-for-closers

Communicator (I Am A Communicator) ~ Subliminal

~ You really can minimize and eliminate the anxiety attached to public speaking!

Many polls have shown that public speaking is the number one most feared event that people may face in their lives. This fear inhibits performance as a result and can manifest itself in the presentation by way of lost lines, forgotten material, elevated perspiration, and more. Yet in order to be successful, there will come a time when one must get up in front of people and make a presentation.

This program is designed to minimize and eliminate the anxiety attached to public speaking. You can become a dynamic, persuasive communicator and foster open communication from others by becoming a receptive listener at the same time.

"I am confident. I speak well. I am liked. I like living. Communication is fun. My thoughts flow freely. My speech communicates. I am relaxed. I am at ease. I listen. Speaking is fun. Speaking is sharing. I like sharing. I am positive. I am self-assured. I am good. I like myself. I love life. Life is sharing. Speech is natural," etc.

innertalk-store.com/products/communicator

Also Available In:

Speaking (Public Speaking) ~ Collection

innertalk-store.com/products/public_speaking_collection

Confidence (Soaring Self Confidence) ~ Subliminal

~ You can never be your best until you believe in yourself.

Many people lack the confidence to undertake everything from a new challenge on the job to meeting and mixing with a new group of people. The lack of confidence can be related to a variety of life experiences ranging from acquiring new skills to learning in general. Confidence comes not just from knowing what you're good at but from that unshakable belief in yourself and your ability to learn or master a new skill.

If you have ever felt like you needed a real confidence boost—then this program is for you! Use the program to create the new ultimate you. Project confidence and success. Yes, you can do it.

"I feel good about myself. I exude sincerity and confidence. I am capable. I am positive. I can do it. I am relaxed. I am peaceful. I am confident. I look great. I feel great. I am happy. I like people. I am liked by people. I am calm. I act decisively. I am thoughtful. I am unafraid. I do my best. I do it with confidence," etc.

innertalk-store.com/products/soaring_self_confidence

Also Available In:

Confidence (Soaring Self-Confidence) ~ OZO

innertalk-store.com/products/soaring_self_confidence_ozo

Confidence (Strong Confidence) ~ Power Set

innertalk-store.com/products/strong_confidence-ps

Creative (Infinitely Creative) ~ Subliminal

~ One creative idea can change your life for the better.

You do not need to be a creative artist such as writer, painter, musician and the like to enjoy and benefit from the power in creativity. Even those among us not involved in the creative arts need creativity to develop new ideas and insights needed to advance our lives.

It only takes on good idea to change the world. Creativity is the source of all those great ideas. One creative idea can change your life for the better. Whether a matter of prosperity or a solution to a problem, accessing the reservoir of creative juices within is a natural way to improve your life.

"I am creative. I am imaginative. I consider alternatives. I see solutions. I feel solutions. I sense solutions. Creativity is natural. Creativity is fun. Creativity is exciting. I like creativity. My imagination is powerful. I relax. I channel inspiration. I breathe deeply. I am confident. I succeed. I apply myself. I can do anything. I image. I see clear mental pictures. I see details. I see vivid mental images. I solve problems," etc.

innertalk-store.com/products/infinitely_creative

---

*"I listened to your **Creativity** program and prayed to allow the messages to be absorbed into my subconscious. Three months later, I was in Washington, D.C. presenting my paintings to the President and being honored. It was a dream come true. Thank you."*

Also Available In:

Creativity (I am Creative) ~ Platinum Plus

innertalk-store.com/products/creativity_pp

Creativity is Natural ~ Power Imaging/Hypnosis

innertalk-store.com/products/creativity_is_natural_pi

Disciplined (Self Disciplined and Determined) ~ Subliminal

~ Don't let life's trials side-track you from achieving your goals.

Vince Lombardi once said, *"The difference between winning and losing is quitting."* History teaches us that great men and women are their best through continued self-discipline and dogged determination.

Whatever your goal or ambition, to succeed you will need that mind set which carries with it the energy and ambition to persist, the discipline to remain doggedly determined about your success, and the belief in yourself that you can and will do it!

Don't let life's little trials sidetrack you from achieving your goals. Obstacles are opportunities there to overcome. Many confident and competent people miss their goal because they simply quit too soon. You're not destined to be one who quits five minutes before the miracle. You deserve to win!

"I am motivated. I am a doer. I do it now. I have will power. I apply myself. I apply my energies. I organize my efforts. I plan my day. I set goals. I achieve my goals. I am in control. I accept responsibility. I am responsible for myself. I am confident. I am stress free. I am enthusiastic. I am capable. I use time wisely. I enjoy self-discipline. I am self-disciplined," etc.

innertalk-store.com/products/self_disciplined_and_determined

Employment (Finding the Right Employment) ~ Subliminal

~ When you have the right attitude, potential employers will love you!

What happens when we grab that first job offer often leads to unhappiness. If you're going to be happy in the work force, you must first do something you enjoy and that you can feel good about at the end of the day. In other words, finding the right employment begins within yourself. It is therefore critical that you believe in yourself, your abilities and talents, and possess the confidence to project both during the interview process.

There are many forms of preparation appropriate before undertaking a job application and interview, and they are easily found on the Internet. What you can't find on the Internet is the needed mindset for both the selection of your perfect employment, and for the presentation of yourself during the process of earning the position you are seeking.

When you have the right attitude, potential employers will love you. Obtaining that perfect fit where your employment is satisfying and rewarding is something you deserve.

"It's easy to find employment. It's easy to find the right employment. I know what I enjoy. I know what I am good at. I enjoy life. I love working. I love achieving. It's easy to project my very best. It's easy to do my best. It's easy to be confident. It's easy to be interviewed. I interview well. I am poised and confident. I am ambitious and prepared. I sincerely want the best for my employer. My employer's best interest is my best interest. I am grateful for work. I am enthusiastic about my employment. I act and find employment now. I take my best attitude and win the job. I enjoy employment. I enjoy

associations. I look forward to each day. I look forward to every day. I expect good," etc.

innertalk-store.com/products/finding_employment

Enthusiastic and Motivated ~ Subliminal

~ Life just has a special sparkle when you are feeling enthusiastic and motivated.

Enthusiasm is contagious and is the fuel of nearly every successful endeavor. Life is full of opportunities and when we seize them enthusiastically, our success is almost guaranteed. Every day we meet opportunities, sometimes in our workplace, sometimes in our homes, often just by chance—how do you meet those moments? Enthusiasm gets things done!

The old ho-hum attitude leads to ho-hum results. As Aldous Huxley once remarked, "The secret of genius is to carry the spirit of the child into old age, which means never losing your enthusiasm." It matters not what you undertake, when you do so with enthusiasm your efforts are easier, and the outcome is improved. Life just has a special sparkle when you are feeling enthusiastic and motivated.

"I am positive. I am enthusiastic. I am motivated. I do. I do it now. I decide. I trust my decisions. I act. I follow through. I feel great. I love life. I think positively. I think enthusiastically. I make things happen. I am a doer. I can do anything. I am lucky. I enjoy my efforts. I act enthusiastically. I set goals. I follow the steps to my goals. I am an achiever," etc.

innertalk-store.com/products/enthusiastic_and_motivated

Also Available In:

Motivation (Maximum Motivation) ~ OZO

innertalk-store.com/products/maximum_motivation_ozo

Motivated ~ Power Set

innertalk-store.com/products/motivated_ps

Entrepreneur (Accessing the Entrepreneur Within) ~ Subliminal

~ Innovation often drive the prosperity of the future.

There are many rewards to becoming an entrepreneur including autonomy, purpose, flexibility, legacy, and of course, financial rewards. To be successful though you must truly believe in yourself and your ideas. You must become almost single minded about your goals. It takes tenacity, courage, long hours and hard work—and all of this begins and ends in the mind. You may have to learn new skills, take on challenges that test your conviction, sacrifice weekends and holidays, and more.

The mental edge is what every entrepreneur needs and InnerTalk is here to provide the technology for just that. Remove nagging fears and doubt, harness the real power of your mind, focus on your goals, and innovate your way to the success you deserve,

"I am ambitious. I am daring. I am willing to work hard. I am willing to be dedicated to my success. I feel the pioneering spirit within. I hear the sound of success. I am worthy of success. I accept my worthiness. I am an entrepreneur. I am willing to study. I am willing to make a detailed plan. I am willing to listen to others. I am willing to invest in my ambition. I accept the entrepreneur spirit. I study. I make a plan. I invest my time and money in my ambition. I am confident. I am courageous. I am honest. My integrity is impeccable," etc.

innertalk-store.com/products/accessing_the_entrepreneur_within

Failure (Eliminating the Fear of Failure) ~ Subliminal

~ Many people refuse to even try for fear that they will fail!

One of the biggest blocks to achieving success is the fear of failure. When someone is afraid of failing, they can expend a lot of time, energy, and focus on being afraid of what will happen if they fail. Does failure mean the end of opportunities? Does it mean losing someone's respect, or maybe losing respect for yourself? What would happen if you turned this thinking around—if you put all your energy into succeeding, and could look at the possibility of failure as a way to learn how to succeed the next time?

Don't let the fear of failure hold you back and prevent you from even trying, or maybe even starting in the first place. The most successful people have a trail of failures behind them. They did not allow the fear of failure to hold them back. They held on to their dreams, held the vision of success, and moved forwards. Are you ready to move forwards yourself?

"I believe in myself. I believe in my worthiness. I believe I deserve success. I know I deserve success. I know I can succeed. I deserve to succeed. I always do my best. I support myself. I believe in myself. I believe in my abilities. I am confident in myself and my destined success. I am calm and at peace with myself. I am at peace with the world around me. I am happy. I am grateful. I have many opportunities. I take advantage of my opportunities. I am focused. I am ready to succeed. I accept that I will succeed. I prepare to succeed. I practice my success. I visualize my success. I know I will be successful. I am confident of my certain success," etc.

innertalk-store.com/products/fear-of-failure-subliminal

Goal Power ~ Subliminal

~ Goal setting is the first step toward success.

It's been said that setting a goal is the first step in turning the invisible into the visible. It's also been argued that failing to set a goal is like setting out to sea and allowing the winds and current to take you wherever.

Successful people will tell you that realizing a goal is all about your mind set. You must be prepared to invest in your goal with your energy, but you must get that energy from your mental commitment. If you wear down mentally—you'll typically abandon your goal. To realize a truly worthwhile goal, you must believe in yourself and your abilities. The mind sets the body in action. It takes action, not just dreaming, to be successful.

"I set goals. I crystallize my thinking. My goals are realistic. My goals are meaningful. I apply myself. I apply my best. I succeed. I accomplish my goals. I am confident. I am positive. Goal setting is fun. Goal setting is the first step towards realization. I realize my goals. My thought power is strong. Thought is the greatest force in the Universe. My thoughts are clear. I see my success. I see the achievement of my goals. I am achieving. I am a winner. I

am a self-generating force. Thought is the fabric of reality. My reality is great. I create my reality. My goals aid the creating of my reality. I focus. I sense success," etc.

innertalk-store.com/products/goal_power

Icon (Building Your Personal Icon: Finding Your Path in Life) ~ Subliminal

~ Improve your life by remaking your personality

Today, science insists that one of the best ways to improve your life is to remake your personality. Imagine doing just that, consciously choosing the characteristics you desire and then incorporating them into your very own personality.

If you were to take the best characteristics of those people you truly admire and would like to model yourself after, the icons of their fields, put those characteristics together in yourself, would you have created a personal icon so strong that you became those things? This program is designed to help you build the personal icon that is who you are capable of being.

"I have unique gifts. I have special talents. I can be me better than anyone. I can do many things well. I am aware of my gifts. I am aware of my abilities. I list my talents. I list my likes. What I like to do I do very well. I like to do many things. I focus my thoughts. I focus my energy. I can do many things. I choose to do my best at what I do. I choose to do what I enjoy doing. I admire others. I admire the gifts and abilities of others. I choose the aspects of those I admire and emulate them. I build an inner Icon of me as I really am. I build a perfect Icon of me at my best," etc.

innertalk-store.com/products/personal_icon

Also Available In:

Icon (Building Your Personal Icon: Finding Your Path in Life) ~ Platinum Plus

innertalk-store.com/products/personal_icon_pp

Intention (Power of Intention) ~ Subliminal

~ Decide on the intention that will guide your life plan!

A plan begins with an intention. Have you decided on the intention that will guide your life plan yet? Success is a journey, not a destiny, as is life itself. Success follows the path of intention. Success of all kinds, whether business, relationships, spirituality, and all else—all follow a clear intention. It's as if intention itself cannot or will not be manifest until and unless we make it known at least to ourselves. There is some evidence to suggest that the simple act of setting an intention actually leads to manifesting the opportunity to fulfill the intention.

"My mind is powerful. My thoughts are powerful. I can focus my thoughts. I can energize my thoughts. I can emotionalize my thoughts. I choose when to empower my thoughts with creative force. I cancel thoughts I do not like. I cancel thoughts I do not wish to create. I empower only good thoughts to create. My creative thoughts are empowered by deliberate intention. I focus intention in my creative thoughts. Load my creative thoughts with emotion and energy. I empower my thoughts with intention, emotion and energy. It's easy to concentrate those thoughts with which I choose to create. I empower my chosen thoughts with the force of good," etc.

innertalk-store.com/products/power_of_intention

Intuition (Empowering Intuition) ~ Subliminal

~ Einstein reported that his greatest discoveries came from intuition received while in an altered state.

Intuition combines intellect with imagination, conscious and subconscious considerations, in a way that transcends the sum of the parts. Our intuition is an internal guidance system. Lives have been saved, health issues resolved, creative breakthroughs discovered, and so much more as a matter of listening to our intuition. **Einstein reported that his greatest discoveries came from intuition received while in an altered state.**

"Intuition is natural. Intuition is wise. I trust my intuitions. I relax. I become still. I listen to my intuitions. I decide quickly. I trust my decisions. I feel my intuition. My intuition perceives. I have insights. I am creative.

I trust. I am confident. I am rational. I trust my first impression. I sense my impressions. I am wise. I integrate reason and intuition into wisdom. My judgement is keen. I solve problems. Problems are opportunities to be solved. I make wise choices. I think and feel my decisions. I am a child of the universe. I have spiritual gifts," etc.

innertalk-store.com/products/empowering_intuition

Leader (I Am A Leader) ~ Subliminal

~ Enhance and improve your leadership skills today.

Dwight D. Eisenhower defined leadership this way, "Leadership is the art of getting someone else to do something you want done because he wants to do it." It's often said that leaders are born, but the truth is, leadership is a skill to be developed and honed.

Leaders are inspiring—they set goals, establish visions, motivate followers, and continually strive to improve their own leadership skill set. Great leaders achieve success because they work hard. In John Maxwell's words, "A leader is one who knows the way, goes the way, and shows the way. Ultimately, leadership is not about glorious crowning acts. It's about keeping your team focused on a goal and motivated to do their best to achieve it, especially when the stakes are high and the consequences really matter." Enhance and improve your leadership skills today.

"I am in charge. I am a good follower. Leaders listen. Leaders are fair. Leaders are just. I am a leader. I lead wisely. I am a great leader. I like leading. I am capable. Leadership is natural. I am confident. I am comfortable. I make wise decisions. I breathe deeply. I deliberate carefully. I remain calm. I deliberate quickly," etc.

innertalk-store.com/products/leadership

Mental Blocks (Releasing Mental Blocks) ~ Subliminal

~ Clear the clutter out of your mind. Allow the answers to flow in.

Most of us experience mental blocks of some kind or another. Perhaps it is a particular name that we can never remember, or maybe it is an entire field of study. Sometimes it's our creativity that is blocked. We have all experienced this troublesome issue at some time in our lives. When you think you cannot remember something, then chances are you won't. When you don't believe that you can find a solution to a problem, then you won't.

Mental blocks are often the result of self-doubt, indecision, stress, and uncertainty. Retraining your inner dialogue, that stream of consciousness that informs you of your uncertainty, reminds you of the accompanying stress, and so forth, is necessary to removing mental blocks.

"I enjoy creativity. I enjoy problem solving. I enjoy research. I prepare well. I am mentally tough. I think clearly. I move through mental blocks easily. My mind is sharp and alert. I am productive. I love productivity. I truly enjoy being productive. I love learning. I enjoy new knowledge. I enjoy reading. Life is wonderful. I love life. I evaluate ideas. I love creative ideas. I follow through. I enjoy my life. I am grateful. I have a gratitude attitude. My mind accesses memories easily. My mind is clear. My thoughts are clear. Remembering comes easily to me. I like remembering. I enjoy connecting the dots. Mental blocks dissolve. I see clearly. I see easily. I remember new information easily. I like making the effort to remember," etc.

innertalk-store.com/products/releasing-mental-blocks-subliminal

Millionaire Orbit ~ Subliminal

~ You can't create abundance in your life until you believe you can.

Are you ready for abundance in all things—financial, personal, career, etc. Are you prepared? Do you really want it? You can't create it until you think you can. The universe does not discriminate in providing abundance. Only your self-limiting beliefs hold you back from that which you truly desire. You are worthy. Your wealth does not limit the supply of abundance available for any other being. Go for it! There is enough for all.

"I am a winner. Living is winning. I am infinitely alive. I am infinitely adaptable. I am one with the universe. The light of the universe is life. I have infinite power. Universal power flows through me. Universal thought flows through me. Ideas are mine. Creativity is mine. I attract success. Love and abundance are mine now. I am helpful. I am generous. I radiate love. I am a gift from the universal. I live to the glory of the universal. My mind is the

universal mind. I have many talents. I use my talents. I like living. I like creating. I like working. I succeed," etc.

innertalk-store.com/products/millionaire_orbit

MLM (Living the MLM Dream) ~ Platinum Plus

~ Energy in its potential!

Please note: This title is only available in the Platinum Plus format. It is being included in the Subliminal-Success section just for completeness.

The program was created specifically for the MLM industry and many have reported outstanding great success. Indeed, some MLM creators provide copies of the program to their sales force. As with every form of sales, a good salesperson exemplifies product knowledge, enthusiasm, and sincerity. They are proud of their vocation and the product they represent. They care about their customer and network their associations to build new contacts, leads, and sales. All of this effort begins as a mental conviction—energy in its potential, and this program is designed to facilitate just that.

"I network my relationships. I share my goals and vision. I help others by sharing. I help others by teaching. I assist others while earning and learning. I introduce everyone to my down-line. I am confident. I am a great speaker. I am good on the phone. I am good in person. I offer advantages. I offer benefits. I offer others freedom. I create my own freedom. I create the best downline. I create from my vision. I have a vision. My vision is strong and powerful. I have the vision of super success. My vision is unstoppable. I am unstoppable. I can do it. I can visualize success," etc.

innertalk-store.com/products/living_the_mlm_dream_pp

Money Management ~ Subliminal

~ Build a secure future for you and your loved ones!

Money is a representation of your energy. In a sense, it is literally stored energy. You work hard for what you earn but for many, there is nothing to show for their efforts when those monthly bills are met. And yet, we all know the importance of saving and investing wisely. The art of money management begins by recognizing that you want your stored energy to continue to work for you, not disappear into things we typically forget about in a very short time.

This program is all about motivating you to use your money wisely. It will encourage you to save for, as the saying goes, a penny saved is a penny earned. It will also provoke the initiative to manage your debts effectively, eliminating interest payments that make others wealthy. You will discover new strategies to save as opportunity presents itself and in so doing, you will begin to build a secure future for you and your loved ones.

"I am energy. I am responsible. I am thrifty. I use energy wisely. I make wise decisions. I am calm. I am stress free. I am whole. I am enough. I am relaxed. I am in control. I am self-responsible. I create my future. I am patient. I am honest. I am happy. I am confident. I am capable. I am respected. I respect myself. I respect all others. I am prosperous. I create my success. I appreciate my success. I have many blessings. Money is good. I save regularly," etc.

innertalk-store.com/products/money_management

Musicians (Especially for Musicians) ~ Subliminal

~ Music makes you smarter, happier and more productive!

Music affects the brain in many positive ways. It makes you smarter, happier and more productive at any age. Listening is good, playing is even better. There are many more inherent gains that come as a result of music, and you may not be aware of all of the advantages or care, you just love music and performing it. This program was specifically created to both enhance your experience as a musician and sharpen your skill set. Today is a great day to add a whole new dimension to your performance ability, make practice and performing much more fun, and motivate your overall skill development.

"I can improvise effortlessly. I have a great stage presence. I play with great confidence. I love my work. I'm getting better and better at playing every day. I can easily find other healthy musicians to work with. I can get into any band that I want. I choose a fun, healthy, creative band with great music and great members. I am intelligent. I can learn any new song quick and easy. I have a great memory. I create new music effortlessly. I am very

talented. I love to practice. I look forward to practicing daily. I find new connections in the music business easily," etc.

innertalk-store.com/products/especially_for_musicians

Organized and Efficient ~ Subliminal

~ When you are organized, life just proceeds more efficiently!

Is it time to unclutter your life? Is it time to become more efficient? Does it seem like you're going in circles sometimes, getting little or nothing done? If you'd like to relax, release some stress, find more time for recreation or simply enjoying your family, then it's time to get organized and in the process become more efficient.

Watch your competence seem to magically rise as your organizational skills begin maximizing your output today with this program. When you are organized, life just proceeds more efficiently. Freedom is one click away.

"I am great. I am confident. I am certain. I am self-assured. I am enthusiastic. I am motivated. I am relaxed. I perform well. I perform relaxed. I am efficient. I am enthusiastic. I am organized. I am thoughtful. I am deliberate," etc.

innertalk-store.com/products/organized_and_efficient

Performance Anxiety (Freedom from Performance Anxiety) ~ Subliminal

~ Turn fear into the fuel that energizes your performance today!

Performance anxiety is typically caused by negative thoughts about one's ability to perform well. While many assume that performance anxiety is relatively rare, it's actually one of the most commonly reported symptoms among all social fears. It takes on many colors. Performance anxiety can be attached to everything from public speaking and theatrical endeavors to sexual performance.

Our mental fears can seriously hold us back from the life we deserve. Using InnerTalk, you can enjoy your passion for creativity in whatever form and do so confidently with all eyes on you. You really can gain the confidence to deliver your finest performances and using this powerful program will facilitate your success!

"I am a great performer. I am liked. I am appreciated. I appreciate my talents. I am very talented. I like myself. I am comfortable with myself. I like my body. I look terrific. I feel good. I like to perform. I love audiences. I am calm and relaxed. I enjoy working the audience. I enjoy performing. It's easy for me. It's easy to be calm and relaxed. It's easy to be free of tension or nervousness. It's easy to excel. I excel. I am a great performer," etc.

innertalk-store.com/products/eliminating_performance_anxiety

Performing (Peak Performance for The Performing Arts) ~ Subliminal

~ Now it is time to put on your best performance ever!

Stage fright or performance anxiety is common among performers of all ages and in all areas of performance. Learning to excel under pressure is a mental skill set that all performers require if they are to be truly successful. This skill begins with confidence and that confidence is partially the result of hard work, practice—practice made perfect.

All of this begins with our intention to perform at our very best and once again the mental training comes into play. This program is designed to facilitate your success by assisting in the mental conditioning necessary to maximize your opportunities. Now it is time to put on your best performance ever. You deserve the very best—why not give yourself the mental edge and begin using this program today!

"I am relaxed when I perform. I am confident. I am poised. I perform well. I practice my performances. I steadily improve in every way every day. I am comfortable performing. I prepare well. My peers recognize me as an outstanding performer. My audiences love me. I play to my audience. I enjoy pleasing my audience. I enjoy their cheers. I love the support of my fans. I am warm and personable as a human being. I remain humble. I am grateful. I love to perform. I love being in front of an audience. I am grateful for each

opportunity to share my talents. I am continually improving. I seek only my very best in every performance. I am sincere. I am genuine," etc.

innertalk-store.com/products/performing_arts

Planning (Strategic Planning and Peak Performance) ~ Subliminal

~ Set a goal. Devise a plan. Make it happen!

Every coach out there will inform you that first step in achieving a goal is making a plan. Once you have your goal, then devising a strategy by which you will achieve that goal is essential. Often the best approach is to design the steps necessary to realize your ambition, and then set about accomplishing them one at a time. On the other hand, we can have a goal and our plan, but then we postpone action—procrastinate. Peak performance is always an essential element is manifesting your ambition in its highest best form.

If you're an executive or a person on your way up, if you own your own business, if you are in sales, if you invest in the market, if you are concerned about bringing any plan to successful fruition, then this program is for you. If you just need to get something done, to achieve a particular goal, complete a task you have been avoiding, then this program is invaluable! Begin today by making things happen.

"I can make a plan. I can evaluate the options. I can optimize my performance. I can be prepared. I can consider alternatives. I can accept guidance. I can be open minded. I can be motivated. I choose to make a plan. I choose to consider the possibilities. I choose to evaluate alternatives. I choose to develop a strategy for success. I choose to be thorough. I choose to listen. I choose to be a peak performer. I choose to excel. I choose my best. I choose to improve. I will always choose to improve. I will always choose to learn. I will always make a plan. I will always do my best. I will always improve in every way every day. I will always stay informed. I will always keep up with new information. I create my future. I choose to create the best future. I create my opportunities. I create preparedness in myself," etc.

innertalk-store.com/products/strategic_planning_and_peak_performance

Power (Unlimited Personal Power) ~ Subliminal

~ When you are feeling empowered, your life can be great!

Psychology Today addresses personal power this way, "Personal power is based on strength, confidence, and competence that individuals gradually acquire in the course of their development. It is self-assertion, and a natural, healthy striving for love, satisfaction and meaning in one's interpersonal world. This type of power represents a movement toward self-realization and transcendent goals in life; its primary aim is mastery of self, not others."

Within you is a giant. This program taps your inner resources and unleashes incredible feelings of self-confidence and mastery.

"I accept myself. I accept my creation as a miracle. I am a miracle. I was created perfectly. I accept the perfection. I accept the gift. I accept the power. I am powerful. I am a leader. I am an example. I can do anything. I know I am gifted and creative. I expect good. I expect greatness. I allow creativity. I accept inspiration. Success is mine. I sense opportunities. I seize opportunities. I trust myself. I am good to myself," etc.

innertalk-store.com/products/personal_power

Practice (Power of Practice) ~ Subliminal

~ Decide how good you want to be and go to work becoming just that.

If you want to improve in anything, practice is the proven method. Why? Practice actually rewires your brain. The more we do something the more brain itself develops patterns to facilitate and enhance the doing.

This program was designed to instill a mind-set determined to practice—to practice regularly, to incorporate practice into your life as part and parcel of your routine. We know that practice makes perfect. Make the process of practicing easy, effortless and productive.

"Practice improves me. I like to practice. Practice perfects my skills. I practice my skills daily. I do my best. I rehearse my skills by practicing. Practice improves me. I am good and getting even better. I improve in every way every day. Regular practice is good for me. I enjoy practicing. I enjoy improving. I enjoy perfecting my skills. I love what practice does for me. I

simply love practicing. Every day I improve. Every day I practice. I balance my practice times with the rest of my life. I choose to use my time wisely. I am alert to ways and methods for improvement," etc.

innertalk-store.com/products/power_of_practice

Procrastination (End Procrastination) ~ Subliminal

~ Enjoy a sense of pride instead of making excuses.

Just as you may wish to engage some hot energy fuel by becoming highly motivated, you may also experience the companion to an absence of motivation. That companion is procrastination. Many can be enthusiastic and motivated but still find ways to procrastinate. You probably have known those that talk a great story—but fail to realize the content of their vision. This program was demonstrated effective in a clinical study. Look forward to completion and accomplishment.

"I decide. I decide now. I act. I act decisively. I have energy. I am energetic. I use my energy. I am positive. I am involved. I am motivated. I am a doer. I do it now. I am an agent of action. I am a mover. I make things happen. I like myself. I am confident. I calculate carefully. I am aware. I make decisions. I put action into my decisions," etc.

innertalk-store.com/products/ending_procrastination

Also Available In:

Procrastination (End Procrastination) ~ Power Set

innertalk-store.com/products/end_procrastination_ps

Procrastination (End Procrastination) ~ OZO

innertalk-store.com/products/end_procrastination_ozo

Prosperity and Abundance ~ Subliminal

~ Get out of your own way so that financial success can come to you!

Prosperity and Abundance will help you eliminate the fears that cause you to sabotage your own success. It will remove the subconscious beliefs that are keeping prosperity away, such as '**Money is the source of**

all evil,' '*Rich people are all crooks,*' or '***I'm always messing things up, what says this time won't be any different?***' This program will help you realize that there are always new chances and endless opportunities to achieve success. You will be prepared and courageous to open yourself up to your higher power and opportunities will flow to you. Appreciate the things you already have and create a vibe that makes it easier to attract prosperity and abundance today! Let go of the negative mental programming that prevents you from experiencing prosperity. Abundance is naturally yours!

"I am prosperous. I appreciate my success. I have many blessings. I focus on my blessings. I become a magnet attracting prosperity. Prosperity is attracted to me. Abundance and prosperity flow to me now. I naturally receive. I deserve prosperity. I invest my time. I work hard. My energy is stored in money. I use money in good ways. I know abundance exists throughout nature. I am a child of the universe. Abundance is naturally mine. I am already successful. I realize my prosperity. My mind magnetically attracts prosperity. I hold prosperous thoughts. I visualize my prosperous reality. I deserve money. I deserve success. I have more money. I am a magnet attracting prosperity," etc.

innertalk-store.com/products/prosperity_and_abundance

---

*"I have had amazing success with the **Prosperity** program. On the days that I listen to it on my way to work, my stock portfolios go up in value. Sounds crazy, I know, but this happens predictably and consistently. At first, I dismissed this as dumb luck, but after months and months this phenomenon continues like clockwork virtually every time I listen to it."*

Also Available In:

Success Power ~ OZO

innertalk-store.com/products/success_ozo

Success Power ~ Power Set

innertalk-store.com/products/success_power

Prosperity (Ultra Prosperity) ~ Subliminal

~ For the achiever who wishes to achieve even more!

You are doing well. You appreciate your successes and now you wish a more total focus on wealth building, a limitless expectation, a concentrated focus, an ever-alert readiness to capitalize on opportunities and more. Wealth building is all about timing and confidence. Is it time for you to step out of the crowd and distinguish yourself as the wealth builder that you are? If it is, act now!

"I can make a million dollars. I can choose to become a millionaire. I choose to be a millionaire. I choose to make money. I will always choose to be a winner. I will always succeed. I love money. I love success. I love what can be done with money. Money is stored energy. I use my energy to generate money. I create success. I create money. I create abundance. I enjoy money. Generating wealth is easy. Making money is easy for me. I have the power to earn millions. I have more and more wealth coming every day. I am a winner. Living is winning. I am infinitely alive," etc.

innertalk-store.com/products/ultra_prosperity

Real Estate (Successful Career in Real Estate) ~ Subliminal

~ For real success, learn to sell with caring, concern and integrity.

Real Estate Pros know that their business is quite unique among sales professionals. Buying and selling a home is much more than a sale, it involves a special kind of caring, listening, a genuine concern for the client, a sense of fairness and a deep commitment to integrity. The real estate business is very competitive. Learn to stand out in the crowd, get the deals and close the sales.

"I love the real estate business. I eagerly anticipate every day. I am enthused. I enjoy talking with people. I enjoy making telephone calls. I enjoy taking phone calls. I love to share my presentation with others. I am consistent and persistent. I am motivated. I help people. I am charismatic. I have charm. I close sales. I listen well. I use what I hear to close sales. I adapt my presentation to my customer's needs. I provide a valuable service. I am

proud of my profession. I enjoy selling. I am resilient. I know my product and services. I have a powerful memory. I remember everything I need whenever I need it. I remember details. I remember customers. I am a powerful communicator. I speak clearly. I choose my words. I speak with authority," etc.

innertalk-store.com/products/successful_career_in_real_estate

Sales (Networking for Sales) ~ Subliminal

~ Quid pro quo is still an economy everyone understands.

Selling is about making connections, and not just with potential customers. A good salesperson learns the importance of word of mouth, customer referrals, the old silent salesperson—the business card, and of course, recommendations. As such, collaborating with others for the purpose of networking together obviously can lead to great success. Indeed, whether it involves securing employment, generating business leads or seeking professional advice, networking yields immeasurable rewards.

"I am a closer. I am prosperous. I am successful. My confidence is unshakable. My enthusiasm is great. Life is great. Selling is great. Living is great. I am motivated. I generate leads. I close sales. I follow through. I get referrals. I use product knowledge. I make calls. I create success. I am a doer. I make things happen. I do it now. I work the percentages. NO is ON. My success is infinite. I love life. I love living. I love selling. Abundance is mine now," etc.

innertalk-store.com/products/networking_for_sales

Sales (Powerful Telephone Sales) ~ Subliminal

~ Meet people on the phone with an absolutely awesome and involving personality.

You don't need to be in sales to benefit from this program but if you are, you'll definitely want this program! Whether your work is telephone only or just involves the occasional use of the telephone, your ability to radiate enthusiasm, sincerity and share your knowledge is crucial to success. Meet people on the phone with an absolutely awesome and involving personality. Express your ideas and learn to listen intently, turning objections into final closes and therefore sales. Learn to look forward to every phone call and let those rejections just roll off you like water on a duck's back. If you're serious about telephone sales, get this program today.

"I am enthused. I enjoy talking with people. I enjoy making telephone calls. I enjoy taking phone calls. I love to share my presentation with others. I am good at telephone sales. I am consistent and persistent. I work the numbers. I am motivated. I help people. I help myself. I am energetic. I am capable. I am positive. I have power. I am confident. I motivate people. I am a leader. I am prosperous. I am successful. I make things happen. I am lucky," etc.

innertalk-store.com/products/telephone_sales

Selling (Powerful Selling and Closing) ~ Subliminal
~ Good selling techniques gain their real traction as the result of principles of agreement.

You do not need to be in sales in order to benefit from this program. Selling yourself is a required skill - no matter what your vocation. Selling is natural and easy. Build the confidence and acquire the skills to be the best salesperson - without 'high-pressure' and other tasteless techniques. If you are seeking advancement, managing people, selling a product already, or just entering sales and management, we guarantee that you will benefit from this program.

Being successful in sales is a matter of remembering that it is all about the numbers. This can be hard to do for some in a field where there can be a lot of rejection. Refresh your mental processes and prepare yourself for performing to the best of your ability. Many sales organizations throughout the country consider this program their secret weapon.

"I am positive. I have power. I am confident. I motivate people. I am a leader. I am prosperous. I am successful. I make things happen. I am lucky. I am wise. I use my time wisely. I am purposeful. I set goals. I achieve my goals. I am time wise. I am helpful. I like people. I present myself well. I project success. I attract success. I project prosperity. I attract abundance. I share my success. I am charismatic. I have charm. I close sales," etc.

innertalk-store.com/products/selling_and_closing

> *"After listening to the **Selling and Closing** program
> for just a few days, I noticed my sales were improving
> quite a bit. I have no trouble asking for a sale now.
> The more I listen, the better I feel about selling. And
> my closing is much easier! I'm excited!"*

Also Available In:

Sales (Super Sales Power) ~ Album

   innertalk-store.com/products/sales-power-album

Sales (Powerful Sales) ~ Collection

   innertalk-store.com/products/sales_collection

Salesperson (Powerful Salesperson) ~ Video

   innertalk-store.com/products/powerful_sales_dvd

Success (Ultra Success Power: Health, Wealth and the Fountain of Youth) ~ Subliminal

~ You really can live longer, happier and be more prosperous as a result of the thoughts in your mind!

Are you aware that solid scientific research has shown that your mind set, your attitude, the way you talk to yourself and your expectation, are all linked to wellness, longevity, happiness and prosperity at every level of your life? Why not have it all—health, wealth, youth, happiness and an absolutely positive expectation of and from life? Thoughts do become things. Expect the best in everything—you do deserve it!

"I can be successful. I can choose to be successful. I can be better in every way every day. I choose to be better in every way every day. I choose to be successful. I visualize my success. I believe in myself. I have the ability to achieve all my dreams and goals. It's easy for me to meet and talk with people. I always know what to say and when to say it. Every day in every way I improve. Every day I'm getting stronger and healthier. I remember youth. My body remembers youth. My cells reproduce perfectly. My cells are strong and willing. My cells are young and healthy. My cells are perfect. I

relax. I am in control. I choose a healthy life style. I rest peacefully. My sleep is refreshing. I choose healthy foods," etc.

innertalk-store.com/products/ultra_success_power

Also Available In:

Success ~ Collection

innertalk-store.com/products/success_collection

Success Power ~ Power Set

innertalk-store.com/products/success_power_ps

Success (Ultra Success Conditioning) ~ Video

innertalk-store.com/products/ultra_success_conditioning_dvd

Thinking (Breakthrough Thinking) ~ Subliminal

~ Gain focus, creativity, persistence, and an ultimate confidence that you can and will find the way!

Breakthrough thinking is defined as a deliberate, focused effort aimed at developing radically new approaches that overcome constraints, instead of making incremental changes in the older ways of working. Whether inside the box or outside, what is most required is focus, creativity, persistence, and an ultimate confidence that you can and will find the way. That is exactly why this program was created.

Imagine what you may accomplish when you add this skill set to your acumen. Begin today—why wait?

"I am exceptionally creative. I often ask myself, 'What if?' I explore possibilities. 'What if?' can lead to new possibilities. I am reflective. I am patient. I am naturally inquisitive. I question. I listen. I integrate my learnings. Information builds patterns. Patterns are within patterns. From fractals I find patterns. The language of breakthrough thinking is often intuitive. I listen to my intuition. I respect my intuition. I trust my inner vision. I believe in myself and my abilities. Patterns form relationships. I find new relationships in patterns. I somehow see the same thing differently and this provides breakthroughs. Breakthrough thinking is a passion of mine.

I love being creative. I love to convolute the model. I am infinitely creative," etc.

innertalk-store.com/products/breakthrough_thinking

Time Management ~ Subliminal

~ Increase productivity and become happier!

Time management is all about the ability to use one's time effectively. We all know there seems to never be enough time given the many demand in our modern society. The question then is always, "How do I get more accomplished?"

Time management is everyone's concern. When you plan your time correctly, you will be a lot more productive. When you are not always missing deadlines, or being late, everyone will just be happier, and you will be free of the stress and pressure that so many feel!

"I am time wise. I am punctual. I am organized. I am efficient. I am thorough. I am relaxed. I am calm. I breathe deeply. I am alert. I am attentive. I use time wisely. I use time efficiently. I am motivated. I am confident. I am enthusiastic. I am good. I am aware. I have a keen sense of time. Time is energy. I use energy positively," etc.

innertalk-store.com/products/time_management

Visualization (I Visualize Successfully) ~ Subliminal

~ What you can see in your mind, you can achieve!

Visualization is defined as the formation of a mental image of something; the representation of an object, situation, or set of information as a chart or other image. Visualization is a power tool used for a variety of goals ranging from manifesting peak performance to solving mathematical problems. It is a key power advantage used by athletes, artists, business people and successful individuals in all walks of life. What you can see in your mind, you can achieve.

"I see mental images. I visualize pictures. I see color. I remember pictures. I remember scenes. I remember dreams. I remember impressions. I construct visual pictures mentally. I image in detail. I image in color. Imaging is mental movies. I direct the movies of my mind. I see. My mental movies are

positive. I sense my mental movies. I relax. My imagination is powerful. Imaging is easy. Imaging is fun. I concentrate. Concentration is easy. I hold images," etc.

innertalk-store.com/products/visualization

Work (Joy of Work) ~ Subliminal

~ Work is the pathway to the fulfillment of our dreams.

Work need not be a four-letter word. Think of work this way, *"Dreams don't work unless you do!"* Work is the pathway to the fulfillment of our dreams. When you decide to focus on the dream instead of the work in front of you, when you choose to enjoy the job at hand, everything magically changes. Learn to enjoy your work. The time will pass more quickly, and you will feel better for it.

"I enjoy employment. I enjoy associations. I look forward to each day. I expect good. I am positive. I am motivated. I am sincere. I am enthusiastic. I work well with others. I do my best. I take pride in my best. I am proud of myself. I am proud of my efforts. I set goals. I achieve my goals. I succeed. I am happy. I create my happiness. I am responsible. I make it happen," etc.

innertalk-store.com/products/joy_of_work

Writer (I am a Writer) ~ Subliminal

~ Writing is a window into your inner-self!

Are you aware of the many psychological and physical wellness benefits that come from writing? Is there something inside you needing to be expressed? Writing is an outlet while at the same time it is a window into your inner-self. Many writers report that they have made many discoveries about themselves and their opinions by articulating them in writing. Whether your journaling or writing the newest best-seller, this program will facilitate both the skill set and the tenacity prudential for success.

"I enjoy sharing ideas. I develop ideas and plots easily. I write regularly. I write something every day. I read other's writings. I get ideas from others. I study successful writers. I read other writers alert to their method and style. I study writing skills. I develop and improve my own writing skills. I

am a writer. I enjoy writing. I love writing. I develop writing exercises. I practice writing exercises. I expand my vocabulary. I learn new words every week," etc.

innertalk-store.com/products/i-am-a-writer

Writing (Creative Writing) ~ Subliminal

~ Open up to those creative juices and express them in written form!

Ever wish you could write? Write in such a way that the words came alive, that the reader couldn't put the material down, or just write in a vivid creative way that everyone enjoyed? Within every human being there exists a creative surge waiting for an opportunity to express itself. This program is designed to facilitate opening up to those creative juices and expressing them in written form while providing confidence in your ability to express novel ideas in new ways, with fresh stories and spectacular narratives.

"I am creative. It's easy for me to create. I have great ideas. I experience creative inspiration regularly. I organize my thoughts. I develop outlines. I plan plots. I feel the characters. I sense the story line. I experience the creative flow. I love to write. I write every day. I record my thoughts. I keep a creative notebook. I write for fun. I write for relaxation. I dream of writing. My dreams give me ideas. I love to write. I am a good writer. I pay attention to detail. I read others' writings," etc.

innertalk-store.com/products/creative_writing

Better Life

For our most complete success related packages, please see:

Happiness (The Master Secret: Happiness is Success)
~ Library

      innertalk-store.com/products/master_secret_library

Abuse (Healing from Abuse) ~ Album

    innertalk-store.com/products/healing_from_abuse_album

Esteem (Reclaiming Your Inner Power: Ultimate Self-Esteem)
~ Album

    innertalk-store.com/products/ultimate_self_esteem_album

Luck (Becoming Lucky: Attracting and Enhancing Good Luck) ~ Album

    innertalk-store.com/products/becoming-lucky-album

Self-Sabotage (Eliminating Self-Sabotage) ~ Album

    innertalk-store.com/products/eliminating_self_sabotage_album

Stress (Eliminating Stress: Experiencing Joy) ~ Album

    innertalk-store.com/products/eliminating-stress-album

Esteem (Soaring Self Esteem) ~ Collection

    innertalk-store.com/products/esteem_collection

Loneliness (Overcoming Loneliness) ~ Collection

  innertalk-store.com/products/overcoming-loneliness-collection

Relaxation (Deep Relaxation) ~ Collection

innertalk-store.com/products/deep_relaxation_collection

Stress Management ~ Collection

innertalk-store.com/products/stress_management_collection

Abuse (Survivors of Abuse) ~ Subliminal

~ It is time to release the hold the abuse had over you!

No matter the type of abuse, all survivors struggle with feelings of guilt, shame, poor self-worth, and blame. In many instances, they often blame themselves for causing the abuser to be abusive. The abused individual often does not feel worthy of happiness or respect, and these feelings can continue, long after the abuser has left their lives. The fact is, you are worthy, and you do deserve to be happy. It is time to release the hold the abuser had over you, to let go of the programming that causes you to sabotage anything good that comes into your life.

"I am loved. I am accepted. I accept others. I am positive. I am confident. I am whole. I am sufficient. I am free of guilt. I am free of shame. I am free of blame. Life is miracle. I am a miracle. Life is a teacher. I learn from life. I love living. Life is wonderful. I am good. I am capable. I am in control. Pain is gone. Anxiety is gone. Stress is gone. I breathe deeply. I am calm. I am relaxed. I am comfortable. I release anger," etc.

innertalk-store.com/products/survivors_of_abuse

Also Available In:

Abuse (Healing from Abuse) ~ Album

innertalk-store.com/products/healing_from_abuse_album

Ahimsa (Ahimsa: Respect for Life) ~ Subliminal

~ When you live in honor of all life, then all life will live in honor of you!

When we live our lives in respect for *all* life, we enrich our minds and bodies to become aware of the interconnectedness we all have with each other. The beauty about this world is that we are never alone. Every living thing is a part of the universe and has a life force that we can benefit from. We can recognize that all life freely gives and in return, we ourselves can know that we are not insignificant at all! Although we may feel like a small grain of sand, we can draw from the strength of those around us knowing how we all are part of life's miracle.

"I respect all life. I am aware of life's significance. I sense the life force in life. I appreciate nature's bounty. I choose my foods wisely. All life matters. I treat all life with honor and dignity. Life is a miracle. All life has cycles. I am aware of how foods are prepared. I am aware of how foods are grown. I choose foods treated with dignity. No life is ever to be wasted. No life is insignificant," etc.

innertalk-store.com/products/ahimsa

Alert (Be Alert, Stay Safe) ~ Subliminal

~ Train your mind to pay attention to details!

Being safe means being alert and aware. While this program was created especially for children and senior citizens, we can all benefit from paying attention to our surrounding. Staying safe includes paying attention to where you walk, doorway heights, stair steps, and so forth.

In this day and age, remaining alert is critical to all of us. It has become more and more important that we all pay careful attention to details that formerly were far less important such as abandoned packages and the like.

Additionally, we all must remain more alert as we drive. More and more people are using their smart phones, texting, talking and even web searching while they drive. This can pose a sudden and unexpected behavior by other drivers that can lead to dangerous accidents.

Learn to be cautious without being afraid. Train your mind to pay attention to details and to keep you safe, wherever you are.

"I breathe deeply. I breathe properly. I am calm. I am peaceful. I am attentive. I listen to my hunches. I heed my intuition. I feel my instincts. My reflexes are good. My judgment is wise. I make wise choices. My senses are alert. I am confident. I trust my body. I notice differences. I notice newness. I concentrate easily. I am aware. My mind is keen. My mind is alert. My mind is powerful. I respect myself. I respect others. I rest properly. I eat

properly. I am cautious. I stay safe. I remain alert when appropriate. Safety is always on my mind. Safety is important," etc.

innertalk-store.com/products/be_alert_stay_safe

Anger (Releasing Anger) ~ Subliminal

~ Anger serves no one

Anger can be thoroughly debilitating. It can be your enemy. However, you really can eliminate angry responses and stop damaging relationships.

Are you easily triggered by your feelings of annoyance or hate that lead you to make physical and/or emotional outbursts? Perhaps you hide and repress your anger by making snide remarks, being overly critical, avoiding, or expressing sarcasm towards others.

Anger can also be very unhealthy as it puts stress on your immune system, making you sick and more susceptible to depression and other mood disorders.

At the very least, anger can just take the joy out of life. Let go of your anger and open yourself up to finding the real solution for your problems! Or just simply let the anger go, forgive yourself and others, and move on—because anger serves no one. Living in harmony includes the fact that you have to release all anger and jealousy towards other beings. You can be positive, loving, patient, peaceful, balanced, harmonious, and humble. You can reach your greatest potential when you see the best in others—just take the first step.

"I release all anger. I forgive myself. I forgive others. My emotions are positive. My expectations are loving. I am patient. I live in peace. I am peace. I am balance. I am harmony. I release all guilt. I release all shame. I release all anger. I am calm. I am at peace. I am in control. I see the best in myself. I see the best in others. I breathe deeply," etc.

innertalk-store.com/products/releasing_anger

Also Available In:

Anger and Fear (Freedom from Anger and Fear) ~ Video
innertalk-store.com/products/freedom_from_anger_and_fear_dvd

Animals (Connecting with Your Animal Friend) ~ Subliminal

~ Feel the special relationship and energy you share with your animal friend!

Animals play an important role in many people's lives. They are family members, therapy pets, service members, emotional companions, and dear friends. Research has shown the many benefits of spending time with animals, both to health and emotional issues. Animals have been used as healing helpers for combat soldiers, inmates, seniors, troubled youths, cancer patients, and more. The fact is, we all feel better when we are around our animal friends. With *Connecting with Your Animal Friend,* you will be able to pay closer attention to your animal friend's feelings and body language.

"I trust my senses. My senses are keen. I am alert. I sense the energy of those around me. I can feel the energy of animals. I sense and feel the feelings of my animal friends. I am empathic to the needs of my animal friends. I am sensitive to the vibrations emitted from my animal friends. I allow myself to feel their thoughts and expressions. I trust my feelings. I take time to listen to my friends. I am able to articulate the feelings and thought of my animal friends," etc.

innertalk-store.com/products/connecting_with_your_animal_friend

Anxiety (Releasing Anxiety: Discovering Self-Peace) ~ Subliminal

~ You can do much better than just cope with anxiety, you can free yourself of it!

Anxiety is a common emotion many feel from time to time. For some, anxiety can become something they deal with much more often than occasionally. Whether it's event anxiety or the more troublesome sense of daily anxiety, this program is designed to help you. Learn to eliminate unhealthy anxiety and armor plate yourself against triggers that have led to discomfort in the past. You can do much better than just cope with anxiety, you can free yourself of it, and this program is designed to provide the cognitive tool-kit to do just that.

"Living is fun. I make decisions. I make decisions easily. I am comfortable in my own skin. I like myself. I make wise choices. I am confident. I am positive. I am anxiety free. Anxiousness is gone. I feel great! I trust. I allow. I let go. I have fun. I like to play. I enjoy my work. I focus on the positive. I am optimistic. I relax all over. I am trusting. I exercise. I take walks. I enjoy the outdoors and nature. I sleep easily," etc.

innertalk-store.com/products/releasing-anxiety-subliminal

Attitude (Positive Mental Attitude) ~ Subliminal

~ Creating success in all aspects of your life starts with a positive attitude.

The power of positive thinking cannot be overstated. Studies have shown that positive thinking is a natural remedy to many of the discomforts we might encounter in life. When you have a positive attitude, you will be able to see all the good that is in your life and recognize opportunities when they appear. Plus, a positive mental attitude will also do wonders for your health and sense of wellbeing.

"I am positive. I am capable. I can do anything. I like myself. I like others. Others like me. I think positively. I act positively. I expect only positive. My reality is positive. I have energy. I am motivated. I attract the positive. I exude positiveness. I am a winner. I take charge. I create my reality," etc.

innertalk-store.com/products/positive_mental_attitude

Begin Anew ~ Subliminal

~ Find new meaning and purpose to your life.

Sometimes life brings you situations where you have to start all over again, maybe even rebuilding your life from scratch. Not having a clear picture of your future can cause a great deal of angst. Stress can have you failing to take control of the situation—making the life adjustment a harder process to go through. It is important to believe in yourself, to know you have the ability to create a new and wonderful life for yourself. This program will assist you in finding the inner strength and fortitude you need to get through this situation. Transform your crisis into an opportunity for adventure and fun!

"Every day is a new beginning. Each day holds fresh opportunities. I meet each day with excitement. I look forward to building a new life. All of my tomorrows begin today. I have a new plan. I have adjusted. I am accepting. I know that everything comes to me for some good reason. I trust in the grand scheme of it all. I enter each day with enthusiasm. I bring my very best to each new day. I love living. I love life. I find joy in life. I laugh. I have fun," etc.

innertalk-store.com/products/begin_anew

Believe (I Believe) ~ Subliminal

~ What you believe really does matter—for yourself and for the world around you!

Belief is a powerful force. When you truly believe that success is possible, you're likely to succeed. When you believe from the innermost core of your being that peace, balance and harmony are feasible—you inevitably enjoy more of it. The world changes one person at a time, one small act at a time, one belief at a time. Hold fast to the idea that appreciation, gratitude, love, and peace are genuinely in our future, and watch the world follow suit.

"I believe in peace. I believe in the sacredness of life. I believe there is a future for our children. I believe in caring for our planet. I believe in caring for others. I believe in promoting peace, balance and harmony. I accept peace for myself. I accept balance and harmony. I am calm and peaceful. I am rational and peace oriented. I love life. I believe life loves me. I love living. I enjoy every moment. I think of peaceful solutions," etc.

innertalk-store.com/products/i_believe

Best (Presenting My Best: From Appearance to Communication) ~ Subliminal

~ Looking you best is a success strategy that leads to improved opportunities!

There is an old adage that a person is judged by their appearance and another that insists first impressions are lasting. Looking your best is therefore a critical factor in everyone's life. It is also a success strategy that leads to improved opportunities. The fact is, dressing well will not only increase your self-confidence but it will also impress and attract other people. This program is designed to make the thought and care automatic—a part of you. Show yourself off. Be proud of your appearance and begin to reap the many benefits. Act now for a future packed with promises!

"I like to look good. I take care with my appearance. I make it a point to stand straight. I pay attention to my posture. I hold my stomach in. I plan my clothing ahead of time. I dress for the occasion. I look sharp. I like being well groomed. I walk confidently. I sit erectly. I present myself well. I speak clearly. I speak confidently. I believe in myself. I smile. I laugh easily. I enjoy good humor. I am calm and capable. I enjoy looking my best. I like people. People like me. I radiate competence," etc.

innertalk-store.com/products/presenting-my-best-subliminal

Care Giver (Positive Care Giver) ~ Subliminal

~ Taking care of yourself is important too!

Caring for another can be stressful and demanding. Most do not realize or appreciate the heavy burden placed on the caregiver. Being a caregiver entails constant readiness, attentiveness to the smallest detail, responsibility pressures, fear of failure, and so forth. But caregivers have needs and desires too. This program was created to assist in balancing one's personal needs with the role of caregiver while providing the best of care for another.

"I can be caring and loving. I can be patient. I choose to be a good care giver. It's easy for me to deal with difficult situations. It's easy for me to be a good care giver. It's easy for me to have empathy. I choose to be empathetic. I create my future. I make my choices. I have a positive outlook. I am optimistic. I am good. I am worthy. I am safe. I am loved. I am supported. I like to support others," etc.

innertalk-store.com/products/positive_care_giver

Change (Accepting Change) ~ Subliminal

~ Nothing changes until you do!

Nearly everyone seeks change at some point in their lives and yet change can be frightening. What is it you wish to change? Take the step today to armor yourself with confidence and courage to make the change you desire. That said, if you're experiencing a change already that is uncomfortable, then this program will help you navigate the process with confidence. Resisting change only makes it more painful. Remember, nothing changes until you do. Enable your inner strength today.

"Change is natural. Change is growth. Change is opportunity. Change is exciting. Change is fun. All things change. I accept change. I accept others. I accept myself. I live in harmony. I choose harmony. I am stress free. I have self-esteem. I breathe deeply. I sleep soundly. I am at peace. I am confident. Life is dynamic. I am whole. I am sufficient. I am enough," etc.

innertalk-store.com/products/accepting_change

Compassion (Developing Compassion) ~ Subliminal

~ Our world is better off when we identify compassionately with others.

Compassion is simply a feeling of deep sympathy and sorrow for another who is stricken by misfortune, accompanied by a strong desire to alleviate the suffering. Compassion is the state of being that leads to responsible actions designed to identify with and ameliorate the suffering others endure. It is a mental readiness to truly relate to others. Relating and understanding others is a near magical path to both personal peace and success in every walk of life.

"I am compassionate. I am sensitive to others' feelings. I care. I am caring. I understand. It's easy to be compassionate. It's easy to be caring. It's easy for me to listen. I listen. It's easy for me to sense others feeling. I respect others. I am honest with myself. I am considerate of others. I can feel compassion safely. I can care about others safely. I can be non-involved and still compassionate. I am sincere. Compassion helps me understand. Compassion is an act of caring," etc.

innertalk-store.com/products/developing_compassion

Complaining (No More Complaining) ~ Subliminal

~ Focus on the positive and discover joy!

What do you get out of complaining? Does it make you feel better or worse? Are you more positive and optimistic when you complain or less likely to feel satisfied and happy with life?

The research is clear, a positive optimistic outlook shared with feelings of gratitude will lengthen your life expectancy and enhance your quality of life. Indeed, excessive complaining has been linked to higher levels of stress and stress can be a killer. Not only that, but complainers tend to find fewer and fewer people who want to be around them. The fact is, complaining robs your life of the joy you deserve.

Train you mind to focus on the positive, and let loose the joy in your life!

"I am free of complaining. I choose to be free of complaining. I am positive. I focus on the positive. I am optimistic. I expect the positive. I seek peace, balance and harmony in my life. I promote peace in my life. I establish the complaint free habit. I catch myself when and if complaining begins. I arrest myself from complaining. I live a complaint free life. Being complaint free is liberating. I seek out the positive in life," etc.

innertalk-store.com/products/no-more-complaining-subliminal

Control (Self Control) ~ Subliminal

~ Be positive, energetic, healthy, grateful, and responsible!

Sometimes life pushes you around in many different ways that make you feel like you have no control over what you do and say. But you can always choose to respond differently—in ways that support your goals. You can have an optimistic response and see it as a way to learn and grow stronger. Your reality is your own and you can have control over them! This program will bolster your enthusiasm to be positive, energetic, healthy, grateful, and responsible.

"Attitude creates reality. Attitude forms expectations. My attitude is great. My attitude is positive. My attitude is optimistic. I am positive. I am enthused. I am energetic. I am healthy. I am optimistic. I am joyous. I am eternal. I am

a gift. I am grateful. I love life. I love living. Life is wonderful. Life is fun. I see good in all. I see the Divine in all. My reality is wonderful," etc.

<u>innertalk-store.com/products/self_control</u>

Courage (I am Courageous) ~ Subliminal

~ Courage is a mental discipline.

There are many times in our lives that we all need some extra courage. It takes courage to change. It takes courage to put yourself at risk in any endeavor. Courage is required if you are to develop a strong sense of confidence or ever emerge as a leader. Courage is regarded as an admirable personal trait, providing benefits for people personally, socially and professionally. Begin programming your life today to fully embrace the courage within!

"I am fearless. I am a winner. I am enough. I am courageous. I am smart. I am confident. I am charismatic. I am powerful. I am loving. I am patient. I am humble. I am strong. I am decisive. I am wise," etc.

<u>innertalk-store.com/products/courage</u>

Criticism (Accepting Constructive Criticism) ~ Subliminal

~ Not all criticism is an attack.

Many people have difficulty discerning between constructive criticism and negative feedback and therefore reject any value that may exist in remarks taken as critical. Improvement comes as a matter primarily of two factors: the first is practice and the second is criticism. Without the feedback that can lead us, without the coaching that counsels, without the constructive criticism that demands we improve—we will fail to do so! If accepting criticism is holding you back, then begin to change that now.

"Life is a school. Living is learning. I choose to learn. I choose to improve. I improve every day in every way. I will always improve. I will always learn. I am flexible. I am teachable. I am a great learner. I am patient. I am discerning. I can accept criticism. I know constructive criticism. I recognize

constructive criticism. It's easy to accept constructive criticism. It's easy to learn from others. It's easy to learn from mistakes," etc.

innertalk-store.com/products/accepting_constructive_criticism

Curiosity (Unleashing Curiosity: Expanding Possibilities) ~ Subliminal

~ Curiosity is the fuel behind the greatest discoveries!

Curiosity is the fuel behind the greatest discoveries in science. Think of curiosity this way, in the words of Bernard Baruch, "Millions saw the apple fall, but Newton asked why." Or maybe this way, in the words of John Locke, "Curiosity in children, is but an appetite for knowledge. The great reason why children abandon themselves wholly to silly pursuits and trifle away their time insipidly is, because they find their curiosity balked, and their inquiries neglected." In which way was your curiosity mentored? Curiosity is the cure for boredom, the ignition for discovery, the excitement behind pioneering ideas, and at least a co-founder to the mother of invention. Why not regain the magic of curiosity and add some spice to your life? Who knows what you might discover?

"Curiosity is natural. Curiosity is helpful. Curiosity is the foundation of arts and science. I came into the world curious. Curiosity asks questions. Curiosity seeks solutions. Curiosity is powerful. Curiosity solves problems. I am curious. I am a curious person by nature. I was born curious. I have an inquiring mind. Curiosity is an adventure. I love adventures. I cultivate my curiosity," etc.

innertalk-store.com/products/curiosity-subliminal

Decluttering Your Life ~ Subliminal

~ When your environment is clean, neat, and clutter-free, you will find it easier to relax.

Is the clutter in your life out of control? Do you avoid cleaning and straightening because the job is overwhelming? Are you tired of shoving stuff into a drawer or closet just so that you can gain some extra surface space? Having a clean environment is part of living a healthy life. Clutter can be distracting and unhealthy. Sort through what is important and useful from the items you do not need. You can enjoy cleaning and being tidy! **This program** will help you find cleaning and organizing your home to be a very joyful and liberating experience. You will enjoy being able to find what you need when you need it, and you will feel a sense of self-pride at your own organizational abilities. Enjoy the freedom that comes when you finally de-clutter your life!

"Cleanliness is important. I enjoy being clean. I like cleanliness. I enjoy cleaning. I maintain a clean environment. I enjoy a clean home. I organize my things. Everything has a place. I pick up after myself. I am a tidy person. I like being tidy. I straighten the clutter. I enjoy organizing where everything goes. I see that everything is in its correct place. I pick up the trash. I straighten the house. I enjoy living in a clean, neat, clutter free home," etc.

innertalk-store.com/products/decluttering_your_life

Depression (Up from Depression) ~ Subliminal

~ Replace that negative, depressing, self-talk with self-talk that uplifts and inspires!

Demonstrated effective, this program helps you lift the cloud of depression helping you to enjoy life with energy and enthusiasm. At Progressive Awareness, we refer to this program as our *Being Cheerful* program and often play it in the office when someone is just feeling down. Life is just that much more fun when you are in a positive, upbeat frame of mind.

"I love life. I love living. I feel great. I laugh. I find humor. I am in control. I enjoy people. I enjoy myself. I am lucky. I am blessed. I am relaxed. I am calm. I choose happiness. I choose joy. Living is joyous. Life is great. I think positive. I feel positive. I am positive. I sense good in all. I see good in all. I forgive others. I forgive myself. I am forgiven. I contribute to life," etc.

innertalk-store.com/products/up_from_depression

Also Available In:

Depression (Freedom from Depression) ~ Video

innertalk-store.com/products/freedom_from_depression_dvd

Dreams (Ending Bad Dreams) ~ Subliminal

~ Engineer positive outcomes from all of your dreams!

Dreams help us process emotions, consolidate memories, and teach us the truth of our being. Nightmares often occur as a way to force ourselves to resolve a conflict we have in our lives. Learn to recognize the balance and harmony within all your dreams and resolve the conflicts in your life. Discover how to engineer positive outcomes from all of your dreams— whether good or bad. You can eliminate your bad dreams and turn them into a great learning experience! Take control of your dreams today and discover how refreshing sleep really can be.

"My dreams teach me. I release conflict. My dreams reflect the truth of my being. The truth of my being is LOVE. I live in peace. I live in balance and harmony. I choose to forgive all. I am forgiven My dreams reflect harmony and balance. The past is over. My dreams are positive experiences. I engineer the positive outcome of my dreams. I make wise peaceful choices in my dreams," etc.

innertalk-store.com/products/ending_bad_dreams

Driving (Safe Driving) ~ Subliminal

~ Be alert, drive defensively

There is no substitute for attention or proper rest when it comes to driving. Most drivers are fully aware of this but nevertheless find themselves drifting on in thought and/or feeling tired and sleepy. This program is designed for use while you drive, and for young drivers as well. Be alert, drive defensively, be aware of peripheral information, drive safe!

"I choose to be a safe driver. I choose to be cautious. I am proud of my driving ability. I am alert. I enjoy being alert. I enjoy driving safely. I will always drive safe. It's easy to stay alert. It's easy to pay attention. I am a defensive driver. I am a safe driver. I am a good driver. I am calm when driving. I am patient with traffic. I abide by the speed limits. I pay attention to traffic signs," etc.

innertalk-store.com/products/safe_driving

Eating (End Picky Eating) ~ Subliminal

~ Variety is the healthy food of life!

Picky eating can become a habit that young people never outgrow. Picky eating can lead to weight loss, nutritional deficiencies, and more. We live at a time when the availability of healthy food is abundant all year. Eating the same restricted diet week after week no longer makes any sense. One of the best ways to eat healthfully is to eat a variety of foods. While this program was originally designed for children, it will help everybody to enjoy eating a varied, healthy diet.

"I enjoy chewing my food. I enjoy eating healthy foods. I enjoy trying new foods. I enjoy eating vegetables. Vegetables taste good. I love new tastes. I expect food to taste good. I expect to enjoy my meals. I like trying new foods. I enjoy my meals. I love healthy foods. I really love fresh vegetables and fruits. I enjoy natural foods. I choose healthy foods. I chew my food slowly," etc.

innertalk-store.com/products/end_picky_eating

Ecology Awareness ~ Subliminal

~ Make ecology awareness a natural part of who you are.

We live at a time when our planer faces many threats. For generations planet resources have been taken for granted and that gives rise to the need for new habits and practices by all. Ecological Awareness is the scientific study of the relationships that living organisms have with each other and with their natural environment. For the each and every one of us, this translates into an aim to cause minimal damage to our environment. How do we do this? By beginning to recognize the problem and then by disciplining ourselves to adopt new patterns of behavior. Use this program to facilitate both a new awareness and new habits.

"I am responsible. I assume responsibility for my role in ecology. I conserve resources. I minimize waste. I choose products that are environmentally sound. I recycle materials. I think first in terms of ecology. I think about the impact to the planet. I am involved in ecological planning. I know that ultimately ecology and economy are the same. I am aware of the necessity to preserve nature. I do my part to save the environment for future generations," etc.

innertalk-store.com/products/ecology_awareness

Emotion (Coherent Emotion) ~ Subliminal

~ Balance your emotions for clearer thinking, optimized health, increased happiness, and enhance creativity!

There is much a buzz today about the positive influence of coherent body states. Clinics are teaching coherent heart and brain wave states through sophisticated bio-feedback means. Software is being written for home use and neuro-feedback devices are beginning to feature the advantages of brain/body coherence. Many optimal states are reported as accompanying this coherent heart/brain state called simply emotional coherence. This program is designed to assist you in experiencing this state for yourself.

"I am calm. I am relaxed. I am at peace. I am at peace with my emotions. I am at peace with my body. I love my body. My body is good. I am good. My emotions are peaceful. My emotions are coherent. Bliss is mine. I live in bliss. Joy is mine. Serenity is mine. I will always know love and bliss. I choose bliss. I choose coherent emotion. I choose peace, balance and serenity," etc.

innertalk-store.com/products/coherent_emotion

Also Available In:

Bliss: Coherent Emotion ~ Platinum Plus

innertalk-store.com/products/bliss_coherent_emotion-pp

Coherence: Brain/Body Balance ~ Video

innertalk-store.com/products/coherence_dvd

Emotional Pain (Healing Emotional Pain) ~ Subliminal

~ Release the past emotional pain that still controls your life!

Emotional pain is something most of us have tucked away in the dark corners of our minds. This is not a place that we like to go, but occasionally, something takes us there. It can be a thought that reminds us of the past and it might be something that just occurred. Emotional pain is real and sometimes even more debilitating than physical pain. It's time to heal. There are powerful strategies in this program that facilitate that healing process. Begin the healing today. You deserve more!

"I like giving. I enjoy giving. I like loving. I enjoy loving. I like being loved. I enjoy being loved. I like receiving. I enjoy receiving. I like challenges. I enjoy challenges. I accept challenges. I release the past. I look to the future. I live in the moment. I have joyful anticipations. I like laughing. I like having fun. I am relaxed. I am at peace. I release all tensions. Exhaling releases tensions. Exhaling releases fears. Exhaling releases the past. I think positive thoughts. I tell myself I am good," etc.

innertalk-store.com/products/healing_emotional_pain

Enthusiasm (Ultra Enthusiasm) ~ Subliminal

~ Enthusiasm is the fiery spirit that ignites the quintessential best in our lives!

Life is meant to be enjoyed! Engage it with a passion and witness the glory life brings forth. Living is a miracle! When the level of enthusiasm you seek about life and living turns to pure excitement, an absolute passion, it feels as though fireworks fill your being. It's wonderful. Every day is full of new opportunities and new excitement. If you're one of those TGIF people, do yourself a favor and get this program. You'll love and cherish every moment of living.

"Life is a miracle. Every breath is a wonder. Every moment is infinitely divisible. Every person is important. Every day something new comes to me. Every day life becomes more wondrous. Life force is awesome. Life force is sacred. Living is so wondrous. I am in awe of life. I am in love with living. Every breath is more joy. I am passionate about life. I seize life's every moment. I take advantage of life to live the richness of its glory. I am a miracle. I meet every day with enthusiasm. I meet every day with excitement. I meet every day with gratitude," etc.

innertalk-store.com/products/ultra_enthusiasm

Also Available In:

Passion (On Fire with a Passion for Life) ~ Platinum Plus

innertalk-store.com/products/passion_for_life_pp

Esteem (Soaring Self Esteem) ~ Subliminal

~ A strong self-esteem informs us we can succeed, lifts our confidence and presses the persevere button when needed.

Self-esteem is critical for success in every endeavor, whether in personal relationships or business. A healthy sense of self-esteem becomes the first step in recognizing our own self-worth. This program is considered to be the single most important step to building a happy and whole life. Esteem comes from knowing who you are and a willingness to accept yourself. Positive feelings of self-worth can empower you to succeed in all that you do and reap the rewards of satisfaction and fulfillment. Use this program and watch the transformation.

"I am in control. I am positive. I am honest. I am responsible. I am happy. I am confident. I am capable. I can do anything. I am one with the Divine. Honesty is oneness. I live in oneness. I like myself. I like others. I respect myself. I respect others. I love all. All is oneness," etc.

innertalk-store.com/products/soaring_self_esteem

---

*"I bought the **Self-Esteem** CD some months ago. I didn't feel any different at first but after a week people around me at work started responding much more positively towards me. I can honestly say that your products work."*

Also Available In:

Esteem (Reclaiming Your Inner Power: Ultimate Self-Esteem) ~ Album

innertalk-store.com/products/ultimate_self_esteem_album

Relaxation and Esteem Building ~ Video

innertalk-store.com/products/relaxation_and_esteem_building_dvd

Peace (Personal Peace) ~ Power Imaging/Hypnosis

innertalk-store.com/products/personal_peace

Peace and Serenity ~ Power Set

innertalk-store.com/products/peace_and_serenity

Esteem (Powerful Esteem) ~ Echo-Tech

innertalk-store.com/products/powerful_esteem

Peace (Inner Peace) ~ OZO

innertalk-store.com/products/inner_peace

Esteem (Soaring Self Esteem) ~ Collection

innertalk-store.com/products/esteem

Fears (Freedom from Fears) ~ Subliminal

~ Let go of your fear and discover the peace and harmony within!

Fear is a mechanism of the mind designed to keep you safe—but sometimes it can get out of control. *Freedom from Fears* will allow you to free yourself from the hold your fears have over you. It will help enable you to experience life to the fullest. You will feel in control, relaxed, and confident to handle fearful situations so that nothing can hold you back from living the happy life you deserve.

"I am confident. I am poised. I am judicious. I am relaxed. I am free of fear. I remain calm. I remain relaxed. I am in control. I remain in control. I retain control. I breathe deeply. I breathe regularly. I live in harmony. I am strong. I am courageous. I am brave. I control my inner environment. I am in charge of myself. I am unafraid," etc.

innertalk-store.com/products/freedom_from_fears

Also Available In:

Anger and Fear (Freedom from Anger and Fear) ~Video

innertalk-store.com/products/freedom_from_anger_and_fear_dvd

Flying (Freedom from the Fear of Flying) ~ Subliminal

~ Experience the joy of flying!

As many as 25 percent of all Americans suffer some nervousness about flying. If you're uncomfortable flying, this program was designed for you. Whether you are traveling for business or for pleasure, a fear of flying can really ruin the trip. Eliminate the fear of flying and bring the joy back.

"I am confident. I am poised. I am relaxed. I love to fly. Flying is relaxing. Planes are safe. Flight attendants are helpful. I can nap while flying. I can enjoy reading while flying. I sit back and relax on the plane. I look forward to flying. I remain calm. I remain relaxed. I am in control of myself. I am powerful. I can do anything," etc.

innertalk-store.com/products/freedom_from_the_fear_of_flying

Forgiving and Letting Go ~ Subliminal

~ You know you have forgiven yourself and others when the memory no longer gives you pain or anger.

Learning to let go with love is exceedingly challenging to most. Yet not to do so is to bind ourselves and our growth in resentment and anger. Research shows that we'll live healthier if we release the anger, guilt, shame and fear that is healed by forgiveness. Although *Forgiving and Letting* was one of our best-selling titles, in 1990 Eldon Taylor decided this issue was so important to everyone that he decided to make this program free of charge. You can therefore download a *free* version of this program by going to www.eldontaylor.com/forgiveness.html (If you would prefer a free CD version of this program, please call our offices: 1-800-964-3551. Please note: shipping and handling charges will apply.)

Life is too short to waste any energy on not forgiving. Forgive others, forgive yourself, allow others to forgive you, and be forgiven!

"I am a gift. Love created all. The Divine exists in all. I see the Divine in all. Good exists in all. I see good in all. Life is a miracle. I am a miracle. Living is wonderful. I am forgiving. I am appreciative. I am positive. I am confident. I am balanced. I live in peace. I live in harmony. I live in now. Now is all there is. I have all I need now. I am free of addictions. I emulate the highest. I am understanding. I love unconditionally. I care without

reward expectation. Form is function. I am non-resistive to life. I forgive myself. I forgive all others. I am forgiven." etc.

innertalk-store.com/products/forgiving-and-letting-go-subliminal

Gossip (Freedom from Gossip) ~ Subliminal

~ Break the gossiping habit and become the kind of person you would like to be.

Think about the intent of most gossip. It is to harm the reputation of another person, to intrude into their lives, or harm their relationships. Ask yourself, what value is there to gossip? How is it helpful? Then ask yourself what kind of person you want to be.

Be kind. Gossiping is a horrible habit that many get sucked into in order to join the grapevine. You do not like people talking about you behind your back so why would you do it to others. Break this habit and become the kind of person you would like to be. Begin today!

"I am responsible. I take responsibility for everything I say. I am aware of the Golden Rule. I do unto others as I would have them do unto me. I act toward others as I would have them treat me. I avoid gossip. I see good in others. I focus on the good in all. I choose to see good. It is my choice. I am safe and comfortable. I am secure in myself. I am confident. I need prove nothing. I have no enemies. I am at peace with myself. I accept others. I accept myself. I practice living in harmony," etc.

innertalk-store.com/products/freedom_from_gossip

Gratitude (Owning A Gratitude Attitude) ~ Subliminal

~ When you live in a state of gratitude, life can seem to become magical!

More and more research in recent years has pointed to the importance of gratitude in our lives. Just acknowledging each day with gratitude sets up an expectation that leads to brighter days. The smile is hardwired to the brain. When you smile, even fake that smile, your brain releases endorphins, the body's own natural opiates, and this literally makes you feel better.

A gratitude attitude opens doors to you that may not otherwise be available. It enhances your relationships, improves self-esteem, and adds many other riches to your life. The data suggests that grateful people live longer healthier and happier lives.

"I am grateful. I appreciate my life. I appreciate all that I am and can ever be. I recognize a Divine Source from which I come. I recognize that I am a gift. I accept the gift. I give thanks for my being. I love life. I love living. Life is wonderful. I find good in all. Living is a miracle. I am a miracle. I am happy. I am joyful. I am optimistic. I give thanks. I give thanks every day. I start my days with 'Thank you.' I close my eyes at bedtime with 'Thank you,'" etc.

innertalk-store.com/products/gratitude_attitude

Grief and Trauma (Healing from Grief and Trauma) ~ Subliminal

~ Release the fear and begin the healing process today!

If you've experienced trauma, then you've also experienced grief, and probably anxiety. These often go hand in hand. Grief can take many forms, but you need not be trapped by it. A traumatic experience can leave a lasting impression that literally can seem to haunt an individual. Severe sufferers should seek professional help for traumatic grief can be thoroughly debilitating. If you are currently under the care of a professional, seek their advice before using this program.

This program was designed to facilitate the healing process necessary for releasing grief and dealing with tragedy. Sometimes you only need be present during a tragedy to suffer its pangs. Some tragedies and traumas can literally engulf a person with fear. Release the fear and begin the healing process today.

"Life is a gift. Life is eternal. Life is an experience. Spirit is essential. Love is the Divine energy. Love energy flows through me. I accept Love energy. I accept the Divine. Unconditional LOVE is who I am. Who I really am, is eternal. My perfect will is God's will. I accept God's will. God's will be done. Eternal Spirit dwells within me. Eternal Spirit combines in me to animate me. Love is my true being. I accept. I let go. I allow. I trust in God's will. Life is a lesson ground. Life is to experience the lessons. I remember the Eternal. I allow it to awake in me. I am at peace," etc.

innertalk-store.com/products/healing_from_grief_and_trauma

Guilt (Releasing Guilt) ~ Subliminal

~ Free yourself from guilt by gaining the proper perspective!

Guilt punishes in many ways. In addition to the emotional pain, guilt can cause headaches, suppress the immune system and otherwise weaken our natural defenses against disease. Guilt can have a toxic effect on our relationships as well. The fact is, guilt reminds us of something we feel we did wrong, but to hold on to guilt imprisons us both in the moment and the future. Free yourself from guilt by gaining the proper perspective—a healing healthy perspective that acknowledges the lesson but ends the self-imposed punishment.

"Life is a teacher. I am loved. I am responsible. I exude love and acceptance. I am forgiven. I forgive myself. I forgive all others. My choices are wise. My choices are positive. Good exists in all. Good comes from all. I see and sense good in all. I am good. I am happy. Life provides learning opportunities. I am a co-creator. I am non-judgmental. I love myself. I am free of guilt. I am free of shame," etc.

innertalk-store.com/products/releasing_guilt

Happiness is Success ~ Subliminal

~ When you choose happiness, success naturally follows.

Happiness begins in the mind. It is a skill set that can easily be developed once you commit to it. Other people cannot make you happy—this is a personal and private opportunity. While other people can add to your happiness, you must be ready to receive before you can give back. As the old saying goes, "You cannot pour from an empty cup!"

Happiness is really a choice. You may not be responsible for the stimuli in your life, but you are responsible for how you respond. When you choose happiness, success naturally follows. Why wait?

"Happiness exists within. Happiness is my birthright. Happiness is peace. Happiness is balance. Happiness is wholeness. Happiness is harmony. Happiness comes in acceptance. Happiness comes from sharing. Happiness comes from giving. Happiness comes with forgiveness. Forgiveness is Grace. I live in Grace. I am a gift. Life is a gift. All life is a miracle. I am a miracle.

I am grateful. I am loving. Love is the Universal language. Love is the Universal truth. I am loved. I am accepted. I am whole and sufficient," etc.

innertalk-store.com/products/happiness_is_success

Also Available In:

Happiness (The Master Secret: Happiness is Success) ~ Library

innertalk-store.com/products/master_secret_library

Have It All ~ Subliminal

~ If you believe that you deserve the best that life has to offer, then you have taken the first step in actualizing it!

What would a life full of joy, happiness, love, prosperity, health, and inner peace be like? What would it be worth? Have you ever just desired to find a path to such a place?

You can have it all. You can learn to open to a fresh new creativity that prospers your sense of well-being while fostering a strong sense of safety, trust, and the literal cornucopia of possibilities open to all who open their hearts and minds.

If you believe that you deserve the best that life has to offer, then you have taken the first step in actualizing it. Begin today with this powerful program!

"I enjoy life. I have fun. I am humorous. I enjoy humor. I am positive. I am charismatic. I am enthusiastic. I am energetic. I am powerful. I am humble. I am a genius. I am creative. I am a leader. I am intuitive. I am good. I am great. I am important. I am honest. I am truthful. I am proud. I am a gift. I am patient. I am forgiven. I am whole. I am sufficient. I am enough. I am prosperous. I am lucky. I apply myself. I can do anything," etc.

innertalk-store.com/products/have_it_all

Also Available In:

Have It All ~ Echo-Tech

innertalk-store.com/products/have_it_all_et

Hoarding (Freedom from Hoarding) ~ Subliminal

~ Take control of your possessions, eliminate those you no longer need, and enjoy the calm that follows.

Are you one of those people who hates to throw things out? Do you keep hold of 'stuff' just in case you may need it someday? How would you like to have a more orderly home, one that is clean, neat and tidy? Would you like to be able to invite friends and family over without becoming embarrassed by the piles of 'stuff' lying around. This really is possible.

"I like things neat and tidy. I am selective about what I keep. I remove junk and clutter from my home. I am neat and tidy. I dispose of junk and clutter. I am unafraid of letting things go. I do not need to keep everything. I find it easy to dispose of things. I am relaxed when getting rid of items. I sell or dispose of unnecessary items. I keep my home clean," etc.

innertalk-store.com/products/freedom-from-hoarding

Hopelessness (Releasing Fear, Doubt and Feelings of Hopelessness and Helplessness) ~ Subliminal

~ Take back your personal power today.

Nothing seems so debilitating as a sense of hopeless/helplessness. Indeed, hopeless/helpless feelings have been connected with many mind/body dysfunctions varying from failures in the immune system to an absolute sense of despair (giving up). Hope is essential to a sound mind and body. Take back your personal power today.

"I believe in a Divine plan. I am part of that plan. I am important. I accept change. I accept Divine Will. My perfect Will is Divine Will. Thy Will be done. I am eternal. I am positive. I am grateful. I meet every situation with gratitude. Good comes from all. I am powerful. I am capable. I live completely in the moment. I live in Now. I am safe. I am comfortable. I trust in the Divine plan. I let go and live in now. I sense joy and peace," etc.

innertalk-store.com/products/fear_doubt_hopeless_and_helpless

Housekeeping (I am a Good Housekeeper)
~ Subliminal

~Enjoy the peace that comes from a well-kept home!

It doesn't matter if it's your home, your office, or just your room, when your personal space is clean, neat, and organized, life just flows better. But keeping your space clean is a lot more than just having a periodic spring clean, only to have the mess return gradually and relentlessly. Good housekeeping is all about creating those little habits that stop problem areas from even starting. When done correctly, good housekeeping does not take time and effort. With the right mind set, a couple of minutes here and a few moments there can soon have your space looking the best it ever has. And when your personal space is clean and neat, your productivity increases, and your relaxation becomes truly restful.

"I take pride in myself and my things. I take pride in my home. I like my home warm and comfortable. My home is special to me. I like things clean and neat. Housekeeping matters. I matter. My home matters. My home is clean. I keep my home clean. I put things away. I pick up as I go along. I maintain a clean neat home. I am a clean neat person. I keep all my spaces clean. I am a good housekeeper when I'm home. I am a good housekeeper on the job. I like my space clean and neat. I like my space organized. Everything has a place where it belongs. I clean from top to bottom. I treat stains right away. I pay attention to my clean neat environment. I enjoy putting things away. I enjoy tidying up," etc.

innertalk-store.com/products/good-housekeeping-subliminal

Humor (Joy of Humor) ~ Subliminal

~ Humor is essential for balance in life!

Laughter has amazing healing powers and humor enhances all social skills. Laughter has been shown to strengthen the immune system. Humor has been demonstrated to relax muscles, decrease blood pressure, increase memory function, aid in learning, build likability, diffuse conflict, and so much more. This program will make it easier for you to have a sense of humor, or, if you are just in a bad mood, it will snap you out of it!

"I enjoy humor. I love life. Life is fun. Life is exciting. Living is wonderful. Life is humorous. I see humor. I sense humor. Life is a miracle. I am a

miracle. I enjoy laughing. My sense of humor is keen. I enjoy living. I enjoy life. I enjoy my friends. I enjoy my family. I enjoy my associations. I am free of self-consciousness. I share humor. I smile. I like smiling," etc.

innertalk-store.com/products/joy_of_humor

Inadequacy (Eradicating Inadequacy: Unleashing My Strengths) ~ Subliminal

~ Set yourself free today and enjoy a new buoyant self, ready to be everything you can be!

Feelings of inadequacy are common today in a world where on a 24-7 basis we are inundated with super models, fancy fast cars, stylish personally tailored clothes, and so forth. The fact is, no one is perfect and sometimes our inadequate feelings are the result of believing that we should be.

This program was created to assist you in eliminating the disparaging thoughts that you're just not good enough—that somehow you are inadequate. We all have these feelings from time to time, but they need not control us. Set yourself free today and enjoy a new buoyant self, ready to be everything you can be!

"I am more than adequate. I am capable. I am wise. My life is important. I am important. I contribute to the world. I make a difference. I am unique. My talents are unique. I am confident. I am validated by others. I accept their validation. I accept myself. I am effective. I am a good listener. I validate others. Life is a gift. I am a gift. I am a miracle. I am aware of my influence. I use my influence wisely. I commend others. Others commend me. I am trust-worthy," etc.

innertalk-store.com/products/eradicating-inadequacy-subliminal

Integrity (Living with Integrity) ~ Subliminal

~ Discover what true self-respect feels like!

Integrity is a great concept, but while everyone admires it, most people have problems living up to it. In a world where there are so many who care only about themselves and what they can get out of life, it can just be easy to cut some corners in your own life – at least from time to time.

Can you imagine what the world would be like if everyone lived with integrity? While we are not responsible for the choices others make, we are responsible for our own. Try this program and discover what true self-respect feels like.

"I am humble. I am courageous. Integrity is important to me. Integrity comes first. My words match my actions. My actions match my words. I am thoughtful. I am considerate. I am open to learning. I enjoy learning. I set high standards. I live by my principles. My convictions are strong. I do the right thing. I hold to my values. I am continually evaluating my principles. I apologize when I'm wrong. I'm honest about my feelings," etc.

innertalk-store.com/products/living-with-integrity-subliminal

Invalidation (Healing from Invalidation) ~ Subliminal
~ Learn to appreciate yourself and the world will follow suit.

You are your own validator. Stop feeling that you don't matter. You do! You are important and special. You are a unique individual with lots to offer to the world. Learn to appreciate yourself and the world will follow suit. This program was built especially for those who have been treated in an ill dignified way resulting in feelings of inadequacy. You can recover your dignity and replace those feelings of invalidation with a whole new level of confidence, but it all begins in your mind.

I'm okay. I'm good. I'm worthy. I'm deserving. I'm capable. I accept myself. I have learned from my mistakes. Life is a lesson ground. I know I am worthy of dignity and respect. I respect myself. I respect others. I now feel good about me. I choose to be happy. I choose to accept my worth. I am a valid human being. What I think matters. What I feel matters. Who I am matters. I am a gift. Life is a miracle. I am part of the miracle. I love myself. I care for my needs. I respect my being. I let go of the past. I empower today. I live in now. I forgive myself," etc.

innertalk-store.com/products/healing_from_invalidation

Joyous Day ~ Subliminal

~ Choose to be happy!

Joy sometimes eludes us even when we need it most. In every difficulty or failure in life, there is a lesson and an opportunity. It is in these moments that one has to actively participate in finding it, choosing it, and making joy a flame that burns brightly when all other light goes out.

Joyous Day teaches you to stay positive, enthusiastic, and open to success. Have a wonderful day every day and show everyone that joy comes from within! Appreciate the life you have been given and manifest your dreams better than ever before.

"I live in now. Now is all there is. I have all I need now. I have high self-esteem. I am optimistic. I am positive. I am enthusiastic. I am whole. I am enough. I am good. I am liked. I am loving. I am loved. Life is a miracle. Life is fun. Life is a teacher. I improve. I grow. Every day in every way I learn. Every day in every way I improve. Every day in every way I succeed," etc.

innertalk-store.com/products/joyous_day

Also Available In:

Joy (Boundless Joy) ~ OZO

innertalk-store.com/products/boundless_joy_ozo

Joy (Living in Joy) ~ Power Set

innertalk-store.com/products/living_in_joy_ps

Loneliness (Resolving Feelings of Loneliness and Isolation) ~ Subliminal

~ The first step to overcoming loneliness is believing in yourself.

It's not uncommon for everyone to feel somewhat lonely from time to time, even when seemingly they are in a crowd. There are seven types of loneliness according to Gretchen Rubin writing for *Psychology Today* and they include: New Situation; I'm different; No sweetheart; No pet; No time-for-me; Untrustworthy friends; and Missing presence of someone*

This program was created to deal with the common factors to all forms of loneliness. If you feel lonely and/or isolated, then begin to change your life today.

"I care about my relationships. I build new relationships. I like people. I enjoy being with others. I stay in touch with my friends and family. I encourage friendships. Friendships are important to me. I engage with others. I attend events and make new friends. I go out of my way to help others. I feel good about myself. I am liked. I recognize when someone is being friendly. People care about me. People respect me. People like me. I am a good friend. I am capable. I enjoy my friends. I enjoy connecting with people." etc.

innertalk-store.com/products/loneliness-and-isolation-subliminal

Also Available In:

Loneliness (Overcoming Loneliness) ~ Collection

innertalk-store.com/products/overcoming-loneliness-collection

Loss of a Loved One ~ Subliminal

~ Turn the energy of grief toward the beauty of love today!

Regardless of whether a death is unexpected or not, the loss is still very real. However, the death of a loved one need not leave you emotionally and spiritually disabled. Using this tool can help you "over the hump."

"God has already forgiven all. I release myself from guilt. I release myself from blame. I am forgiven. I am at peace. I am a child of love. Love and light are one. I am one with love and light. I am one with all. My loved ones are at peace. My loved ones are with God. My loved ones forgive me. I am released. My loved ones are released. I am at peace. I enjoy living. I am one with the light. The light and love are one. I enjoy living. I am healed," etc.

innertalk-store.com/products/loss_of_a_loved_one

Lucky (I am Lucky) ~ Subliminal

~ Expecting good things is the perfect way to always attract good luck in your life.

It is often said that good luck is just preparedness meeting opportunity. With *I Am Lucky*, you will be able to see the good things that come your way, take chances to attract success, and 'Seize the Day,' as they say. You will be open to receive an abundance of both materialistic and spiritual prosperity. You will be prepared to tune in to everything going on in your life and notice how its synchronicity supports your success and personal goals.

"The Universe brings me good. The universe brings me plenty. I am deserving. I am worthy. I am a creation of the Divine. I am created perfectly. I am lucky. Luck is not an accident. I am prepared. I am ready. I am alert and willing. I accept the good that comes to me. I attract all that I need whenever I need it. I am loved. I love life. I love living. I am inspired. I am here for a purpose. I accept the calling as it is revealed to me. I pay attention to synchronicity. I am alert to coincidence. I am in tune with my purpose," etc.

innertalk-store.com/products/lucky

Also Available In:

Luck (Becoming Lucky: Attracting and Enhancing Good Luck) ~ Album

innertalk-store.com/products/becoming-lucky-album

Mellow (I Am Mellow) ~ Subliminal

~ Mellow people can chill when others are stressed out!

Mellow people are calm. Mellow people sleep better and have stronger social lives. In modern parlance, they chill when others are stressed out. You too can have the sense of presence to know what you can change and what you cannot and remain calm and mellow in either event.

"I am mellow. I am calm. I am relaxed. I laugh. I have fun. I enjoy life. I enjoy myself. I enjoy others. Living is wondrous. Life is a miracle. I respect all life. I am loving. I am appreciative. I am thoughtful. I am reflective. I am patient. I feel great. I feel good about myself. I feel good about others. I am joyous. I am grateful," etc.

innertalk-store.com/products/mellow

Nail Biting (Freedom from Nail Biting) ~ Subliminal

~Allow your hands and nails to be beautiful.

This is a favorite program and the stories we have heard from our customers is the reason. For example, a customer who purchased this program informed us that they had a complaint. The program had worked so well that now they needed to buy a Memory program so that they could remember to buy nail clippers.

Nail biting is not an attractive habit and it can leave your hands looking dreadful. Break this habit and allow your hands and nails to be beautiful.

"I am free of nail biting. I am calm. I am relaxed. I breathe deeply. I care for myself. I like myself. I care for my hands. I care for my fingers. I care for my nails. I present myself well. I look great. I like looking great. My hands look great. I am busy. I am energetic. I am a producer. I am capable. I am whole. I am in control. I am aware. I am aware of my hands. I am aware of my fingers. I am self-assured. I have high self-esteem," etc.

innertalk-store.com/products/freedom_from_nail_biting

Narcissistic Control (Overcoming Narcissistic Control) ~ Subliminal

~ End the need to please the narcissist and take control of your own life.

Narcissists believe they are the most important and that the world should revolve around them and their needs. When you spend any time with a narcissist, it is only too easy to start to believe this too—and if they are the center of the universe, then of course your needs are secondary. Narcissists do all of the taking in a relationship and can totally undermine your core values.

You are an important person in your own right, with needs and desires of your own. Learn to believe in yourself again, to respect your own needs and values, and to regain control over your own life and the choices that you make. You are an important person in your own right, with needs and desires of your own.

"I choose to be free of controlling relationships. I am fee of coercively controlled relationships. I choose to be free of coercion. I reclaim myself. I

have reclaimed all those things I like. I have freed myself from limitations. I am free to go and do as I wish. I am free to speak to whomever I wish. I respect myself. I expect to be treated with respect. I deserve respect. I am a good person. I am a whole person. I am a healthy person. I choose to be happy and healthy. I release old feelings of inferiority. I am capable. I am worthy. I am respected.," etc.

innertalk-store.com/products/overcoming-narcissistic-control-subliminal

Neat and Tidy ~ Subliminal

~ Less mess equals less stress, improved productivity, better health, and peace of mind.

Clutter and lack of organization are often manifestations of the way we live our lives. A lack of organization and tidiness has been shown to increase anxiety and decrease productivity. Research has shown that clearing away the clutter can help you make healthier choices, improve your relationships, and reduce stress. Life just goes more smoothly when you are in a neat and tidy environment. Things are easier to find, and the sense of organization brings its own feeling of calmness and tranquility. Make your personal space neat and tidy today!

"I like myself. I am good. I am liked. I am cooperative. I am patient. I am helpful. I am motivated. I am positive. I am efficient. I am orderly. I look good. I appear good. I feel good. I like neatness. I like being tidy. I love order. I love cleanliness. I am proud of myself," etc.

innertalk-store.com/products/neat_and_tidy

Optimism Plus ~ Subliminal

~ An optimistic attitude will enhance nearly every area of your life!

Optimistic people live longer, enjoy healthier lives, experience less stress, develop enhanced coping skills, and enjoy increased productivity. Optimistic people enjoy more happiness, better relationships, and a greater peace of mind. Self-esteem is boosted by optimism, as are daily mood states. In short, optimism works to enhance nearly every area of your life.

"I am healthy. I am young. I am strong. I am fit. I am powerful. I am positive. I am confident. I am enthused. I am motivated. I am loving. I am sharing. I am patient. I am honest and truthful. I am efficient and organized. I am comfortable. I am considerate. I am calm and relaxed. I am brilliant and capable. I am intuitive and creative. The mind, body and spirit are one," etc.

innertalk-store.com/products/optimism_plus

Past (Healing the Past) ~ Subliminal

~ Don't let the past sabotage your present and future.

The past is over. Its lessons are learned. It's time to release it. Don't let the past sabotage your present and future. Allow yourself to heal from the pains of yesterday. Change your life for the better and begin now

"I can let go of the past. I can accept the past as a life teaching. I can choose to heal the past. I create my future. I create forgiveness in my heart. I create joy in my life. I create happiness and harmony. I create peace and balance. I will always choose peace and balance. I will always choose happiness and harmony. I love living. I enjoy life. I enjoy myself. I love myself. I am willing to let go of the past. I live in now. The past is over. The past is powerless. Only now has relevance on my being," etc.

innertalk-store.com/products/healing_the_past

Patience (I Am Patient) ~ Subliminal

~ Adopt the pace of nature: her secret is patience!

Patience provides the opportunity to listen. Patience offers that sometimes-critical moment to catch our thoughts and abate an action that we might otherwise regret. Patience affords an escape from those traffic jams, crying babies, hormone raging teens, and so forth. Patience makes us better people.

If you're like most, you find yourself often regretting that you didn't have just a little more patience. This program will help you find patience natural and easy, whether dealing with family, friends, business associates or rush hour traffic.

"Patience is power. Patience is understanding. Patience tames passion. Patience is caring. Patience is genius. Patience is persistence. Patience communicates. I am patient. I am understanding. I am caring. I am loving. I am good. I am calm. I am relaxed. I breathe deeply. I feel great. I achieve meaning," etc.

innertalk-store.com/products/patience

Personality (Magnetic Personality) ~ Subliminal

~ Radiating charisma, charm, self-confidence, and trust will influence all around you.

This program is designed to facilitate adding new dimensions to your personality; dimensions like added energy, listening skills, motivational awareness, optimism, awareness, and imagination. These characteristics exist in the person possessing a magnetic personality. There is a definite attractor factor that advantages those with a magnetic personality so why not begin to build your own attraction factor today?

"Life is fun. Life is exciting. People are varied. People are good. We are all growing. We are all learning. We are all gifts. All I can be is a gift. I see the Divine in all things. I have humor. I sense the humorous. I am balanced. I am at peace with myself. I am at peace with the world. I am loving. I am caring. I am sharing. I am loved. I am confident. I am optimistic. I am in control. Joy is mine. Peace is mine. Balance is mine. Harmony is mine. My relationships are positive. All that comes to me comes for good," etc.

innertalk-store.com/products/magnetic_personality

Post War Syndrome / PTSD (Recovery from Post War Syndrome) ~ Subliminal

~ Leave all the trauma and discomfort behind

Post-Traumatic Stress Disorder (PTSD) affects those who have experienced or witnessed life-threatening situations. It can also affect some people who have experienced a shocking, scary, or dangerous event. The result can be heightened states of arousal, fear, nightmares, and more.

You can learn to leave all this discomfort behind, and you do deserve to do so. This program has provided help for many in dealing with the runaway emotions and has aided them in stabilizing their lives—turning their state of mind to the peace, balance, and harmony so many seek.

"I am whole. I am a gift. I am loved. God loves me. God forgives me. I forgive myself. I forgive all others. I am forgiven. I release fear. I release guilt. I release stress. I release anger. I release tension. I release blame. I release shame. I am relaxed. I am free of punishment. I am free of guilt. I am free of fear. I am free of anger. I am free of blame. I am free of negativity. I am free of negative expectations. I am free of negative experiences. I am free of negative dreams. I am in control," etc.

innertalk-store.com/products/post_war_syndrome

Profanity (Freedom from Profanity) ~ Subliminal

~ There comes a point when it is time to leave the profanity behind.

Is profanity an issue with you or someone you care about? People begin using bad language for many reasons—to fit in with their peers, to feel cool, to shock others, to strike out against conformity etc. However, there comes a point when it is time to leave the profanity behind. You sound much more intelligent using language correctly and others will respect you more. You can change this behavior beginning today.

"I speak well. I speak clearly. I speak with dignity. I am free of foul language. I am free of filth. I am free of bitterness. I am free of anger. I select my words. I expand my vocabulary. I am confident. I am patient. I am free of cussing. I am free of cursing. I express myself with dignity. I have self-esteem. I respect myself. I respect others. I am honest. I am truthful. I am forthright. I am responsible. Foul language is self-degrading. Filthy language is offensive," etc.

innertalk-store.com/products/freedom_from_profanity

Reflective (I Am Reflective) ~ Subliminal

~ Reflective thinking encourages a stronger sense of identity and leads to forming deep and lasting relationships.

Being reflective is a state of relating to, or of characterized by, deep thought. A reflective person is one who thinks things through. Doing so allows one the opportunity to make sure they are making the right choices. People enjoy relationships with someone who is thoughtful, reflective and considerate. Reflective thinkers gain a broader understanding of the world they live in. Reflective thinking encourages a stronger sense of identity and leads to forming deep and lasting relationships.

"I am reflective. I am thoughtful. I am creative. I am confident. I am capable. I make decisions. I consider alternatives. I consider advantages. I think forwardly. I want the best for all. I want the best for me. I deserve the best. I am powerful. I succeed. I think rapidly. I think carefully. I think thoroughly. I act on my decisions. I make good decisions. I make wise decisions. Thinking is destiny. Thoughts are seeds. Seeds are true to themselves. My thoughts are good thoughts. My thoughts are wise thoughts. I am positive. My thoughts are positive," etc.

innertalk-store.com/products/i_am_reflective

Relaxation ~ Subliminal

~ Take a mini-vacation from the day's tensions.

True relaxation is a state free of tension and anxiety. Both of these can build up slowly, so slowly that we easily become accustomed to heightened states of arousal and worse, we soon become unaware of this state of being until suddenly it whacks us. Tension and stress can lead to many manifestations of illness or dis-ease ranging from back and neck pain to cardiac difficulties. Take a mini-vacation from the day's tensions. You'll feel a sense of calm and peace, refreshed and renewed. If you have trouble sleeping, play this program at bedtime or throughout the night. You will notice the difference in so many important ways!

"I am calm. I am relaxed. I breathe deeply. I remain calm. I perform relaxed. I am impervious to tension. I am impervious to anxiety. I am impervious to stress. Relaxed I perform well. Relaxed I solve problems. Relaxed I respond well. Relaxed my reflexes are faster. Relaxed my thoughts are clear. I act relaxed. I am in control. I am strong. I am healthy. I am worry free. I am stress free. I am tension free. I am at peace. I am at peace with myself. I am at peace with the world around me," etc.

innertalk-store.com/products/relax_now

Also Available In:

Relax Now ~ Power Imaging/Hypnosis

innertalk-store.com/products/relax_now_pi

Relaxation (Deep Relaxation) ~ Collection

innertalk-store.com/products/deep_relaxation_collection

Relaxation and Esteem Building ~ Video

innertalk-store.com/products/relaxation_and_esteem_dvd

Rescripting the Child Within ~ Subliminal

~ Re-script your inner child and walk joyously confident into your future today.

As children, we would often formalize a criticism, taking it to heart, and creating defense strategy that remained in our subconscious. Within each of us is our inner child and often that child makes choices that no longer serve us. The choices are based on old programming that is not relevant in our lives today. Discover the joy of learning to love, heal, and accept your wounded inner child.

"I accept myself. I accept others. I forgive myself. I forgive others. I release guilt. I am happy. I am capable. I am whole. I am enough. I love life. I love living. I love myself. I love others. I am positive. I expect positive. Life is a school. I have many learnings. I accept my learnings," etc.

innertalk-store.com/products/rescripting_the_child_within

Resilience (Developing Resilience) ~ Subliminal

~ Winners are invariably those who simply tried one more time!

Some people fall apart whenever things go even slightly wrong, whereas others just jump right back up and try again. Excuses are easy and quitting is often easier than pursuing.

Resilience is the capacity to recover quickly from difficulties. Resilience is that quality that permits some people to be knocked down by life and come back stronger than ever.

"I am strong. I recover quickly. I am resilient. I spring back quickly. I overcome obstacles. I overcome tragedy. I remain strong. I remain confident. I am optimistic. I am positive. I adapt. I am free of stress and anxiety. I relax. I live in now. I think positively about the future. I have goals. I pursue my goals. I enjoy living. I am decisive. I like learning about myself. Life is a miracle. I am a miracle. I am hopeful. I am trusting. I am grateful. I have a gratitude attitude. I learn from the past. I have a positive expectation. I am truly resilient," etc.

innertalk-store.com/products/developing-resilience-subliminal

Responsibility Syndrome (Freedom from Responsibility Syndrome) ~ Subliminal

~ Learn to shift responsibility around in positive ways that free you of feeling always responsible for everything!

Responsibility Syndrome (RS) is often defined as a condition where "you believe you're responsible for everything because you alone are the only one who can do it. People who get caught up in RS are exhausted from their workload. Learn how to do your best and then let go of the rest. This program was designed to assist in creating a mind-set that while encouraging your best efforts, also diminishes your need to inspect everything, set goals that are too high, and seek perfection in everything you do.

"I do my best. I can let go. I manage my time. I manage wisely. I allow. I do what I can do and then let go. I am worry free. I am stress free. I shed stress. I am reasonable. I have reasonable expectations. I sleep well. I take care of myself. I like to exercise. I exercise. I take time to relax. I enjoy relaxing. I enjoy my private time. I am free of worry. I am confident. I accept help. I relegate often. I share responsibilities. Others help me. I accept the help," etc.

innertalk-store.com/products/responsibility_syndrome

Self-Destructive (Ending Self Destructive Patterns) ~ Subliminal

~ Self-sabotage is often the way your subconscious protects you from being hurt again.

Are there things in life you want but feel unworthy or unprepared to receive? Do you sabotage your own attempts at success? Without being consciously aware of it, most have some self-sabotaging mechanism operating at some level with regards to some things. Whenever you see a "repeat performance" of things gone bad, and you are the only common denominator, it's probably due to some self-sabotaging mechanism, some unconscious belief. This program will help you get out of your own way.

"I am calm. I am relaxed. I accept myself. I am good. Life is good. Living is a miracle. I am a miracle. I deserve the best. I deserve success. I believe in myself. I trust myself. I am confident. My abilities are awesome. I desire success. I desire the best. I am ready to succeed. I succeed now. I make success happen. I allow luck to assist me. I am lucky. Luck is good. I plan my success. I use my energy to succeed. I am committed," etc.

innertalk-store.com/products/ending_self_destructive_patterns

---

*"In response to my request for assistance in my business and life, you said, 'I suggest using **Ending Self Destructive Patterns** first. This may assist in uncovering any self-sabotaging strategies that hold prosperity from you.' Things are working! My seminars are starting to get off the ground...thank you so much for your program!"*

Also Available In:

Self-Sabotage (Eliminating Self-Sabotage) ~ Album

innertalk-store.com/products/eliminating_self_sabotage_album

Self-Destructive Patterns (Ending Self-Destructive Patterns) ~ Echo-Tech

innertalk-store.com/products/self_destructive_patterns_et

Sabotage (Stop Self Sabotage) ~ Power Set

innertalk-store.com/products/stop_self_sabotage_ps

Serenity ~ Subliminal

~ Experience a hush of peaceful tranquility pouring over every cell of your being.

Imagine remaining in a state of calm repose, unruffled quietude, clear and free of unpleasantness. That is the state of being serene. Serenity has been sought by the mystics as a path of enlightenment. It is often sought by all for no more reason than the quality of the experience. Many of our customers have indeed reported using this program when they simply felt stressed out.

"I am relaxed. I am safe. I am calm. I remain calm and composed. LOVE is what I am. I am a gift. I am grateful for the gift. I am blessed. I accept the Divine plan. The Universe is purposeful. I am serene. I acknowledge the good in all. I am non-judgmental. I am caring and sharing. I am loving. I am compassionate. I am detached from worldly woes. I recognize the illusion. Only the eternal is real. I invest myself in the eternal. I am infinite wisdom. I am infinite composure. Serene and calm," etc.

innertalk-store.com/products/serenity

Also Available In:

Peace and Serenity ~ Power Set

innertalk-store.com/products/peace_and_serenity_ps

Stress (Freedom from Stress) ~ Subliminal

~ Take control of your stress and achieve a state of calm and well-being.

You can learn to condition your mind to become virtually stress free. Remain relaxed and composed in almost any circumstance—prepared, ready, but without tensions, anxiety or stress. Research shows that as much as 80% of all illness is stress-related. Within each of us is the power and ability to reinterpret our stressors and to experience much less stress and anxiety. The health benefits are enormous!

"I am calm. I am relaxed. I am confident. I am stress free. I release stress. I release anxiety. I externalize stress. I desensitize stimuli. I breathe deeply. I have a proper perspective. I am in charge. I am in control. I am at peace with myself. I am at peace with the world around me. I am comfortable. I like myself. I like others. I love living. I like exercise. I exercise. I like relaxation. I relax regularly. I am tranquil," etc.

innertalk-store.com/products/freedom_from_stress

---

*I have had an extremely difficult year, both professionally and personally. Consequently, I felt useless to others and couldn't find my way through it. I started to use the **Freedom from Stress** CD and soon had fantastic results. I am now experiencing a good night's sleep and no longer have frightening anxiety attacks. I look forward to every day and have, at last rediscovered my long-lost enthusiasm!"*

Also Available In:

Stress (Eliminating Stress: Experiencing Joy) ~ Album

innertalk-store.com/products/eliminating-stress-album

Stress (Free of Anxiety and Stress) ~ Power Imaging/Hypnosis

innertalk-store.com/products/anxiety_and_stress_pi

Stress and Anxiety (Freedom from Stress and Anxiety) ~ Video

innertalk-store.com/products/stress_and_anxiety_dvd

Stress Free Living ~ Power Set

innertalk-store.com/products/stress_free_ps

Stress Free ~ Echo-Tech

innertalk-store.com/products/stress_free_et

Stress Management ~ Collection

innertalk-store.com/products/stress_management_collection

Stuttering (End Stuttering) ~ Subliminal

~ Stuttering does not need to hold you back. Are you ready to open up new horizons in your life?

Stuttering can affect many areas of your life and is invariably worse at the times it is most important to speak clearly. This can severely limit your choices of career and social activities. Amazing results have been reported with this program. Stuttering does not need to hold you back.

"I breathe deeply. I relax. I remain relaxed. I am calm. I am composed. I speak clearly. I sense the right side of my body. I sense the right side of my body when speaking. I breathe through my right nostril when speaking. I shift my weight to the right side when speaking. Words are effortless for me. I am confident. I am accepting. I am patient. I am whole. Sentences form easily. I speak well. I speak with confidence. I speak relaxed. Speech is natural," etc.

innertalk-store.com/products/end_stuttering

Technophobia (Freedom from Technophobia) ~ Subliminal

~ Keep up with technology and have fun doing it!

In today's information age, with an almost daily advance in technology, who hasn't from one time to another been just a little intimidated by technology. For some, this intimidation is actually a deep fear—a fear they may ruin something, they may somehow "mess up big time." Whether it's the new VCR or the new computer, many are unwilling to use the units to the utmost of their abilities for fear of something. Technology will only continue to advance, but we can choose to keep up while having fun doing so. This program is designed to aid in just that.

"I can learn easily. I can enjoy equipment. I can be technical. I can enjoy technical equipment. Technology is wonderful. Technology is liberating. Technology is fun. Technology is exciting. I can enjoy technology. I can choose to learn new things. It's easy to learn. It's easy for me to learn. I can play with technology. It's easy to enjoy technology. I am grateful for technology. I learn easily. I enjoy learning. Learning is fun. Learning is play. I choose to learn," etc.

innertalk-store.com/products/freedom_from_technophobia

Television (Freedom from Television) ~ Subliminal

~ Turn off the television and get back your life!

The polls and data often are at odds. It would seem that many people watch much more television than they would like to admit. The numbers for children run anywhere from 4 to 7 hours each day. Adults do no better on average. Have you ever found yourself watching more television but enjoying it less? Did you ever think that you could have done something else and had more fun? Are you addicted to your TV? This program is designed to give you back your time.

"I can enjoy myself. I can use my time wisely. I can read. I can play games. I can enjoy talking. I can enjoy friends and family. I can be active. I can avoid television. I choose to avoid television. I choose to use my time wisely. I choose to enjoy family and friends. I choose to enjoy reading. I choose to enjoy being all that I can. I enjoy self-improvement. I enjoy self-help. I enjoy becoming better and better in every way every day. I create my future," etc.

innertalk-store.com/products/freedom_from_television

Thoughts (Think Nice Thoughts) ~ Subliminal

~ "Be the change you wish to see in the world."

Have you given any thought to the nature of civility today? How long has it been since you heard or saw uncivil behavior, whether in a movie or real life? When we are surrounded by nasty thoughts and ideas, it is very easy to find ourselves sucked into this sort of thinking ourselves.

It was Gandhi who said, "Be the change you wish to see in the world." This program is the perfect way to start this process. Try it for yourself today.

"I treat others with respect. I think nice thoughts. I cancel thoughts I don't want. I speak nicely. I avoid rumors. I say nice things. I am positive. I am a positive person. I add joy to the world. I spread civility in the world. I treat others as I wish to be treated. I am humble. I am honest. I am caring. I train myself to think good thoughts. I train my mind to think nice thoughts. I intentionally cancel unkind thoughts. I go out of my way to be kind. I am a thoughtful person. I practice the Golden Rule. I enjoy sharing

positive thoughts. I enjoy being kind and thoughtful. I discipline myself to be kind," etc.

innertalk-store.com/products/think-nice-thoughts-subliminal

Toilet Anxiety (Overcoming Toilet Anxiety) ~ Subliminal

~ Discard the fears that underlie your toilet anxiety

Toilet anxiety is a lot more common than most people think, and it is particularly hard when it comes to using public restrooms. For some, it is the fear of embarrassing noises and smells. For others it is a fear of germs and other people's 'dirt.' And there are others who are just more comfortable when they can 'go' at home.

There are many social ramifications to toilet anxiety. Some people avoid social events in case they need to go, while others refuse to use the restroom and allow their personal discomfort to increase. As the discomfort increases, their ability to interact with others decreases. In more extreme situations, the discomfort of 'needing to go' can cause a person to become short tempered and curt in their interactions.

Discard the fears that underlie your toilet anxiety and discover a whole new freedom.

"My body processes are normal. I am comfortable with all of my body processes. I am free of fear. I am free of anxiety. I am confident. I am capable. Toilet duties are normal. Toilet duties are safe. I am safe. Public restrooms are safe. I am relaxed in the bathroom. I am relaxed urinating. I am relaxed defecating. I trust my body. I am comfortable with my body. My body provides plenty of warning before I need the bathroom. I am okay with using the bathroom. Using the bathroom is natural. Everyone uses the bathroom. There's nothing to fear. Bathroom noises are normal. I am comfortable with the sounds in the bathroom. I am comfortable with the noise attached to using the bathroom. I am comfortable with clean restrooms. Most restrooms are clean," etc.

innertalk-store.com/products/toilet-anxiety-subliminal

Violence (Non-Violence) ~ Subliminal

~ Cultivate a non-violent mental mindset!

This program was originally designed to create an attitude of non-violence in the workplace. This Non-Violence program obviously crosses many borders . . . from relationships and child development to the workplace. By virtue of our attention in our entertainment, we often program violence without even being aware of it. Use this program as an antidote for the whole family.

"Violence begets violence. Violence is non-productive. Violence generates fear and anger. Fear and anger produce more fear and anger. Fear and anger generate self-alienation. Violence is not of God. An act of violence does violence unto all. Violent thoughts are imprisoning. Imprisoning oneself is absurd. I release violent thoughts. I am free of violent tendencies. I release the false in favor of the true. I am eternal. I am a gift. I am a miracle. I am grateful for the miracle. All that I can ever be is a gift. I accept the gift. I hold onto the virtue of good," etc.

innertalk-store.com/products/non_violence

Worry (Freedom from Worry) ~ Subliminal

~ Release worry, enjoy a restful mind, and improve your health!

Worrying takes a lot of energy and robs you of your ability to think clearly. If you cannot thing clearly, then it is very difficult to find solutions. As such, worrying about a problem is counter-productive. In addition, worrying puts a lot of stress on the body, which of course can create other problems. Free yourself from worrying, enjoy a restful mind and improve your health!

"I relax. I let things go. I allow. I am positive and optimistic. I enjoy life. I laugh. I am trusting. Life is fun. I like to play. I exercise. I like to take walks. I focus on the positive. I think about the good. I can find good in all. I expect good. I expect joy. I accept the good. I accept happiness. I accept peace of mind. Peace of mind is mine now. I am relaxed. I am at ease. My mind is at peace with itself and the world around me," etc.

innertalk-store.com/products/freedom-from-worry

Relationships

For our most complete success related packages, please see:

Relationships (Positive Relationships) ~ Album
innertalk-store.com/products/positive_relationships_album

Loving Relationship ~ Collection
innertalk-store.com/products/loving_relationships_collection

Love (Attract Your Perfect Partner) ~ Set
innertalk-store.com/products/your_perfect_partner_set

Love (Enhancing Your Love Relationship) ~ Set
innertalk-store.com/products/enhance_the_romance_set

Co-Dependence (End Co-Dependence) ~ Power Set
innertalk-store.com/products/end_codependence_ps

Boundaries (Setting Healthy Boundaries: Saying No with Grace) ~ Subliminal

~ You can become comfortable asserting your own rights!

Are you one of those people who find it hard to say no? Do you find yourself agreeing to things such as plans that don't sound like fun to you or would deprive you of something you would rather do?

If you experience boundary issues this program is for you. Isn't it time you became comfortable asserting your own rights? Isn't it time you shaped your own life, made your own commitments because it's what you want to do instead of trying to satisfy another? Isn't it time for you to change the self-talk inside that stops you from asserting yourself? Isn't it time for you to begin to live a life of your choice?

"I value my time. I value my worth. I value myself. I value my schedule. I value my priorities. I can say no gracefully. I practice saying no with a smile. I don't apologize for saying no. I can say no to anyone. It is my time, my life, and my priorities. It is my space and my body. Saying no does not mean I'm a bad person. Saying no is sometimes necessary. I value my peace of mind. I value my health. I am unique, valuable, and important. I am direct when saying no. I am polite when saying no. I need no excuse to say no. I am guilt free. I am honest. I know my limits. I accept myself. I love and respect myself," etc.

innertalk-store.com/products/healthy-boundaries-subliminal

Charismatic (I Am Charismatic) ~ Subliminal

~ People always remember the charming and charismatic.

True charisma radiates an undescribed form of magnetism that consistently draws people closer. It is rare form of charm that seems irresistible. What could your life become if you added a dab of charisma to your personality? This ability to attract, charm, and influence people could change your life. Why not put a little magic in your personality. People always remember the charming and charismatic.

"I am charismatic. I am charming. I am witty. I am humorous. I am confident. I am poised. I am calm. I am comfortable. I am relaxed. I am positive. I am strong. I am loving. I am caring. I am sincere. I am understanding. I am patient. I love people. I love myself. I love life. Life is wonderful. Relationships are rewarding. Friends are fun. People are my friends," etc.

innertalk-store.com/products/i_am_charismatic

Co-Dependency (End Co-Dependent Patterns) ~ Subliminal

~ Become whole in yourself and start creating healthy relationships!

Classic co-dependence is destructive and manipulative and often leads to addictions. Co-dependents need to be needed, even if they must create or exaggerate the reason for the need. If you or yours fit this description or behave in an addictive, compulsive manner, this program can be very beneficial and enlightening. Its uses range from family relationships to chemical dependency.

"I am whole. I am independent. I am accepting. I am forgiving. I value myself. I am of value. I am worthy. I am deserving. I am positive. I am secure within myself. I need only myself. I am loving. I love myself. I am okay. I am sufficient. I am enough. I respect myself. I expect respect. I give respect. I am respecting. I enjoy myself. I enjoy life. I am responsible for me. I am only responsible for me," etc.

innertalk-store.com/products/end_codependency

Also Available In:

Co-Dependence (End Co-Dependence) ~ Power Set
innertalk-store.com/products/end_codependence_ps

Co-Dependent (End Co-Dependent Patterns) ~ Echo-Tech
innertalk-store.com/products/codependence_et

Communications (Gentle Communications: Speaking from the Heart) ~ Subliminal

~ Speaking from the heart demonstrates our inner strength!

Have you ever listened to the way in which you communicate with others? Are you aware that your communications are often harsher than you intended? Have you ever stopped to think about the consequences of this? The fact is, harsh communications have become the norm and we see this in families, across the political arena, and in our children.

Hard communications can demoralize the listener, suck away their self-esteem, cause them to give up on their own beliefs and dreams, and build up anger and resentment. This is no way to treat your loved ones, friends, colleagues, or any of the myriad of other people you interact with.

"I listen to myself when speaking. I choose my tone of voice deliberately. I choose to speak with a gentle voice. I choose to speak with a sincere voice. I speak with a caring voice. I speak with an understanding voice. I watch my tone of voice. I am careful about my tone of voice. I train myself to use a

comforting tone of voice. My tone of voice communicates care and concern. My tone of voice discloses my true character. I choose to be honorable. I choose to be wise. Arguments betray true communication. My tone of voice seeks understanding. My tone of voice disengages arguments. My tone of voice is strong but gentle. I choose a tolerant and optimistic perspective," etc.

innertalk-store.com/products/gentle-communications-subliminal

Cooperative (I Am Cooperative) ~ Subliminal

~ Cooperation leads to more success.

Cooperation is defined as the process of working together to the same end. The range of benefits can include everything from building lasting personal relationships to cross-pollinating ideas. Cooperation can be critical to our own personal development. The fact is: cooperation is important because it allows people and groups to work together to achieve a common goal and/or derive mutual benefits. Cooperative behavior leads to harmony in all relationships. This program is great for children and adults alike.

"I am cooperative. I am patient. I am an excellent listener. I listen intently. I am calm. I am relaxed. I am composed. I am whole. I am complete. I am capable. I am good. I respect myself. I respect others. I am respected. I build associations. I am friendly. I am courteous. I am respectful. I like others. I like myself. I like working with others. I like cooperating. I enjoy cooperating. I like companionship," etc.

innertalk-store.com/products/cooperative

Envy (Releasing Envy) ~ Subliminal

~ Release the little green monster and focus on all the good in your own life.

Envy, like anger, can play havoc with your life in many ways. It can lead to anxiousness, insecurity, and stress thereby damaging your health and relationships. It can be the unspoken source of much emotional angst that can provoke acts of anger and meanness. The feelings of insecurity can actually lead to stronger feelings of incompetence and failure, thereby sabotaging your goals and ambitions. Living in envy of is neither healthy, wise, nor spiritual. Release the little green monster and focus on all the good in your own life. Begin today!

"I am worthy. I am deserving. I am good. I celebrate the success of others. I enjoy witnessing others success. I celebrate my own successes. I am successful. All things in time. I am accepting. I am patient. I admire success. I am happy. Happiness is a choice. I choose happiness. I find good in all. I enjoy life. I love living. I am capable. I accept myself. I accept all others. Envy is a form of greed. I am a giving person," etc.

innertalk-store.com/products/releasing_envy

Get-Even (Eliminating The 'Get-Even' Response) ~ Subliminal

~ Plain and simple, revenge is unhealthy!

When you attempt to get-even, you sabotage your own self-growth. Vengeance can literally eat up our energies and in many ways damage not only our relationships but also our health. Just the thought of revenge can increase blood pressure, release neurochemicals that interfere with the optimal operation of our immune, endocrine and autonomic nervous system. Remember who you are and the person you would rather be. Don't give into the *get-even* response. Train your mind to remain in control while desensitizing any emotional stress.

"I am a good person. I like myself. I enjoy others. I am allowing. I am forgiving. I am humble. I accept others. I accept myself. I respect others. I respect myself. I am in control of my feelings. I know how to let things go. I am non-judgmental. Retribution is silly. Revenge is self-destructive. Reprisal is foolish. I am a wise person. I am a confident person. I am a capable person. I am comfortable with me. Anger accomplishes nothing. I am peaceful," etc.

innertalk-store.com/products/eliminating_the_get_even_response

Honesty (I Am Honest) ~ Subliminal

~ When you lie, you cheat yourself!

Exaggeration and "little white lies" are harmful. Outright dishonesty is dangerous. This habit shows its face from childhood on through adulthood and into business and relationships. Even though one may not intentionally set out to deceive others, people begin to question your integrity and sincerity.

"I am honest. I am sincere. I am courageous. I am whole. I like myself. I respect myself. I am good. I am proud. I am forgiving. I love living. I choose to be truthful. I am smart. I am wise. I am honorable. I am responsible. I am confident. I am accountable. I am upright. I am open. I am forthright. I am frank," etc.

innertalk-store.com/products/honesty

Intimacy and Relationships ~ Subliminal

~ Create more intimacy in your relationship and have fun in the process.

Intimacy begins with honesty—genuine honesty. It requires open trust and communication. When you can be who you are without regard to ideas of rejection, you have the foundation for a truly intimate relationship. Intimacy of this nature allows you to explore your partner both physically and mentally. You are open to touch, to experiences you may not otherwise consider, and in the process your shared intimate moments secure your shared bond.

This program contains some messages that refer to sex with your partner. We therefore urge you to be aware of the affirmations and the presence of children when you play it.

"I am trusting. I am open. Intimacy is fun. Intimacy is rewarding. I am relaxed. I am calm. I am creative. My sensations are pleasing. I am loving. I am loved. Intimacy is good. I enjoy sex. I enjoy my partner. I am sharing. I like to touch. I like being touched. My body is beautiful. I am natural. I am accepting. Creative intimacy is exciting," etc.

innertalk-store.com/products/intimacy_and_relationships

Jealousy (Freedom from Jealousy) ~ Subliminal

~ Become secure within yourself and experience a whole new freedom and happiness.

Jealousy can ruin relationships and spoil your sense of peace. Understanding this powerful emotion is important to learning more about yourself with the ultimate goal to eliminate these negative effects from your life. This programmed is designed to facilitate this process.

"I believe in myself. I accept myself. I accept others. I am good. I am secure in myself. I choose my destiny. I know that I am whole and sufficient. I know that I am a gift. I know that I am eternal. I am confident in myself. I like me. I respect myself. I respect others. I need nothing. I have within me the kingdom. I release fear and doubt. I own no one. No one owns me. I feel good about my freedom. I am free of pettiness. I am free of suspicion. I am free of jealousy. I celebrate others' happiness. I allow others their choices," etc.

innertalk-store.com/products/jealousy

*"I purchased the **Jealousy** CD a couple months ago and listened to it for about an hour a day. I soon found that little things that used to irritate me no longer would. I used to get jealous of other women if I considered them very attractive; this does not happen anymore. I even try to put myself in positions where I used to get jealous to see what happens. The CD really does work! I don't feel that sick feeling in the pit of my stomach anymore. To any ladies out there who don't want to have these negative feelings towards other women because of how they look, this is the CD for you. It worked for me and I am sure it will work for you."*

Listening (I Listen Intently) ~ Subliminal

~ Many misunderstandings can be avoided when you really hear what the other person is saying.

Altogether too often, people fail to really listen. Instead they begin to prepare their response before they have heard everything trying to be said. Developing good listening skills is critical in relationships of all kinds. Listening can lead to effective problem solving and creative innovations. We all learn much more when we listen than when we speak! Is it time for you to build good listening skills?

"I am a great listener. I remember what I hear. I sense what is told me. I listen intently. I speak when others finish speaking. I think about what others say. I think about what I say. Listening is learning. Listening is power. Listening is meaningful. Listening is fun. Listening is exciting. Listening is sharing. Listening is helpful. Listening is caring. Listening is an act of loving. I am caring. I am helpful. I am exciting. I am confident. I am positive. Life is fun. I like living," etc.

innertalk-store.com/products/listening

Love Relationship (Attracting the Right Love Relationship) ~ Subliminal

~ Cultivate the authenticity and confidence you need to attract the right kind of match for you!

Most people want to have that perfect someone in their lives. Oftentimes we block love from coming in. This program will help you see all the possible relationships out there and recognize how easy finding your perfect match really is. You will be able to feel comfortable in your own skin and send off friendly and approachable vibes to potential partners. You will feel deserving and capable of having love. People will enjoy your authentic companionship. You will encounter new dating possibilities that you were previously unaware of. Your confidence and unique personality will attract 'the one' for you and accepting their love will feel natural.

"Love is natural. I am good. I am caring and sharing. I am deserving. I like myself. I am considerate. I am kind. I am friendly. I am attractive. I am intelligent. I am an interesting person. People enjoy my companionship.

I attract good to me. I attract good people. People like me. I like people. I attract my perfect mate. My perfect mate is attracted to me. I am willing to give. I am deserving of gifts. Love is the highest gift. I deserve to be loved. I accept love in my life. I love myself. I am loved. It's okay to love and be loved," etc.

innertalk-store.com/products/attracting_the_right_love_relationship

Opposite Sex (Confidence with the Opposite Sex) ~ Subliminal

~ Build the composure and confidence appropriate for making and cultivating positive relationships with the opposite sex.

Do you ever lose confidence when speaking with someone of the opposite sex? Do your inhibitions prevent other people from seeing the *real* you? Would you like to be able to relax in the company of someone of the opposite sex? This program is designed to build the composure and confidence appropriate for making and building upon positive relationships with the opposite sex.

"I am attractive. I am desirable. I am open and honest. I appreciate openness. I appreciate honesty. I am appreciated. I am mature. I accept the opposite sex. Women are good. Men are good. I respect the feminine. I respect the masculine. I treat each person with dignity. I treat all with respect. I remain centered. I remain balanced. I am calm and at ease. I am comfortable with the opposite sex. I accept that there are differences. I allow for differences. I am confident in myself. I am confident in my sexuality. I admire the opposite sex. I see beauty and strength in both sexes," etc.

innertalk-store.com/products/confidence_with_the_opposite_sex

Rejection (Releasing the Fear of Rejection) ~ Subliminal

~ The fear of rejection can prevent us from even trying.

The fear of rejection is one of our deepest held fears. This fear can actually become an expectation and that expectation shades our perception, so it's not uncommon for someone to feel rejected when no such intent exists.

The fear of rejection can also prevent us from ever taking advantage of desirable opportunities. Release the fear and maximize your opportunities.

"I am good. I am capable. I do my best. My best is accepted. I am accepting. I am accepted. I allow. I am aware of my abilities. I am confident. I am sufficient. I am optimistic and positive. I release fear. I release anger. I treat myself with respect. I treat others with respect. I expect the best. I am grateful for all I have experienced and learned. I create happiness and joy. I turn things over to my higher self. I listen to my higher self," etc.

innertalk-store.com/products/releasing_the_fear_of_rejection

Relationships (Positive Relationships) ~ Subliminal

~ Open the channels to understanding and acceptance.

Relationships are the key to joy. Research has shown that people with positive relationships live longer healthier lives. Business success almost always depends on strong relationships. The fact is, no matter the endeavor, relationships play an important role in success and happiness. This is as true with our loved ones, as it is with those others in our lives who are there to support and encourage us. Learn to give and receive with trust and positive expectations in all of your relationships and watch your life flourish.

"I have positive relationships. I am confident. I am loving. I have self-esteem. I am trusting. I listen intently. I am patient. I am caring. I am giving. I am understanding. I love living. I love life. I am positive. Relationships are fun. Relationships are positive. Relationships are rewarding. Relationships are meaningful. I enjoy my relationships. I am confident in myself. I am independently secure. I am independently happy. I share my happiness. Life is sharing," etc.

innertalk-store.com/products/positive_relationships

Romance (Enhancing Romance, Intimacy and Love) ~ Subliminal

~ Bring back the magic in your relationship.

Has your intimate partnership lost its sparkle? Would you like to bring more romance into your life? Relationships take work, and over time it can be easy to take each other for granted. Bring back the magic in your relationship. Rekindle those warm feelings of love, respect and companionship. Relight the fire of passion. Listen and be heard. Let your own personality shine. This program contains some messages that refer to sex with your partner. We therefore urge you to be aware of the affirmations and the presence of children when you play it.

"I enjoy my intimate relationship. I enjoy my partner. I am open with my partner. I am honest with my partner. I am relaxed with my partner. I love my partner. I respect my partner's individuality. I respect my partner's desires. It's okay to be an individual. I am happy being me. I enjoy touching my partner. I enjoy sex with my partner. It's okay to want your own space. I am secure in my relationship. I am safe. I enjoy being intimate with my partner. I enjoy relaxing with my partner. I trust my partner. I enjoy sharing with my partner. I communicate openly. I communicate honestly. I express my feelings. I respect my partner. I respect myself. I choose to be honest," etc.

innertalk-store.com/products/enhancing_romance_intimacy_and_love

Shyness (Overcoming Shyness) ~ Subliminal

~ Be your personal best and exude confidence.

innertalk-store.com/products/overcoming_shyness

Shyness is the tendency to feel awkward, worried or tense during social encounters, especially with unfamiliar people. Is your fear of people holding you back from meaningful relationships and success opportunities? Help yourself be your personal best and exude confidence with members of both sexes. Learn to communicate in groups and create new relationships.

"I am comfortable around people. I am calm during introductions. I look forward to meeting people. Contact with people is fun. I make contact easily. I enjoy people. I am liked by people. I release the fear of people. Conversation is easy. Conversation is relaxed. Conversation is fun. I control my moods. I am comfortable with my facial expressions. I am secure with my appearance. Self-imposed limitations are gone. Negative barriers are gone. Fear is gone," etc.

innertalk-store.com/products/overcoming_shyness

Health and Wellness

For our most complete success related packages, please see:

Health and Wellness ~ Library

    innertalk-store.com/products/health_wellness_library

Young (Forever Young) ~ Album

    innertalk-store.com/products/forever_young_album

Pain Management and Relief ~ Collection

innertalk-store.com/products/pain_management_and_relief_collection

Sleep (Peaceful Sleep) ~ Collection

    innertalk-store.com/products/sleep_collection

Younger and Healthier ~ Power Set

    innertalk-store.com/products/younger_and_healthier

Cardiac Care and Recovery ~ Video

    innertalk-store.com/products/cardiac_care_and_recovery_dvd

ADHD (Adult ADHD) ~ Subliminal

~ Learn to focus and watch the rest of your life thrive!

Do you find yourself having trouble concentrating and keeping focus? Are you zoning-out, overlooking important details, or having a hard time remembering important events and conversations? Is your impulsivity causing you to become addicted to certain things or habits? Do you feel over-emotional and restless about your current situation? Are you tired of people telling you that you are unproductive or absent-minded? Learn to control your impulsive behaviors, manage your time and money, organize your life, boost your productivity, manage your stress and impulsivity, and communicate your desires clearly.

"I am organized. I plan my days. I like planning. I like accomplishing my plans. I think ahead. I contemplate my speech and action. I am a thoughtful person. I am patient. I pay attention. I listen and hear. I follow directions. My attention and focus is keen. My mind is sharp and alert. I feel good. I am calm and peaceful. I feel happy. I am busy. I like to exercise. I exercise often. I like being active. I like play. I have fun. I am fit and healthy. I meditate. I take time to quiet my mind and be mindful of my thoughts. Meditation is rewarding. I enjoy exercising my mind. I like mental tasks. I enjoy solving riddles and puzzles. I exercise my brain and mind regularly. I am a good learner. I enjoy learning. Learning is an important part of life. I am a perennial learner," etc.

innertalk-store.com/products/adult_adhd

Allergies (Freedom from Allergies) ~ Subliminal

~ Take charge of your allergies and learn to breathe more easily!

There are many mental factors involved in allergies. Research has shown that even slight stress and anxiety can substantially worsen a person's allergic reaction to some routine allergens. You may no longer need to dread springtime pollens, household pets or other allergy-causing substances. Customers have reported a definite reduction in allergy induced breathing issues using this program. Try it—you may be astonished at the results.

"I am free of allergies. I am relaxed. I breathe easily. I breathe deeply. I breathe effortlessly. My body is perfect. My cells generate perfectly. I am a gift. I love life. Allergies are unnatural. I am natural. I forgive myself. I forgive others. I am forgiven. I am loved. Breathing is natural," etc.

innertalk-store.com/products/freedom_from_allergies

Arthritis (Freedom from Arthritis) ~ Subliminal

~ Maximize your mind/body connection and heal your body.

Most people are unaware that stress can aggravate arthritis symptoms. Indeed, the mind plays a significant role in our ability to manage pain as well as promote healing. Research has repeatedly demonstrated that the body-mind connection can lead to body-mind health. Through the incredible directive of your mind, you can find relief from this sometimes-crippling disease. Maximize your mind/body connection and heal your body rather than allowing it to attack itself.

"I am free of arthritis. I am free of unnecessary calcium deposits. I eat proper foods. I eat at regular meals. I like water. I drink water. Water cleanses me. My body regenerates itself. My body regenerates perfectly. My brain, body cooperate. My mind cooperates. I will healing. Health and enjoyment are my birthright. Miracles happen. I am well and healthy. My joints are free. Movement is easy. Pain is gone. I exercise. Exercise is therapeutic. I exercise wisely. I visualize healthy joints. I visualize a healthy body. I maintain an ideal weight," etc.

innertalk-store.com/products/freedom_from_arthritis

Back Pain (Freedom from Back Pain) ~ Subliminal

~ Relax and end the back-pain cycle!

Pain is often identified as a cycle attenuated with fear. That is, we feel the pain, expect it to worsen, it worsens, we therefore expect it to grow even more severe, it does, and so forth. In part, this is both a self-fulfilling prophecy and the result of the tightness and tension we bring to the affected area. Pain is a signal. It can be managed. When one is relaxed and calm, out of the pain cycle, both healing and pain management can be facilitated.

"I will always choose to relax my muscles. Relaxed, allowing, comfortable--me now. I enjoy the comfort. I enjoy being at peace. I enjoy relaxing my muscles. I love life. I love living. My body heals perfectly. I care for my back. I have good posture habits. I let stress and tension go. I have the power within to heal perfectly. My back is strong. My back is free of tension.

My back muscles are healed. It's easy for me to relax. It's easy for me to be comfortable," etc.

innertalk-store.com/products/freedom_from_back_pain

Blood Pressure (Lowered Blood Pressure) ~ Subliminal

~ Create a more peaceful state within your heart and lower your high blood pressure.

Any kind of anxiety, depression, or unhealthy habit can exacerbate high blood pressure and can put extra stress on your heart, and your health in general. This program works as a biofeedback tool. Biofeedback is a technique that trains you to improve your health by controlling involuntary bodily processes, like blood pressure, through relaxation techniques and mental exercises. By harnessing the power of your mind and becoming aware of what is going on inside your body, you can gain more control over your health.

"I breathe deeply. I inhale through my nose. I exhale through my mouth. I relax. I remain relaxed. I remain calm. I remain composed. I am okay. I am in control. I choose peaceful thoughts. I think of joyful experiences. I think of tranquil times. I enjoy quiet. I am happy. I am whole. I am sufficient. I am worry free. I am stress free. I love life. I love living. I laugh. I expect good. I expect health. My blood pressure is normal. My systolic blood pressure is normal. My diastolic blood pressure is normal. I visualize perfect health. My cardiovascular system is healthy," etc.

innertalk-store.com/products/lowered_blood_pressure

Also Available In:

Blood Pressure (Relaxed: Lower Blood Pressure) ~ Video

innertalk-store.com/products/lowered_blood_pressure_dvd

Bruxism (Freedom from Bruxism) ~ Subliminal

~ Learn to relax while sleeping and eliminate your bruxism.

Occasional teeth grinding, medically called bruxism, does not usually cause harm, but when teeth grinding occurs on a regular basis the teeth can be damaged and other oral health complications can arise. Usually bruxism occurs during sleep so it can be difficult to identify except by symptoms such as headache, aching jaw, sore gums, etc. Try this program and see how much better you feel in the morning.

"I relax. I let go. I breathe deeply and evenly. I let my muscles totally relax. I let all tension go. I release stress. I release stressful thoughts. I think of good things. I relax my jaw muscles. I care for my teeth and gums. I care for myself. When I go to bed, I take a moment to let everything go. I breathe through my mouth for a few minutes. I open my jaws slightly and loosen my neck and jaw muscles. I sleep peacefully. I awake refreshed and rested. During sleep, I am aware of my mouth and jaws. My awareness eliminates grinding my teeth. It is easy for me to relax and let go," etc.

innertalk-store.com/products/freedom_from_bruxism

Caffeine Addiction (End Caffeine Addiction) ~ Subliminal

~ You really can kick the caffeine habit!

Caffeine can really help you get going in the morning or when you find yourself slowing down. But too much caffeine is not good for you. If you find that you cannot function without your regular doses of caffeine, you may have a caffeine addiction. Don't try to kick the habit alone—this program will make it a lot easier.

"I make a plan to eliminate caffeine from my diet. I systematically reduce the amount of caffeine I drink. I enjoy decaffeinated drinks. I choose decaffeinated drinks. I wean myself from caffeine. I let caffeine go. I feel better without caffeine. I like caffeine free drinks. I choose to eliminate caffeine. I find it easy to drink non-caffeine drinks. I reward myself by letting go of caffeine. I sleep well. I awake from sleep refreshed. I am relaxed. I am calm. I am peaceful," etc.

innertalk-store.com/products/end_caffeine_addiction

Cancer (Spiritual Healing for Cancer Remission)
~ Subliminal

~ This is a spiritual healing program for cancer and is not a replacement for professional health care.

In a longitudinal study, many physicians and patients involved in the use of these programs have reported excellent results. This program is only available free of charge, but it requires either a note from the attending physician or the patient, stating they are aware this program is not a replacement for professional health care. (Shipping and handling fees still apply. Educational property only.) There is also only one program per customer.

"I am a gift. I am created perfectly. I am loved. I love myself. I forgive others. I forgive all others. My mind is powerful. My life force is eternal. My consciousness is alive. My consciousness exists throughout my body. My cells are conscious. My mind is conscious. My cells form perfectly. My body rejects alien intrusions. My body does so perfectly. My healthy cells multiply. My cells rejuvenate. I am healthy. I am strong. I am positive. I am confident," etc.

innertalk-store.com/products/cancer_remission

Dental Anxiety (Freedom from Dental Anxiety)
~ Subliminal

~ You really can enjoy your next dental appointment!

One of the most common fears in America is the dreaded visit to the Dentist. It need not be that way. Clean white healthy teeth can make a real difference in one's appearance and confidence. This program was actually put to the test in a study conducted by the Mexican government's Health Care Department of Social Services and found to be so effective that they took 5000 units to distribute throughout their dental care facilities.

"I am thankful there are dentists. I am grateful for my health. I care for myself. I am thankful care is available. I am grateful for health care professionals. I appreciate my dentist. I appreciate the care my dentist provides. I care for my teeth and gums. I am proud of my teeth and gums. I smile. I enjoy smiling. I look good. My dentist cares for me. My dentist is

helpful. My dentist can be trusted. I trust my dentist. I relax in the dental chair. I remain calm and relaxed with my dentist. I enjoy looking and feeling good. I enjoy my dental visits. Calm and relaxed. Patient and comfortable. Trusting and confident. I express my gratitude to my dentist," etc.

innertalk-store.com/products/freedom_from_dental_anxiety

Also Available In:

Dental Anxiety (Freedom from Dental Anxiety) ~ Video

innertalk-store.com/products/freedom_from_dental_anxiety_dvd

Energetic (I Have High Energy) ~ Subliminal

~ Live each day with abundant vitality and enthusiasm!

Ever feel down with no energy, or perhaps a low level of energy? Have big plans, goals, etc. and just lack the initiative to begin. Managing your energy is akin to managing your time. Lightening the load is beneficial, prioritizing assists, and rest, exercise and more will provide more energy. You can begin to establish new habits and behavioral patterns that will not only give you more energy but will also enrich your life in the process. Imagine living each day with abundant vitality and enthusiasm. Listening to this program will give you energy to spare for all the work, sports and social activities you would like to have in your life.

"I am powerful. I am good. I feel great. I am positive. I love myself. I am energetic. I am refreshed. I am rested. Energy is mine. I do it. I do it now. My body is perfect. My mind is alert. I feel the energy. Energy surges through me. I breathe deeply. Each breath - more energy. I have high energy. I am abundantly energetic. I love it," etc.

innertalk-store.com/products/energetic

Fertility (Enhancing Fertility) ~ Subliminal

~ Create the thought patterns and expectations that are conducive to a relaxed natural conception!

This program was designed with a Medical Doctor for those women who wish to naturally conceive but are fearful of their ability to do so. It is designed to assist in creating the thought patterns and expectations that are conducive to a relaxed natural conception.

"I choose to create joy in my life. I am calm and relaxed. I am confident and secure. I am safe. I am loved. I enjoy life. I am beautiful. I am grateful. I am surrounded by love. I am supported. I have creative power within. I am at peace with myself. I am accepting and loving. I am fertile. My eggs are strong and healthy. I am blessed with a wonderful body. I am young and strong. In every way every day I improve. Young, healthy, optimistic, confident, calm, loving, nurturing, me now! It's easy to be fertile. It's easy to remain young. It's easy to be optimistic," etc.

innertalk-store.com/products/enhancing_fertility

Hair Loss (Freedom from Hair Loss) ~ Subliminal

~ Customers have reported new hair growth as a result of using this program.

Not all hair loss is hereditary or genetic. Stress, poor nutrition and anxiety often contribute to this disorder. You can reverse hair loss due to many of these causes, especially those associated with stress and anxiety. When you wish to find a natural way to improve hair growth and minimize hair loss, this program may be your answer. It has helped many.

"My body is alive. My mind is keen. My cells are healthy. I am young. Each cell responds to the brain. The brain communicates with the body. My mind instructs the brain. My mind instructs hair growth. New hair grows. More hair grows. Thicker and fuller. Stronger and healthier. My scalp tingles. I am confident and capable. I look and feel great. The brain and body respond. My hair is thick and full. My hair is young and healthy. I have fun and enjoy life. I am alive and vital. Living is wonderful. Life is a miracle. I am grateful," etc.

innertalk-store.com/products/freedom_from_hair_loss

Headaches (Freedom from Headaches) ~ Subliminal

~ Mobilize your mind and body to free you of pain!

Since most headaches are the result of tension, stress, and eyestrain, simple relaxation can relieve the pain quickly. InnerTalk users have reported incredible results with this program. You can learn to deflect tension and stress by altering the way in which you process the stimuli in your environment. This is a cognitive skill well worth developing, and with InnerTalk, the training is easy.

"I relax. I relax my scalp. I relax my facial muscles. I relax my throat. I relax all over. I smile. I breathe deeply. I feel peaceful. I feel good. I am stress free. I am calm. I am relaxed. I breathe deeply. I am non-resistive. I am comfortable. I control discomfort. I control pain signals. I choose comfort. I choose health. I feel great," etc.

innertalk-store.com/products/freedom_from_headaches

---

*"For a number of years I have been plagued by headaches, taking aspirin to quell the pain. Although it's worked, I have found myself taking between 8 to 10 tablets a day. Using the **Headache Relief** program for just 10 days, the number and severity of my headaches has reduced significantly. I am now down to only 2–3 pain killers a day. Another side benefit includes more energy. I feel strong and resilient."*
—Linda Hoy, Actress

Healing (Accelerated Healing and Well Being) ~ Subliminal

~ Health begins in the mind!

The interaction of mind and body is no longer in question. Indeed, some research suggests that not only can we heal ourselves, we can literally lengthen our lives while increasing our overall quality of life. Accelerate your healing process today and minimize any pain that may accompany the process. Retrain the mind to release the feel good healthy neuro-chemicals involved in optimizing the body's natural intelligence. You can enjoy a healthy long life

"I am positive. My body is powerful. My mind is powerful. I am whole. I am healthy. My body responds. My body is well. My mind expects health. I am happy. I relax. I am comfortable. Pain is a signal. My body heals. I am

healthy. All is well. I smile. I laugh. Pain is gone. Health is within. I am healthy. I am strong. I am ambitious. I feel strength. I release fear. I release dysfunction. I release dis-ease. I release anger. My cells are perfect. My cells replicate perfection," etc.

innertalk-store.com/products/accelerated_healing

Also Available In:

Health and Wellness ~ Library

innertalk-store.com/products/health_wellness_library

Healing (Accelerated Healing and Pain Relief) ~ Video

innertalk-store.com/products/accelerated_healing_dvd

Health (Pain Relief and Health Imaging) ~ Power Imaging/ Hypnosis

innertalk-store.com/products/pain_relief_and_health_pi

Health and Healing ~ OZO

innertalk-store.com/products/health_and_healing_ozo

Healthy Living (The Joy of Healthy Living) ~ Subliminal
~ Make living a healthy lifestyle fun!

We all know that it is wise to choose a healthy lifestyle. There's no secret that diet and exercise increase our vitality and overall wellbeing. Most of also know how important our relationships can be when it comes to health and support. And we recognize the importance of maintaining a healthy social life. We also are fully aware that stress is a killer and some addictive substances are literally poisonous. So, knowing all of that, why don't we practice it? Apparently knowing and doing are not the same thing.

Change the thinking that causes you to sabotage your health for activities that only cause a downward spiral. The many joys of healthy living are in your reach. Begin living a healthy life today!

"Healthy habits are fun. Healthy food tastes good. Healthy living feels good. I enjoy healthy living. I feel good every time I make a healthy choice. I choose

to promote my health in every way every day. I am vigilant about healthy choices. I consciously choose the healthy option. It gives me pleasure to choose the healthy option. I am healthy, healthy, and healthier. I ask about healthy options. I investigate healthy options. I choose healthy foods. I maintain a healthy diet. I am interested in the healthier options. I am wise about my choices. I establish a healthy exercise routine. I do everything I can do to be healthy. Health is important to me. I appreciate my health. I am a gift. Life is a gift," etc.

innertalk-store.com/products/healthy-living-subliminal

Hospice Care ~ Subliminal

~ Making the transition with as much ease as possible!

Whether you're providing home hospice care or moving a loved on to a hospice center, the decision to do so is just the first step in a process that can be heart wrenching and difficult. Leaving this life is but opening a door to a new one. This program was designed to assist you and your loved one in making the transition with as much ease as possible.

"I love God. My life has been rich and rewarding and I feel good about my life. I surrender to the will of God and let go of any need to control the outcome of my life. I trust in the process of life. I am one with my Creator. I am one with all that is. I trust my loved ones to take care of themselves and release them to their own experience of life. I trust that those who care about me want what is best for my highest good. There is no death, only life, and I gracefully move to the next experience. I release any attachment to my body. My spirit flies free! I am free!" etc.

innertalk-store.com/products/hospice_care

Immune (Powerful Immune System) ~ Subliminal

~ Mobilize your body's own natural defenses!

There are many ways to bolster your immune system. Training your expectation regarding wellness is essential when it comes to optimizing your personal best. The mind/body connection is very well established in scientific literature. Now you can use your mind to bolster your immune system and mobilize your body's own natural defenses. Train your unconscious processes to defend against attacks on your wellbeing.

"My immune system is strong. My immune system heals me. My immune system is perfect. My immune system protects me. My body creates helpful antibodies. My immune system maintains health. My immune system creates health. My body is a miracle. I am a miracle. My muscles are strong. My bones are strong. My body is responsive. I breathe deeply. I breathe regularly. I breathe slowly. I breathe rhythmically. I breathe evenly. My breathing is perfect. My body is perfect. My bones form perfectly. My muscles are perfect. Health is within," etc.

innertalk-store.com/products/powerful_immune_system

Also Available In:

Immune (Psychoneuroimmunology: Powerful Immune System) ~ Video

innertalk-store.com/products/powerful_immune_system_dvd

Junk Food (Freedom from Junk Food) ~ Subliminal
~ End your craving for junk food and achieve your health and weight goals.

Processed foods have a powerful influence on the reward centers of the brain. Foods like sugar and wheat involve the brain transmitter dopamine. This heavy dopamine signal can hijack the neurochemistry of the brain and thereby lead to the desire for more. Ending this cycle takes concentrated effort that begins in the mind.

These impulsive and addictive behaviors are rooted in your subconscious. Change the way you think, and you can change the way you live. This program will help you end your craving for junk food and achieve your health and weight goals.

"I feel great. I am good. I take care of myself. I exercise. I breathe deeply. I relax. I eat slowly. I am patient. I take time for myself. I eat healthy foods. I sleep soundly. I sleep peacefully. I love living. I enjoy life. I slow down. I rest. I like fruits. I like vegetables. I drink water. I like water. I balance my nutrition. I eat nutritional foods," etc.

innertalk-store.com/products/freedom_from_junk_food

> *"My favorite program is **No More Junk Food**. After listening for a week, I went to the grocery store and discovered that the junk food was no longer a magnet that drew me to it. To my surprise, I am able to pass it by. Thanks InnerTalk!"*

Menopause (Living Healthy Through Menopause) ~ Subliminal

~ Learn how to be comfortable through menopause!

Living with the changes that menopause brings is more than challenging for many. Apprehension, fear, uncontrollable sweats, irritability, and much more are common problems associated with menopause.

Menopause may be natural but how it impacts you in both its manifest symptoms, and the attitudinal adjustments, feeling of loss, embarrassment and more, can be relieved. Now you too can learn to employ the mind/body connection utilizing this special program to improve your life.

"I am calm. I am relaxed. I allow. I am in touch with me. I am in touch with the spiritual side of me. I trust. I am wise. I am good. I am loving. I am grateful I have a gratitude attitude. I am forgiving. My bones are strong. My body is a miracle. My body serves me wonderfully. My body balances my hormone requirements. My estrogen levels are stable and healthy. I am very healthy. Menopause is easy for me. Menopause is a natural change. I am free of menopause symptoms. I accept change easily. My body accepts change easily. I am comfortable with my body. I live in now. Now is simply wonderful. I look good. I feel good," etc.

innertalk-store.com/products/living_healthy_through_menopause

Nausea (Freedom from Nausea) ~ Subliminal

~ Control the sensation of nausea and put some harmony back in your life!

There are many causes for nausea and some pass quickly while others, such as those associated with pregnancy, vertigo, motion sickness and the like persist for much longer periods. Mind/body research has shown that nausea can be controlled with the proper mental approach.

Take back control and eliminate or minimize nausea. You can program you own mind to treat this physical symptom differently and thereby systemically desensitize its influence on you.

"I am calm. I am relaxed. I breathe slowly. I breathe rhythmically. I am in control. I am tranquil. I am resilient. I am whole and sufficient. I am free of worry. I release anger. I am free of anger. I am positive. I am worthy. I am good. I am loved. I am loving. I am creative. My stomach is settled. My body is a miracle. I am alert. I am mentally active. I am free of nausea. I relax. I take time for myself. I care for myself," etc.

innertalk-store.com/products/freedom_from_nausea

Operations (Pre and Post-Operative) ~ Subliminal

~ Relaxed and positive expectations improve surgical outcomes!

Research has repeated demonstrated that patients with a relaxed positive expectation do better after surgery. Reduce pre-operative worries and create accelerated healing after surgery with a program that has actually been studied and demonstrated effective. This program has proven exceptionally helpful with small children, as well as adults. In a study performed with 360 patients who used our InnerTalk Pre and Post-Operative program, the physician's team reported that anesthetic requirements were reduced by 32% and post-secondary care was also diminished dramatically.

"I am confident. I am positive. I have positive expectations. I love life. I heal rapidly. My body is wonderful. I trust my surgeon. I am confident in my Doctors. My surgery will be successful. I am relaxed. I am calm. When touched—I relax more. When touched—I become calmer. Background sounds relax me. Touching relaxes me. Pressure relaxes me. My body heals perfectly," etc.

innertalk-store.com/products/pre_and_post_operative

Pain (Natural Pain Relief) ~ Subliminal

~ Interrupt the pain cycle and minimize the suffering.

Pain is an important signal system designed to warn us, but solid scientific studies have demonstrated that we have the mental ability to both interrupt the pain cycle and to minimize the suffering. Many users of this program have been able to replace or reduce their pain medication with this natural alternative. Why not acquire the mental training and release some or all of your pain now?

"I am relaxed. I breathe deeply. I am non-resistive. I am healthy. I am alive. I am happy. I am loving. I am patient. I am loved. I am free of pain. Pain is gone. I am comfortable. I control discomfort. I control pain. I choose comfort," etc.

innertalk-store.com/products/natural_pain_relief

Also Available In:

Pain Management and Relief ~ Collection

innertalk-store.com/products/pain_management_and_relief

Health (Pain Relief and Health Imaging)
~ Power Imaging/Hypnosis

innertalk-store.com/products/pain_relief_and_health_pi

PMS Relief ~ Subliminal

~ The body and emotions respond to your positive thoughts.

You needn't suffer a monthly barrage of emotional and physical upsets. You can protect yourself against this discomfort by immunizing your mind. The mind/body connection is strong and one's expectation is powerful. Change the way you think about PMS and you will alter its influence. You needn't suffer a monthly barrage of emotional and physical upsets from your menstrual cycle. The body and emotions respond to your positive thoughts.

"I am good. I am balanced. I like myself. My body is perfect. My hormones are balanced. My cells regenerate health. My mind is clear. My emotions are calm. My health is great. Living is wonderful. I am alive. I love life. I love myself. I love others. I am loved. Change is growth. Growth is positive. I am positive," etc.

innertalk-store.com/products/pms_relief

Posture (Excellent Posture) ~ Subliminal

~ A good posture is fundamental to being your best at all that you seek to achieve.

Posture is a major component in looking your best. However, in addition to being a major contributor to your self-image and self-esteem, it can also affect your health. Developing a good posture is therefore fundamental to being your best at all that you seek to achieve. Sitting and standing erect, training yourself to walk erect, and acquiring all of the skills that underlie proper posture is a matter of motivation firmly establishing the intent of breaking those old sloppy habits.

"I stand erect. I sit erect. Shoulders back. I breathe deeply and evenly. I expand my lungs. I breathe into my chest. I am relaxed. I am comfortable. I move with grace. I move with ease. I am confident. I move with my head up and shoulders back. I make eye contact. I care for my body. I care for myself. I enjoy interacting with others. My body serves me. I move fluidly. I am agile. I am proud. I look forward. I smile. I am happy," etc.

innertalk-store.com/products/excellent_posture

SADS (Relief from Seasonal Affective Disorder) ~ Subliminal

~ Cultivate the correct habits and keep your SAD at bay!

Seasonal affective disorder (SAD), sometimes called winter blues, is described as "a type of depression that's related to changes in seasons. SAD begins and ends at about the same times every year. There are several conscious things that you can actively do to minimize this effect. They include taking Vitamin D, using full spectrum lighting, exercising, laughing, winter sports, visiting your doctor in serious cases, and so forth—but all of this begins when in your mind you decide to consciously do something about the blues.

"I like to care for myself. I choose to care for myself. I exercise. I like exercise. I like the outdoors. I smile. I laugh. I have a keen sense of humor. I enjoy play. I enjoy recreation. I love to exercise. I sleep soundly. I rest easily. I enjoy light. I protect myself with full spectrum light. I use my full spectrum lamp.

I choose healthy foods. I eat healthy foods. I enjoy vegetables. I like natural juices. I enjoy hiking. I love to walk outdoors," etc.

innertalk-store.com/products/seasonal_affective_disorder

Salt (Freedom from Salt) ~ Subliminal

~ Make foods with reduced sodium taste better!

For years we have been warned about salt intake. Too much salt can increase blood pressure and several observational studies have linked high salt intake with an increased risk of stomach cancer. If salt is an issue to you, then this program will help to make foods with reduced sodium taste better and motivate you to avoid excess intake.

"I eat properly. I sleep properly. I balance rest with effort. I have high energy. I am alert. My mind is keen. I care for myself. I drink water. I chew slowly. I eat natural foods. I eat vegetables. I like vegetables. I like fruit. I am free of salt. I avoid salt. I avoid sodium. Food tastes better. Food tastes great naturally. I love natural foods. Natural foods are healthy. I am healthy," etc.

innertalk-store.com/products/freedom_from_salt

Skin (Clear Skin) ~ Subliminal

~ Having a clear complexion always brings its own sense of self-confidence.

The first thing people see when they meet you is your face and most of us would love to have that youthful glow to our skin—one free of complexion problems. Having a clear complexion always brings its own sense of self-confidence. Your skin cells replace themselves very quickly. Your diet, activity, mental attitude and possibly your intention, have all been scientifically connected to cell regeneration. This program is designed to promote your action both consciously and at a subconscious level to foster healthy skin. Your mental healing abilities are called upon as are you to take the appropriate steps to gain and maintain that fresh healthy skin look and feel.

"My body is wondrous. My body serves me. My body responds to me. My mind coordinates my brain and body. My mind is powerful. My mind sees my desires. My mind directs my reality. My body responds to my mind. I see my clear skin. I see my healthy skin. My skin is soft. My skin is elastic. My skin is

clean. My skin is clear. My skin is vibrant. I care for my body. I love my body. My body responds. My mind wills this so. My mind sees healthy skin," etc.

innertalk-store.com/products/clear_skin

Sleep Reduction ~ Subliminal

~ Gain time by making your sleep more efficient!

Do you find yourself sleeping too much? Staying in bed when there are matters you should be attending to. What could you do if you had more hours in the day? Gain some time by making your sleep more efficient with this program.

"I sleep deeply. I sleep peacefully. Sleep is rest. I rest. I am alive. I am vital. I have energy. I sleep to build energy. Body rested - I awake. I awake refreshed. I awake alert. I sleep less. I sleep as needed. I do it now. I sleep to awaken revitalized. I do it. Living is fun. Life is great. I love living. I am active," etc.

innertalk-store.com/products/sleep_reduction

Sleep Soundly ~ Subliminal

~ Sleep well and wake up rejuvenated!

Sleep is a very vital function of life—just as important as eating and breathing! When we sleep, our bodies are busy tending to our physical and mental health and getting us ready for another day. Get that deep restful sleep your body so desperately craves and feel rejuvenated to accomplish more each and every day. Caution: Do not use while driving or operating machinery.

"Sleep restores me. Sleep refreshes me. I sleep deeply. I sleep peacefully. My sleep is sound, peaceful and restful. My sleep revitalizes me. Sleep is rest. I rest. I am alive. I am vital. I have energy. Sleep restores my energy. I sleep to build energy. Sleep is natural. Sleep is effortless. Sleep is easy. Sleep is good. Living is fun. Life is great. I love living," etc.

innertalk-store.com/products/sleep_soundly

> *"Listening to the **Sleep Soundly** CD for one hour a day has turned my life around. Instead of waking up every morning at 4 a.m., wide awake and annoying my husband, I now usually sleep till 6 or 7 a.m. I have also been able to cut down on my alcohol consumption and have lost 10 pounds! Brilliant all round —thank you."*

Also Available In:

Sleep (Peaceful Sleep) ~ Collection

innertalk-store.com/products/sleep_collection

Snoring (Freedom from Snoring) ~ Subliminal

~ Eliminate the snoring and let everyone get a healthy good night sleep.

Snoring can lead to sleep disorders, interrupt breathing patterns, can lead to high blood pressure, strain the heart, and more. It is therefore wise to work on minimizing or eliminating snoring. This program is as much for your partner as it is for yourself. Eliminate the snoring and let everyone get a healthy good night sleep.

"I breathe in through my nose. I breathe out through my mouth. I inhale through my nose. I exhale through my mouth. I breathe deeply. I breathe rhythmically. I breathe easily. I breathe relaxed. I breathe with my chest. I clear my nose before bed. I drink water. I drink water at bedtime. I am calm. I am good. I breathe deeply. I sleep peacefully. I sleep deeply. I sleep aware. My body is perfect. My cells generate perfect health. I care for myself. My nose is clear. My throat is clear. I rotate my sleep positions. I rotate my sleep posture," etc.

innertalk-store.com/products/freedom_from_snoring

Stroke Recovery ~ Subliminal

~ Maintain the proper mental attitude and promote healing.

The National Stroke Association points out that "It is normal to feel angry, anxious or depressed after a stroke. You may feel worried about work, money and relationships, and the tiredness caused by stroke can make things worse." These feelings can actually impede the healing process. It is therefore important to maintain the proper mental attitude to promote healing. Expect to recover and promote a sense of well-being by promoting a positive optimistic attitude. By inoculating yourself with a positive expectation and attitude you will obtain the proper emotional balance that will help you do the other things that assist with recovery, such as exercise, diet, weight, blood pressure changes, and so forth. This approach can not only assist in recovery but facilitate the prevention of another stroke.

"I am alert. I am aware. I am a miracle. My body is a miracle. My brain is a miracle. My body and brain heal miraculously. My body and brain heal perfectly now. My memory is keen. I remember effortlessly. The brain is amazingly redundant. My brain is healthy. My body is healthy. I am healed, healthier and healthier every day in every way. My vision is keen. My speech is strong and clear. I see easily and clearly. I speak easily and effortlessly. My balance is good. My body movements are smooth and easy. My body heals itself now," etc.

innertalk-store.com/products/stroke_recovery

Blood Sugar Control ~ Subliminal

~ Maximize the mind body connection and support the habits necessary for maintaining good blood sugar levels

This program was created to support those who need to watch their blood sugar levels. Maximize the mind body connection and compliment this by supporting the good habits necessary for maintaining good blood sugar levels.

"Life is a miracle. I have miraculous powers within. I can choose to have blood sugar readings that are in control. I choose to be in control of my diabetes. I choose to eat well. I choose to exercise daily. I will always choose to

control my diabetes. Blood sugar is stored energy. I have level and controlled blood sugar and energy. My body is a miracle. My body creates success. I create health. I create blood sugar readings that are in control. I enjoy feeling healthy," etc.

innertalk-store.com/products/blood_sugar_control

Sugar (Freedom from Sugar) ~ Subliminal

~ Free yourself of the dangers in sugar today.

Health professionals around the world are actively expressing their concerns about sugar. Getting away from sugar can be very difficult since almost all prepared foods contain some form of sugar. That said, a conscious approach can free you of this addictive unhealthy substance. If you're aware and trying to eat healthy but still having a problem reducing the amount of sugar you consume, this program will assist you in overcoming the cravings.

"I eat properly. I sleep properly. I balance rest with effort. I have high energy. I am alert. My mind is keen. I care for myself. I drink water. I chew slowly. I eat natural foods. I eat vegetables. I like vegetables. I like fruit. I avoid sugar. I am free of sugar. Food tastes better. Food tastes great naturally. I love natural foods," etc.

innertalk-store.com/products/freedom_from_sugar

Teeth and Gums (Healthy Teeth and Gums) ~ Subliminal

~ Create the good habits that will ensure your healthy teeth and gums.

Many people are simply unaware of the importance of proper oral hygiene. Sure, we all know how nice a smile filled by white teeth is, and how poorly bad breath represents us, but did you know that heart disease is linked to poor oral hygiene as well? So, taking care of your teeth and gums is not only important for a nice smile, it is also vital for your health. Create the good habits that will ensure your healthy teeth and gums. This program is also great for helping children establish good habits early.

"I brush my teeth regularly. I brush after each meal. I floss after each meal. I massage my gums. I use mouthwash. I eat properly. I eat proper foods. I breathe deeply. My body is perfect. My cells replicate perfectly. My blood flows freely through my veins. I brush my tongue. I like my mouth clean. I like my mouth fresh. My gums are healthy," etc.

innertalk-store.com/products/healthy_teeth_and_gums

Vegetarian (Becoming Vegetarian) ~ Subliminal

~ Vegetarian eating patterns have been associated with improved health outcomes including lower levels of obesity, a reduced risk of heart disease and lower blood pressure.

There are plenty of reasons to become a vegetarian. These reasons can range from the health benefits to the desire to live a more humane lifestyle (caring for animals and the way they are farmed in today's world). That said, changing old eating habits can be difficult. This program will help make the process easier.

"I choose to become vegetarian. There are very good reasons to become vegetarian. I choose to give up meat. I respect all life. I am a loving, caring person. I appreciate all life. I respect animals. I am conscientious. I enjoy vegetables. I find great vegetarian recipes. I enjoy fruits. I enjoy nuts. I make substitutions in restaurants for meat dishes. I find it easy to be vegetarian. I find it rewarding. It is my choice. It is healthy. It is wholesome. I enjoy dairy. I plan my protein intake. I enjoy beans. I vary my vegetarian diet. I try new things. I try vegetarian dishes from around the world," etc.

innertalk-store.com/products/becoming_vegetarian

Vision (Keen Vision) ~ Subliminal

~ Change your mindset and see how your vision improves.

For many, vision problems are due to poor habits, dietary deficiencies, stress and attitudinal factors. This program was created to motivate you to use all of your natural abilities to improve your vision. Your vision absolutely can be improved with attention and proper exercise. Begin today to improve your vision by obtaining the skill set and incentive that you will find on this program.

"I have good vision. I exercise my eyes. I care for my eyes. I rest my eyes. I eat properly. I relax my eyes. I appreciate my vision. I see easily. My eyes are strong. My eyes are healthy. My mind and body are one. Images are clear. My vision is perfect. I am a miracle. I am grateful. Life is wonderful. My eyes focus. Images are clear. My vision is keen. My eye muscles are strong," etc.

innertalk-store.com/products/keen_vision

Water (I Like Water) ~ Subliminal

~ Learn to enjoy the taste of water!

There are many advantages to increasing your water intake. They include the improved of physical performance, increased energy, better brain function, an end to some headaches, elimination of constipation, it may even treat kidney stones, and much more! When water is so important to us, why is it that so many of us rarely drink the proper amount of water? Learn to enjoy the taste of water and break the habits that push you towards other drinks.

"I like water. Water is good for me. Water cleanses me. Water refreshes me. Water is my favorite drink. Water tastes good. I choose water as my drink. My drink of choice is water. Water purifies me. Drinking water is healthy. Drinking water is good for me. I love the taste of water. I love the clear look of water. I love the smell of water. I love the feel of water in my mouth. I am refreshed by water. Water quenches my thirst. I enjoy water with my meals. I drink water," etc.

innertalk-store.com/products/i_like_water

Well (Be Well Stay Happy) ~ Subliminal

~ A positive optimistic outlook together with good physical practice can lead to adding many healthy years to your life.

The role of the mind, and our emotions, has been demonstrated to have a powerful impact on both happiness and wellness. For years this mind body connection was ignored by science, but today there exists an abundance of evidence strongly collaborating the importance of our mental state on our overall sense of wellbeing.

While everything may be going haywire around you, you can remain upbeat, happy and content. This program is designed to create expectations within you that will guide your activities and while altering any self-defeating ideas that you may hold regarding happiness and health.

"I am strong and healthy. My body is wise. My body heals itself now. My body optimizes itself now. My body is a miracle. My cells are conscious. My mind and body cooperate. Health is mine now. Healing is natural. I release fear. I release self-punishment. I choose health now. My life is a miracle. I allow and accept the miracle. My body normalizes itself now. My body compensates as necessary to produce perfect health now. My cells are amazingly resilient. All of me loves and accepts all of me now. I am calm. I am at peace with myself. I love life. I am positive and confident. I choose to be optimistic," etc.

<u>innertalk-store.com/products/be_well_stay_happy</u>

Younging (Quantum Younging) ~ Subliminal

~ There need be no "old age" regardless of how long one lives.

This program is designed to facilitate employing the mind to arrest and even reverse the aging process. Building a belief and generating a true expectation has been established as at least one manner in which mind influences body. This is as true for wellness as it is for longevity. If you expect to live that long, there is a real possibility that it may happen. This program will facilitate you in choosing both a personal age that is your mental optimal age and in creating an entirely new expectation regarding your life span.

"I am enough. I am strong. I am healthy. I am young. I will health. I will youth. My body responds. My body remembers. I remember. I remember youth. My body remembers youth. My cells reproduce perfectly. My cells are strong and willing. My cells are young and healthy. My cells are perfect. I feel young. I look young. I am positive. I am enthusiastic. Life is a miracle. Life is wonderful. Living is fun. I eat properly. I exercise. My vision is perfect. My hearing is perfect. I am powerful. I breathe deeply. My body is strong. My

hair is strong. My hair is thick. My stomach is flat. My abdomen muscles are strong. I stand erect. I am proud. I am confident," etc.

innertalk-store.com/products/quantum_younging

Also Available In:

Young (Forever Young) ~ Album

innertalk-store.com/products/forever_young_album

Younger and Healthier ~ Power Set

innertalk-store.com/products/younger_and_healthier_ps

Younging (Fountain of Youth: Remembering Youth to be Young) ~ Platinum Plus

innertalk-store.com/products/fountain_of_youth_pp

Younging (Quantum Younging) ~ Video

innertalk-store.com/products/quantum_younging_dvd

Habits and Addictions

For our most complete habits and addictions-related packages, please see:

Cigarettes (Forever Free of Cigarettes) ~ Collection

innertalk-store.com/products/forever_free_of_cigarettes_collection

Substance Abuse (Overcoming Substance Abuse) ~ Collection

innertalk-store.com/products/substance_abuse_collection

Smoking (Freedom from Smoking) ~ Power Set

innertalk-store.com/products/freedom_from_smoking_ps

Alcohol (Freedom from Alcohol) ~ Subliminal

~ Gain the inner strength, peace of mind, and self-respect necessary to release this unwanted habit.

Whether you are dependent on alcohol or simply just want to consume less, reducing or eliminating alcohol can have a very positive impact on your life. Regardless of the reason why you drink, you can choose to relax once again and have fun without the use of alcohol.

The affirmations in this program will give you the inner strength, peace of mind, and self-respect necessary to release this unwanted habit. Based on the concepts taught by the Alcoholics Anonymous 12-step formula, this program will assist you in remaining alcohol free one day at a time.

"I am free of alcohol. I love myself. I love others. I accept myself. I accept others. I am forgiving. I am forgiven. I forgive myself. I forgive all others. I bless myself. I bless all others. I am a gift. Living is a miracle. I am a miracle.

I am whole. I am sufficient. I am loved. A higher power is with me. I am capable. I am confident. I am enough. God loves me. God gives me strength. God provides peace," etc.

innertalk-store.com/products/freedom_from_alcohol

Gambling (Freedom from Gambling) ~ Subliminal

~ Free yourself of the compulsion for gambling today!

Problem gambling is an urge to gamble continuously despite harmful negative consequences or a desire to stop. An addiction to gambling can be totally destructive. It can ruin your family, your finances and your own self-respect. If gambling is a compulsion, this program is for you.

"I am responsible. I am in control. I am sufficient. I make wise decisions. I exercise discretion. I am reflective. I think things over. I control my impulses. I am free of gambling. I respect myself. I respect all others. I enjoy my family. I enjoy my friends," etc.

innertalk-store.com/products/gambling

Impulse Control ~ Subliminal

~ Take your time to think things through thoroughly.

Many issues that we all deal with in life have their roots in our ability to control our impulses. Indeed, impulse control can be the lynchpin in our ability to control our finances, avoid or end addictions, even lose weight and much more. Learn to resist those temptations and gain emotional regulation. Slow down that impulsive behavior. Whether you are prone to impulsive purchasing or over-reacting, etc., this program can help you take your time to think things through thoroughly.

"I am whole. I am enough. I am in control. I control my body. I control my thoughts. I cancel negative. I am positive. I control my emotions. I forgive myself. I forgive all others. I am forgiven. I respect myself. I respect all others," etc.

innertalk-store.com/products/impulse_control

Internet (Overcoming Internet Addiction) ~ Subliminal

~ Keep things in perspective and eliminate your Internet addiction!

Do you find yourself shopping excessively on the Internet, or playing video games endlessly, or checking posts on Facebook not wanting to miss anything? Does your use of the Internet interfere with your family time or disrupt your other activities like studies? Do you find your mood swings have anything to do with your activities on the Internet? When interrupted, do you find yourself short with people? The Internet is an amazing resource, but real life does not happen in front of your computer screen. Put balance back into your life. Keep things in perspective and eliminate your Internet addiction.

"I enjoy the outdoors. I love to walk. I love the smell of fresh air. I like to be active. I enjoy exercise. I love to read. I use the Internet wisely. I limit my time on the Internet. I am active. I like to move around. I like to stay active. I am free of Internet addiction. I use the Internet sparingly. I prefer to read a book or go for a walk. I am powerful. I am healthy. I am confident. I am capable. I am free of addictions. I use time wisely," etc.

innertalk-store.com/products/internet_addiction

Pornography Addiction (Free of Pornography Addiction) ~ Subliminal

~ End the pornographic indulgence that can destroy lives!

Pornography addiction is on the rise across the globe. If you or a loved one is concerned about their use of porn, its frequency, control over thoughts, fantasies, break in concentration patterns, influence on memory and other cognitive skills, relationship expectations, etc., then this program can facilitate ending the pornographic indulgence that can destroy lives.

"I choose my behavior. I take responsibility for my thoughts. I make wise choices. I make healthy choices. My life is the result of my choices. I am pornography-free now. Appeal for pornography is gone. I stay away from pornography. I conserve my sexual energy. Sex without love is unappealing.

I honor my personal relationships. I direct my sexual energy towards fulfillment of goals that are meaningful and respectful. I respect my sexual energy. I enjoy healthy sexuality with my loving partner," etc.

innertalk-store.com/products/freedom_from_pornography_addiction

Smoking (Stop Smoking) ~ Subliminal

~ Imagine never wanting another cigarette again!

Lots of people smoke to relieve stress and anxiety, experience the false sense of pleasure smoking provides, suppress appetites, and more. Many smokers are addicted long before they become adults, and most don't even think about quitting until they have been smoking for many years. With all of this in place, quitting takes more than your will power to have a clean life free of cigarettes.

Imagine never wanting another cigarette again! Make the process easier for yourself by changing the self-talk that causes you to reach for another smoke. Train your brain to *want* the change.

"I can be happy without cigarettes. I choose to live without cigarettes. I choose to be free of cigarettes. It is my choice. I am able to be happy without cigarettes. It is easy for me to be free of cigarettes. It's easy for me to live smoke free. It's easy to choose life free of cigarettes. I feel free. I feel good. I smell good. I have a keen sense of taste. I will always choose to be free of cigarettes. I have the courage and strength to remain smokeless. I have the will power to free myself and remain free now. I love being free of cigarettes. I love living. I love life. I love myself. I love my body. I love my freedom," etc.

innertalk-store.com/products/stop_smoking

---

*I've been smoking for a number of years, and tried various methods to stop, without much success. I listened to the Stop **Smoking CD** for a week and carried on smoking, it helped with the craving and I smoked less than usual. Within 3 weeks of listening to the CD I'd stopped.*

Also Available In:

Cigarettes (Forever Free of Cigarettes) ~ Collection
innertalk-store.com/products/forever_free_of_cigarettes_collection

Smoking (Stop Smoking) ~ Echo-Tech
innertalk-store.com/products/stop_smoking_et

Smoking (Stop Smoking Now) ~ OZO
innertalk-store.com/products/stop_smoking_ozo

Smoking (Stop Smoking Forever) ~ Power Imaging/Hypnosis
innertalk-store.com/products/stop_smoking_forever_pi

Smoking (Freedom from Smoking) ~ Power Set
innertalk-store.com/products/freedom_from_smoking_ps

Substance Abuse (Freedom from Substance Abuse) ~ Subliminal

~ Substance abuse is often all about self-medicating. It fills an imagined need.

Many people think that substance abuse is all about will power and they couldn't be further from the truth. Substances act upon the brain and this can lead to addiction, for it's the mechanics of the brain demanding more and more satisfaction. This program will assist and facilitate retraining the brain by altering your reward expectation. It will motivate your conviction to become free of addiction. It will augment a new stream of self-talk that will reinforce your progress and shore up your determination to set yourself free.

"I am drug free. I breathe deeply. I breathe smoothly. I am strong and powerful. I make my own choices. I make wise choices. I make thoughtful choices. I make healthy choices. I protect my health. I am healthy. I like exercise. I feel great. I love living. I love life. I am a leader. I am confident. I am happy. I use healthy things. I eat healthy foods. I am relaxed. I am in control. Living is great," etc.

innertalk-store.com/products/substance_abuse_subliminal

> *"I found the OZO Addiction program really powerful!
> I experienced changes the very first time I used it. I
> have tried other self-help recordings and noticed some
> difference, but Dr. Taylors' technology was empowering.
> I saw results right away, whereas, other technologies
> just took too long."*

Also Available In:

Substance Abuse (Overcoming Substance Abuse) ~
Collection

innertalk-store.com/products/substance_abuse_collection

Addictions (Overcoming Addictions) ~ OZO

innertalk-store.com/products/overcoming_addictions-ozo

Addictions (Freedom from Addictions) ~ Video

innertalk-store.com/products/freedom_from_addictions_dvd

Tobacco (Freedom from Chewing Tobacco) ~ Subliminal

~ Learn what it feels like to have a clean, fresh tasting mouth!

Besides the health risks associated with chewing tobacco, there is also the nasty necessity to spit, the vulgar breath, the yellow browning of teeth, etc. It is an unattractive addiction that need not enslave you any longer.

Rid yourself of this nasty habit and learn what it feels like to have a clean, fresh tasting mouth. Your partner will really appreciate this too!

"I am free of tobacco. I like my mouth fresh. I like my mouth clean. I like my teeth clean. I drink water. I breathe deeply. I am relaxed. I remain calm. I am at ease. I like myself. I treat myself well. I do healthy things. My jaws are relaxed. My neck is relaxed. I exercise. I am fit. Tobacco tastes bad. Tobacco stains teeth. Tobacco produces bad breath. I am free of chewing tobacco. My mouth is fresh. My mouth tastes good. My mouth is clean," etc.

innertalk-store.com/products/freedom_from_chewing_tobacco

Video Gaming Addiction (Freedom from Video Gaming Addiction) ~ Subliminal

~ Regain some balance in your life and once again play video game just for fun.

Playing video games can be relaxing and fun. They can also be great for developing hand/eye coordination. However, when you are addicted to playing, other areas in your life can suffer. Eliminate the addiction. Regain some balance in your life and once again play video game just for fun. If you think there is a video game addiction either developing or functioning in yourself or someone you care about, then this program is for you. Don't wait!

"Time is valuable. I use my time wisely. Reading is valuable. Study is valuable. I gain from learning. My life is important. Gaming wastes my time. Gaming is a ritual I can do without. It's easy for me to read and study. It's easy for me to improve my mind. It's easy for me to use time wisely. It's easy for me to be wise. Wisdom dictates learning over gaming. Gaming comes and goes. Investing in my future requires using my time to learn. I choose learning. I use multi-media to gain knowledge and information. I use multi-media wisely. My future is worth investing in now," etc.

innertalk-store.com/products/video_gaming_addiction

Body Image

For our most complete body image related packages, please see:

Weight Loss (Turbo Charged Weight Loss) ~ Library
innertalk-store.com/products/turbo-charged-weight-loss-library

Fit and Healthy ~ Album
innertalk-store.com/products/fit_and_healthy_album

Weight Loss (Healthy Eating for Weight Loss) ~ Album
innertalk-store.com/products/healthy-eating-for-weight-loss-album

Weight Loss (Active Lifestyle for Weight Loss) ~ Album
innertalk-store.com/products/active-lifestyle-for-weight-loss-album

Weight Loss (Maximum Weight Loss) ~ Collection
innertalk-store.com/products/weight_loss_collection

Weight Loss Now ~ Power Set
innertalk-store.com/products/weight_loss_ps

Body (Firm Body) ~ Subliminal

~ Visualize the strength and firmness of your body moving effortlessly.

For many people today a firm body seems to be an almost impossible goal. Toning your body is in competition with many life styles. It takes time and work, tenacity and enthusiasm, to commit to firming your body despite the proven health benefits that are gained. This program is designed to facilitate exactly the kind of change needed to establish the mental toughness to prevail over the flab. Just visualize the strength and firmness of your body moving effortlessly. Strength and vitality can be yours. Create the body you can be proud of and begin today!

"I like myself. I touch myself. My body is perfect. My cells are perfect. My cells generate perfection. My cells regenerate perfectly. My blood flows freely through my veins. I visualize perfect health. I sense health. I expect health. I am healthy. My body is healthy. I visualize cellulite away. I sense heat in cellulite areas. Cellulite is gone. I like my body. I love water. I drink water. Water cleanses me. Fat melts from my body. Excess fat is gone. My metabolism burns fat away. I eat vegetables. I eat fruit," etc.

innertalk-store.com/products/firm_body

Body (I Love My Body) ~ Subliminal

~ Feel good about your body, love it, appreciate it, and your body will respond.

Research has repeatedly demonstrated the appropriateness of feeling good about one's body. Indeed, some findings suggest that by simply recognizing our bodies with love, our bodies look and feel better and even respond with spectacular reversals of conditions that have affected the body in the past. Begin today to train that stream of consciousness to love your body from within and enjoy the many benefits!

"Life is a miracle. I am a miracle. I am worthy. I am deserving. My body is a miracle. My body is wonderful. I love my body. I love all of my body. I enjoy my body. I send love to all parts of my body. I sense the consciousness of my cells. My cells love me. My body is loves me. I care for my body. I touch my body with love. I feel the power of Love fill my body. My body responds to love. My body cares for me," etc.

innertalk-store.com/products/i_love_my_body

Breast (Natural Breast Enlargement) ~ Subliminal

~ "The proof is undeniable!"

Many professionals now believe that there can be a number of psychological reasons leading to the arrestment of normal breast development. Further, a lot of research has demonstrated the effectiveness of techniques employing suggestion, such as hypnosis, for natural breast enlargement. This program has been studied and found clinically effective. Indeed, the results of a UK trial on the InnerTalk program titled Breast Enlargement was published in **What Medicine**, summer 2003 issue. "This trial involved 15 women and resulted in approximately 2cm of breast growth and a fuller cup size within 30 days. Women also reported a 'tingling sensation,' similar to that experienced in puberty."

"I send extra blood flow to my breasts. My body responds. My cells generate growth. My cells multiply perfectly. My breasts are warm. My breasts tingle. My breasts grow full and voluptuous. My breasts are firm. My breasts are alive and growing. My cells are multiplying. Rapidly my breasts fill out. I feel good about myself. I am confident. My body is perfect. My body responds to my mind," etc.

innertalk-store.com/products/natural_breast_enlargement

Metabolism (Using Metabolism to Melt Fat Away) ~ Subliminal

~ You really can accelerate your metabolism to burn excess fat.

When you are doing all those things you are supposed to do in order to lose weight and are still losing the battle, try this program to rev up your metabolism. This program is designed to help you augment all of the mental ways in which you can excite your metabolism, such as drinking more water, increasing physical activity and so forth. Your body has stored fat as an extra supply of fuel. It awaits only the demand to use it. Get going now. Your thoughts will begin to instruct your body to accelerate your metabolism to burn excess fat. Your mental edge will get you physically active and keep you where you want to be.

"I have the power within me to excite my metabolism. I have the ability to direct my metabolism. My metabolism has the ability to melt away excess fat. I will excess fat gone now. I use nutritious foods. I drink water. My metabolism burns excess fat. My metabolic system cooperates, and fat

disappears. Now I am thin and healthy. My mind and body create a fit and healthy me. All excess fat disappears," etc.

innertalk-store.com/products/using_metabolism_to_melt_fat_away

Muscle (Weight and Muscle Gain) ~ Subliminal

~ You can create the body that you have only dreamed about!

Many people are underweight, skinny, and lacking the definition that comes from developing strong muscles. If you are one, then you're not alone. Being underweight can be just as unhealthy as being overweight. If you are into bodybuilding, or you just feel that you are too thin, this program will facilitate your goals. Research has demonstrated that your mind is the edge you need to achieve your goals and your cells respond to your thoughts. You can create the body that you have only dreamed about.

"I am strong. I am healthy. I eat regular meals. I exercise. I build muscle strength. I enjoy food. I accept myself. I like myself. I look forward to exercise. I build a strong and healthy body. I love my body. I listen to my body. I know my perfect weight. I achieve my perfect weight. I look good. I am fit and healthy. My body is perfect. I care for myself. I am proud of my body. I take pride in my body. I feel and sense my health and fitness. I see myself at my perfect weight," etc.

innertalk-store.com/products/weight_and_muscle_gain

Thin (Forever Thin, Fit and Healthy) ~ Subliminal

~ Forever maintain both your thin, fit, and trim shape as well as the motivation that makes it easy to do so.

You have reached your goal weight or are very close, and now you wish to hold onto it. You recognize that you will enjoy a healthier life by remaining thin and fit. You now choose foods more wisely and go for the nutritious diet. Stay motivated—stay thin, fit, and healthy using this powerful mind tool.

"I eat the right foods. I eat at regular meals. I see myself thin. I am thin. I am attractive. I feel good. I use food properly. I like to chew. I chew slowly.

I eat less. I like being thin. Small portions are satisfying. Proper foods are satisfying. Regular meals are satisfying. Chewing slow is satisfying. I am in control. I have perfect will. I lose weight gradually. I relax when eating. I am calm and relaxed. I drink water. I like water. I exercise. I like exercise. I feel good. I am strong and firm," etc.

innertalk-store.com/products/forever_thin_fit_and_healthy

Weight Loss Now ~ Subliminal

~ Eliminate the subconscious programming that sabotages your weight loss goals.

We all know what we are *supposed* to do to lose weight—eat healthy, exercise, diet, reduce sugar intake, drink more water, etc. But sometimes this is just too hard. Unless you address the thinking/subconscious programming that sabotages your weight loss goals, success will just never happen. This program makes losing weight simple and effortless. Many testimonials and clinical studies have proven the effectiveness of this program, and people all over the world are finding the secret to achieving their weight loss goals.

"I am thin, trim, slim and healthy. I am energetic. My body is conscious. My cells are conscious. I exercise. I visualize exercise. I image exercise. My body responds. My body burns off fat. All excess fat is shed from me. My metabolism melts fat away. My blood flows freely through my veins. My heart is strong. I breathe deeply. I eat the right foods. I drink water. I like vegetables. I like fruit. I respect myself. I leave something on my plate. Food is not a reward. Food is not a tranquilizer. I am sufficient. I am enough. My mental images are strong. I image health. I image my ideal weight. My body responds," etc.

innertalk-store.com/products/weight_loss

*"It has been only five days that I've been listening to my **Weight Loss** and **Using Metabolism to Melt Fat** programs, and already I'm noticing a very marked difference in appetite. I'm not as hungry as I used to be and I get full faster. Also, I've been more active in the past 5 days then I've been in the past 2 months.*

Also Available In:

Weight Loss (Turbo Charged Weight Loss) ~ Library

innertalk-store.com/products/turbo-charged-weight-loss-library

Weight Loss (Active Lifestyle for Weight Loss) ~ Album

innertalk-store.com/products/active-lifestyle-for-weight-loss-album

Weight Loss (Healthy Eating for Weight Loss) ~ Album

innertalk-store.com/products/healthy-eating-for-weight-loss-album

Weight Loss (Maximum Weight Loss) ~ Collection

innertalk-store.com/products/weight_loss_collection

Weight Loss ~ Echo-Tech

innertalk-store.com/products/weight_loss_et

Weight (Optimum Weight Loss) ~ OZO

innertalk-store.com/products/weight_loss_ozo

Weight (Optimal Weight Loss) ~ Power Imaging/Hypnosis

innertalk-store.com/products/weight_loss_pi

Weight Loss Now ~ Power Set

innertalk-store.com/products/weight_loss_ps

Weight Loss ~ Video

innertalk-store.com/products/weight_loss_dvd

Sports and Fitness

All athletes, regardless of their sport, know the importance of mental training. With the incorrect mind set, it does not matter how hard you train, you will never perform your best. Train your mind as often as you train your body and watch yourself excel. Most of our programs for specific sports were created in consultation with experts in the particular fields. Use our general sports and fitness programs to get you in the frame of mind to want to work, and then use the specific sports program to help you perform to the best of your ability.

For our most complete sports-related packages, please see:

Fitness (Sports Fitness) ~ Album

>	innertalk-store.com/products/sports-fitness-album

Sports (Optimum Sports) ~ Collection

>	innertalk-store.com/products/sports_collection

Fit and Athletic ~ Power Set

>	innertalk-store.com/products/fit_and_athletic_ps

Sports: Mentally Fit ~ Power Set

>	innertalk-store.com/products/sports_mentally_fit_ps

Baseball ~ Subliminal

~ You can play baseball!

Choosing to play baseball can be a really exciting time in a person's life. Baseball offers the opportunity to be a part of a team, to grow social skills, to master mental discipline, and to become fitter and healthier in the process. Use this program to learn and master the basic skills. Become a hard thrower and a great hitter and have fun doing it. Become the best baseball player you can be. You owe this to yourself and to your team.

"I am a good hitter. I am an aggressive hitter. I am a confident hitter. I am a relaxed hitter. All my power is directed to the ball. I am aggressive to the pitch. I step to the pitch. I can hit any pitcher. I hit all pitches close to the strike zone. I hit a fast ball. I hit a curve ball. I protect the strike zone on a second-strike count. I study the pitcher and learn his motion, his control pitch and his strikeout pitch. Baseball is great. Baseball is terrific. I am a great athlete. I am a winner. I am proud. I am in great condition. I am aggressive. I am tough," etc.

innertalk-store.com/products/baseball

Basketball ~ Subliminal

~ Use the power of your mind to become the best basketball player you can be!

Basketball is a great sport for building team involvement, improving personal skills, and enhancing health. Basketball will improve your endurance, strengthening cardio vascular functions, strengthening muscles and bones, and enhancing cognitive abilities while improving hand-eye coordination. Playing basketball lowers stress levels and enhances social skills. While you may not be a Michael Jordan, you can use the power of your mind to become the best basketball player you can be!

"I perform under pressure. I love basketball. I am alert. My coach is a winner. I am enthusiastic. I am in control. I believe in myself. I believe in my coaches. I am a hustler. I like training. I play well. I make things happen. I seize opportunities. I pass well. I make good passes. I am calm. I play in control. I reach. I concentrate on the rim. I set screens. I play defensively baseline to baseline. I perform well. I am good at basketball. I am a team player," etc.

innertalk-store.com/products/basketball

Body Building ~ Subliminal

~ The mental edge is what makes the difference!

Many want to be a bodybuilder but not everyone has what it takes. Athletes around the world get it—the mental edge is what makes the difference. It is the mental determination, the mental commitment, the mental focus, the pure mental metal that pushes one on to endure hours of hard work and training. Quitting is easy and most do just that. Have you got what it takes to spend the hours and endure the pain involved in building a solid muscled body? Bodybuilding is serious business. Use the power of the mind to make the process easier and more efficient.

"My body is good. My body is powerful. I lift weights. I like weight lifting. I work out. I exercise vigorously. I breathe deeply. I eat properly. I rest properly. I sleep soundly. I drink water. I like water. I am limber. I am fit. I am muscular. My body builds perfectly. I look good. I feel great. I care for myself. I love exercise. I love weight lifting. I love calisthenics. Body building is fun. Body building is rewarding," etc.

innertalk-store.com/products/body_building

Bowling ~ Subliminal

~ Have more fun and gain higher scores today!

Bowling is not only family fun, and a great pastime, but it is also a wonderful sport. This program was co-developed in consultation with professional bowler, Steve Buell. This program will assist you in maintaining the good habits necessary to be a good bowler. You'll be able to master the skill necessary to maintain a consistent tempo on the backswing and forward swing on each delivery. Your hold on the ball and bowling speed will improve. You'll get more strikes and consistently bowl higher scores. You'll find picking up spares easy. Your confidence will grow, and you'll amaze yourself at how much fun the entire process is.

" I can do anything. I am a great athlete. I am a leader. Bowling is fun and exciting. I like to go bowling. I like to practice my bowling. I am confident when I bowl. I have a positive mental attitude when I bowl. I think positive when I bowl. I am lucky. My approach is smooth and fluid. My push away,

footwork, follow through, is smooth and consistent. I always follow through with my release. I always concentrate on hitting my target," etc.

innertalk-store.com/products/bowling

Equine Skills (Developing Equine Skills) ~ Subliminal

~ Connect with your horse on a much deeper level and your equine skills will excel.

Your horse needs to trust you and you want to trust your horse. Nothing builds this trust better than your love. Taking time to groom your horse, all the while speaking to her about what you're doing—talking to your horse as you would a close friend begins this trust. However, to do this, you must trust yourself and love horses. Horses are known to be very sensitive to human feelings. They quickly detect feelings of fear, inadequacy, as well as the lack of confidence felt by the rider. That said, the potential bonding available with a horse is simply awesome.

"I love horses. I sense that horses are special. I love the smell of the horse. I love the feel of the horse. I am comfortable around horses. I trust horses. I am patient with myself. I am patient with the horse. I am gentle. I think about my movement. I am careful not to startle the horse. I move deliberately. I move confidently. I look the horse in the eye. I smile. I sense the horse's mind. Intuitively I know the horse reads me. I acknowledge the specialness of the horse to the horse. I am unafraid to speak to the horse. I speak confidently and caringly. I pay attention to the horse. I watch the head and ears," etc.

innertalk-store.com/products/developing_equine_skills

Exercise (Joy of Exercise and Being Fit) ~ Subliminal

~ The more you exercise, the easier it will become.

There are lots of reasons for exercising beyond just being fit and healthy. Exercise has also been shown to improve your mood and sleep, increase your learning ability, improve memory, and reduces stress and anxiety. However, it can be difficult to find the motivation to stick to any kind of exercise regime. Use this program to re-wire your thinking and make exercising fun!

"I like exercise. Exercise is fun. Exercise is healthy. I am healthy. I choose health. I breathe deeply. I breathe. My cardiovascular system is strong. I am strong. I am good. I like myself. I love my body. I am youthful. I exercise regularly. I walk. I enjoy walking. I rest after exercise. I exercise daily. I love living. Water tastes good. Water cleanses me. Water flushes my body clean. Exercise refreshes me," etc.

innertalk-store.com/products/joy_of_exercise

Also Available In:

Fit and Athletic ~ Power Set

innertalk-store.com/products/fit_and_athletic_ps

Fitness (Optimum Fitness) ~ OZO

innertalk-store.com/products/excel_at_sports_ozo

Fighting Power ~ Subliminal Set

~ This program *will* produce the fighting intent within you.

This dual InnerTalk subliminal set for Wing Chun was created in collaboration with Master Ron Heimberger. This makes learning the art easier than ever before. Internal Power helps produce a flexible, relaxed strength called "spring energy" within the student listening. Fighting Power is for serious martial artists only! Once the desired effects are reached then this program should be listened to no more than once a month.

Fighting Power

"I am moral. I am confident. I am courageous. I am unafraid. I do night fight fair. I am fearless I fight when there is no other choice. I attack fast. I defeat the aggressor. I do not give my opponent a chance to hurt me. I can deal with situations. I never back up in a fight. I go all out. I end fights as quickly as possible. I stop others before they physically hurt me. I move tense less and deliberately. I continue attacking until I can leave safely. My attacks are my defense. I attack continuously. I am humble. I am honorable," etc.

Internal Power

"I am whole. I am enough. I am in control. I control my body. I control my thoughts. I cancel negative. I am positive. I control my emotions. I forgive

myself I forgive all others. I am forgiven. I respect myself. I respect all others. I am respected. I am loved. I am honest. I accept myself. I accept others. Life is wonderful," etc.

innertalk-store.com/products/fighting_power_set

Football ~ Subliminal

~ Create the perfect mental state to play football at level beyond your highest level yet!

Working with winning coaches like Mike Price, this program was created for the individual as well as the entire team. Using InnerTalk football programs, Weber State University won the Big Sky Championship and Washington State University went further, going all the way to the Rose Bowl. Maximize your skill, set your winning intention, and master learning the game with this program.

"Football is fun. I am powerful. I have energy. I have stamina. I am enthusiastic. I am confident. I am courageous. I am capable. I am an athlete. I am the best. I work at it. I like it. I am a team player. I believe in the coaches. I excel. My team excels. I soar. I am smart. I learn easily. I trust myself. I play naturally. I play instinctively. I visualize perfect performance. I perform perfectly," etc.

innertalk-store.com/products/football

Golf ~ Subliminal

~ Research showed this program increased ability and earning power!

Golf is a great game for fitness, relaxation, stress reduction, and fun! Golf is more than just a game; it's also a way to communicate. Business people and leaders around the world often meet on a golf course, where camaraderie is nurtured, plans are made, deals are agreed to, and much more.

Golfers have been shown to live longer, enjoy reduced blood pressure, and less physical damage as compared to faster paced sports. Whether you're a professional golfer or a person who just enjoys the outdoors and the social involvement that comes with golf, you'll benefit from this program.

"I keep my head down. I am a great athlete. I practice. I enjoy golf. Golf is fun. My swing is correct. My swing is powerful. My swing is repeating. My posture is good. My stance is good. One foot is always at a right angle to the line of flight. The other foot is turned out at a quarter of a turn to the left. Golf is relaxing. I am a winner. I am a great golfer. I relax. I am positive. I am good. I play relaxed. Power transfers to my arms and hands. My body generates power. I follow through. My elbows and arms are close together during my swing. My elbows are tucked in during my swing. One elbow points directly at the left hip bone," etc.

innertalk-store.com/products/golf

Also Available In:

Golf Like a Pro ~ Video

innertalk-store.com/products/golf_like_a_pro_dvd

Judo ~ Subliminal

~ The winning strategy for the National Judo Institute!

Developed in conjunction with coach Phil Porter, Ph.D., National Judo Institute (NJI) and shown to have a powerful effect. This program was used by the NJI team to win over 100 medals and for use by athletes in the first ever showing of a US team in the Olympic Games in Barcelona, where athletes collected three medals.

"I am ready. I wage war in Judo. I have an absolute lust to win. Victory is all I know. I attack continuously. I am direct and ruthless. I smother my opponents with a blinding whirlwind of attacks. My opponents are confused and bewildered by my constant unorthodox attacks. I destroy my opponents. I am aggressive in competition. I cut and slash in competition. I am a fierce competitor. I counter every move my opponent makes. I am vicious., I am bold. I attack with tremendous speed and power. I defend with power. When my opponents attack me, I punish them. I grip strongly, always dominating my opponent's grip," etc.

innertalk-store.com/products/judo

Karate ~ Subliminal

~ Karate is valuable in physical development as well as self-defense!

The challenges in Karate will build character, aid in motivating and encouraging an individual to strive for their best. Karate teaches breathing techniques while improving reactionary abilities. And as with all martial arts, Karate teaches the use of energy. Used by professionals and amateurs alike, this program will help you to excel in your ability to focus on your desired athletic goal.

"I am calm and relaxed. My breathing is precise. I am patient. I am confident and capable. I am in control. I am powerful. I am humble. I am unlimited. I focus and concentrate. Concentration is effortless. I receive vivid images. I retain images easily and accurately. I create vivid images easily. I have infinite ability. My mind, body, and spirit are a single harmonious unit. I am peace and harmony, one with myself and all of creation. I am healthy. I am strong. I am healthier and stronger with each and every breath. I move myself with ease. I move myself with speed, strength, and precision. I generate and project KI energy," etc.

innertalk-store.com/products/karate

Martial Arts ~ Subliminal

~ Energy is form that can be projected!

Often forgotten in the study of martial arts is the manipulation of energy. Energy is form that can be projected. This program was developed in conjunction with Doctors Jim Seidel and Tony Markham. Train your mind specifically to excel in martial arts, learn to manipulate energy, remain focused, project movements onto your opponent, etc. and watch your physical skills increase!

"I love martial arts. Martial arts is energy. Energy is form. My mind is strong. I cast away all distractive thoughts. My mind is clear. My mind is the master. I control my mind in all things. I breathe slowly and deeply. I breathe evenly. Breath is life. I enjoy breathing. Breathing is electricity charging. Oxygen is electricity. I like the taste of oxygen. Oxygen is good. I master the use of oxygen. I think electrically. I move electrically. Electricity

is vital energy. I generate vital energy through my breathing. I radiate vital energy. I circulate vital energy. My mind controls my vital energy. Vital energy heals my body. Vital energy strengthens my body," etc.

innertalk-store.com/products/martial_arts

Running ~ Subliminal

~ Run for the sheer joy of running!

Running is a great way to gain fitness, lose weight, use excess energy, relieve stress as well as many other instrumental reasons; but running is also simply something that sooner or later you do because it in itself is pleasurable. This program is good for all skill levels. For the competitive runner, train your mind to do even better. For the young person who just wants to remain fit, it will keep you enthused about running. For the older person who has decided to take up running again, it will get you through the initial hurdles of discomfort and lack of desire and allow you to persist and keep on going.

"I like exercise. I like running. Running feels good. Running gives me a rush. Running is good for me. I pace myself. I care for my body. My body is strong and healthy. I love my body. I listen to my body. I breathe deeply. I breathe evenly. My stride is long. My step is easy. My arms pump my lungs. My arms follow my stride. My legs are strong. My lungs expand. My lungs are strong. My heart is strong. I care for my myself. I practice healthy habits. I use nutritional food. I drink water," etc.

innertalk-store.com/products/running

Soccer ~ Subliminal

~ Make your soccer training instinctive!

Acquire the skill set to be a good soccer player, and the mental fitness to be a truly balanced competitor. Teamwork, patience, skill development, confidence, leadership, work ethic, and physical health are just some of the advantages gained from playing soccer. Make your soccer training instinctive, work as a team, and watch your game improve!

"I love soccer. I move quickly. I am aware of my teammates. I am a team player. I am a good sport. I am a powerful athlete. I play to win. I have

tremendous speed. I am strong. I am fit. I am healthy. I am unbeatable. I am calm. I am relaxed. I play defensively. I am a great player. I listen. I listen to my coach. I listen to my teacher. I use my energy. I use my energy to control my opponent. I use my energy to control the game. I like myself," etc.

innertalk-store.com/products/soccer

Sports (Winning Sports Performance) ~ Subliminal

~ It is the mental edge that maximizes an athlete's potential!

The mental edge is what every athlete knows can make a real difference when it comes to winning and losing. It is the mental edge that maximizes an athlete's potential! It is the passion ignited in the mind that leads to greatness! Elite athletes have proven over and over again that their greatest success stories originated in mental training. This is a program that is great for the individual and the team. Indeed, this program was among a series of programs used by several teams to win championships.

"Sports are fun! I am strong. I am powerful. I have energy! I have stamina. I am enthusiastic. I am confident. I am capable. I am an athlete. I am the best. I work at it! I like it! I am a team player. I believe in the coaches. I excel! I soar! My team excels. I am smart. I learn easily. I play naturally. I visualize perfect performance. I perform perfectly," etc.

innertalk-store.com/products/winning_sports_performance

Also Available In:

Sports (Optimum Sports) ~ Collection

innertalk-store.com/products/sports_collection

Sports (Excel at Sports) ~ OZO

innertalk-store.com/products/excel_at_sports_ozo

Sports (Self Talk Sports) ~ Self Talk

innertalk-store.com/products/self_talk_sports

Sports Performance ~ Power Imaging/Hypnosis

innertalk-store.com/products/sports_hypnosis_pi

Sports: Mentally Fit ~ Power Set

innertalk-store.com/products/sports_mentally_fit_ps

Tennis ~ Subliminal

~ Play your best games ever!

Becoming good at tennis begins with the proper mental attitude. This program is designed to both assist in developing the skills necessary to become excellent at tennis while supporting the mental edge that props up the enthusiasm and determination to excel.

Gain the grip, master the forehand drive, strengthen the backhand, become really good at the groundstroke technique and more. You can become a great tennis player and have so much fun doing so.

"I maintain smoothness and fluidity at all times on the tennis court. I am calm and graceful on the tennis court. My shoulders stay relaxed on the tennis court. I keep my head up and body balanced on all tennis strokes. My footwork is excellent on the tennis court. I love to play in tournaments. I have mastery over my serve and return of serve. I can determine the direction of the ball by watching my opponent. I am graceful and agile. I hit under the ball. I am balanced and in control on the tennis court. I am aware of my environment when I am on the tennis court. I am successful and winning," etc.

innertalk-store.com/products/tennis

Walking for Health ~ Subliminal

~ Walking can literally add vitality, youthful appearance, and much more!

How many times have you heard the virtues of walking extolled? Such a simple and easy exercise can literally add vitality, youthful appearance, and much more. Get the motivation and you'll find the desire to walk regularly for health as just a natural part of who you are. Enjoy all the benefits today. Listen to this program before you walk and while you walk and watch just how much better you feel.

"I love to walk. I love exercise. Exercise is good. It feels good to walk. I walk for fun. I enjoy walking. I enjoy the outdoors. I love the smell of fresh air.

I feel invigorated when I walk regularly. Walking is good exercise. I breath rhythmically and evenly. I do just the right amount of exercise. I treat my body with respect. I love my body. I am strong. I like to be fit. I stay fit. I am in good health. I enjoy life. I am good. Walking is good. Walking relaxes my mind and vitalizes my body. I look forward to walking. I enjoy my walks," etc.

innertalk-store.com/products/walking_for_health

Children, Parenting, and Childbirth

Other Children, Parenting, and Childbirth related titles:

Child (Gifted Child) ~ Album

innertalk-store.com/products/gifted-child-album

Childbirth (Miracle of Childbirth) ~ Album

innertalk-store.com/products/miracle-of-childbirth-album

Child Guidance Series ~ Audible/Subliminal

innertalk-store.com/products/child_guidance_series

ADHD ~ Subliminal

~ Reduce ADHD symptoms while enhancing learning and relationship experiences.

ADHD can cause both physical and mental health problems when symptoms are left untreated. These problems can cause one to use coping mechanisms that are actually harmful. This program was evaluated in a double-blind study and found to have beneficial results. The data from the study suggests that cognitive therapy through InnerTalk persuasion reduces ADHD symptomology while enhancing learning and relationship experiences.

"I am capable. I am powerful. I am in control. I discipline myself. I train myself. I learn easily. I like learning. I am good. People are proud of me. I am liked. I am loved. Everything is okay. I'm okay. I follow rules. Rules are important. I listen and hear. I follow directions. I pay attention. I feel good. I am calm and peaceful. I feel happy. School is good. Learning is fun.

I like to learn. I can sit still. I can be quiet. I think before I act. I control my behavior," etc.

innertalk-store.com/products/a_d_h_d

Bedwetting (Freedom from Bedwetting) ~ Subliminal

~ Help a loved one end the embarrassment and shame that often attends bedwetting!

This program has received nothing but praise from our customers. Many difficult bedwetters have become dry for life in days using this InnerTalk program. This testimonial from Kathleen in Utah is not uncommon, *"My two children have quit wetting the bed after approximately 2 weeks of listening to your recording."*

If bedwetting is an issue you are dealing with, then this program is for you. Act today and help a loved one end the embarrassment and shame that often attends bedwetting. Show them you care.

"I like myself. I am good. I am responsible. I am in control. I use the toilet. I respond to my body's signals. My body signals me. I wake up. I use the bathroom. I am dry. I like my bed dry. I am unafraid. I am smart," etc.

innertalk-store.com/products/bedwetting

---

*"My friend bought a tape for my 3-year-old daughter, who had a **bedwetting** problem. I didn't believe a subliminal program could help, but thought it was worth a try. I gave the program to my daughter, told her it was her bedtime program, and decided not to tell her what was on it. After the first night she was dry. Into the second week she began walking around repeating the affirmations on the program."*

Childbirth (Wonders of Childbirth) ~ Subliminal

~ Recognize the wonder and miracle of childbirth.

More and more research has demonstrated just how important the Mother's attitude and emotions are with regard to delivering a happy healthy child. Childbirth is a miracle and when the wonders of childbirth are recognized, the entire process is both more rewarding and environmentally healthier for Mom and child.

Life begins in the womb. This is a very magical time and you should enjoy every moment. Everything you think and feels affects the new life inside of you. Give your child a positive start.

"Life is wondrous. Life is a gift. Seeds are miraculous. Life begins in a womb. I am a womb. Children are beautiful. Children are innocent. A child resides in my womb. I am gifted. Life springs forth from me. Life is beautiful. I am loved. I am needed. I contribute to life. I am calm. I am relaxed. I am happy. I am grateful. My body is beautiful. My mind is at peace. My emotions are positive," etc.

innertalk-store.com/products/wonders_of_childbirth

Children (Joyful Caretaker of Pre-Verbal Children) ~ Subliminal

~ Radiate the love, care and security your child needs!

Have you ever asked yourself what a pre-verbal infant might say about how their internal states of feeling and emotion? Do they feel loved and secure? Are they picking up your emotions? Caring for pre-verbal children can be a challenge. However, this is a very important stage of their development. Maximize their learning opportunities while you enjoy the process. You can truly feel and radiate the love, care and security your child needs, and do so from the inside out.

"I love children. I enjoy being with children. The beauty of life is miraculous. The glory of innocence is awe inspiring. Pre-verbal children trust me. I am trustworthy. I am patient. I am caring. I am loving. I am peaceful. I am joyful I love life. Life is wonderful. Living is a miracle. I appreciate the miracle. I am a good person. I am a caring person. I am a trustworthy person. I am safe to be with and around. I am safe. Children are safe with me. I love caring and sharing. I love to care for pre-verbal children," etc.

innertalk-store.com/products/joyful_caretaker_of_preverbal_children

Children (Successful Children) ~ Subliminal

~ The optimal parent is one who is involved and responsive, who sets high expectations but respects her child's autonomy.

Raising successful children is not just a parenting responsibility, it is a trust placed in every parent by our entire society. Our children are our greatest asset. No one needs tell any parent just how important their role is with respect to guiding a child to become as great as they can be. That said, saying something and managing to get it done in a world full of uncontrollable stimuli is not an easy task. This program will help you to help your children attract positive experiences, achievement, and satisfaction. When they believe they can be successful, successful is what they will be!

"I make a difference. I am good. I develop naturally. I accept myself. I accept others. I am myself. I am okay. All things change. It's okay to be different. I do my best. Happiness is within me. I am happy. I am honest. I do not blame. I am responsible. I make good choices. I can become anything. I am capable. I am patient. I am attentive. I make friends easily. I am a leader. I am confident. I can do anything. I listen to my elders. I learn easily. I am a good student," etc.

innertalk-store.com/products/successful_children

Also Available In:

Successful Children / Family Dynamics ~ Video

innertalk-store.com/products/successful_children_family_dynamics_dvd

Depression (Freedom from Maternal Depression) ~ Subliminal

~ Believe in yourself and enjoy this special time.

Childbirth can result in a wave of emotions from elation and excitement to fear and anxiety, including the unexpected—depression. The severe and long-lasting form of maternal depression is termed postpartum depression. Maternal depression can affect the entire family in a way and at a time that can leave lasting impressions on everyone. Believe in yourself and enjoy this special time.

"I am a miracle. I gave life to a miracle. I am good. I look good. I have done well. I am respected. I respect myself. I am cared for. I accept myself and others. I am loved. Life is a miracle. Living is glorious. I gave life to a child. I am awed by the miracle. Childbirth is a miracle. Joy fills my being. Joy expresses itself through me in appreciation of the miracle. I laugh. I can laugh at myself. I am safe. I am secure. Life has a newer and deeper meaning to me now. I allow. I accept. I have grown in so many personal ways. I am proud of myself," etc.

innertalk-store.com/products/freedom_from_maternal_depression

Esteem (I Can: Building a Child's Esteem) ~ Subliminal
~ Give children the self-belief that arms them with a positive sense of self-worth!

Children with a high sense of self-esteem come to value others and do better in school. They tend to attract roles in leadership and build positive relationships. Because they like themselves and believe they are worthy of being cared for by others, they are less likely than are people with lower self-esteem to stay in abusive or exploitive situations. They are also more likely to take care of themselves physically and emotionally, and to persist in difficult and effortful pursuits such as completing their education or mastering an occupation.

"I am smart. I am good. I am liked. I am safe. I am protected. I make wise choices. I listen to my teachers. I listen to my parents. I learn easily. It's easy to learn. It's easy to be liked. It's easy to cooperate. It's easy to follow rules. It's easy to be polite. It's easy to be courteous. It's easy to be attentive. I like people. I am liked. I respect others. I respect myself. I am patient. I am teachable. I am a good student. I am pleasant. I am confident. I am capable. It's easy to be likable. It's easy to be pleasant. It's easy to be patient. I will always be safe. I will always be a good learner," etc.

innertalk-store.com/products/building_a_childs_esteem

Leadership for Young People ~ Subliminal

~ The best defense against peer pressure that might lead a young person down the wrong path is to develop their leadership skills early.

Children of all ages can become leaders, and the sooner the better. Leadership skills have many pay-offs in life, whether in business or government. Becoming a leader therefore may usher in advantages and alternatives that others are neither prepared for, nor called upon to demonstrate. If a young person you know deserves a head start on life, leadership training is a great place to begin and this program was created with exactly that purpose in mind.

"I set a positive example. I take pride in myself. I look good. I take pride in my appearance. I stand erect. I am confident. I exude confidence. I am a good student. I follow instructions from my teachers. I listen to instructions. I pay attention in class I do my homework every day. I get good grades. I set an example for fellow students. I respect my elders. I respect myself. I earn respect by giving respect. I respect authority. I appreciate authority. I am grateful for rules. Rules organize society. Rules teach values. I observe the rules. I keep the rules," etc.

innertalk-store.com/products/leadership_for_young_people

Newborns (Just for Newborns) ~ Subliminal

~ Provide an enhanced environment for your newborn!

Science is now proving that newborn infants, though unable to communicate in words, have some understanding of language. Not only that, a stimulating rich environment feeds the development of cognitive abilities. Give your child the opportunity to begin life positive, confident, and with the tools to develop the skills early that a good life requires. Many customers have reported accelerated development in infants who have used this program, such as crawling, walking and speaking sooner.

"I am alive. I am alert. I love life. I breathe easily. I like nourishment. I love mommy. Mommy loves me. I am loved. My body develops perfectly. My mind develops perfectly. I am smart. I smile. I respond positively to stimuli. I sleep soundly. I am good natured. I am patient. I am a miracle. I am secure.

Others love me. I love others. Breathing is miraculous. I am healthy. Life is wonderful. My breathing capacity is strong. God loves me," etc.

innertalk-store.com/products/just_for_newborns

Parenting (Positive Parenting) ~ Subliminal

~ Develop the positive actions that nurture happy, healthy children.

Parenting is not easy. There is no training manual distributed to each of us at the time we become parents. To say that effective parenting is a challenge, is an absolute understatement. Even the best prepared find themselves ready to proverbially "pull their hair out" from time to time.

For parents who want to offer their best! This will help you become aware of words and actions that can have a negative impact on a child and help you develop the positive actions that nurture happy, healthy children.

"I am patient. I am supporting. I am encouraging. I teach my children. I teach my children love. I teach my children through example. I teach my children through love. I assist my children. I respect my children's rights. I enjoy my children. I have fun with my children. I discipline my children in love. I am understanding. Parenting is a joy. Parenting is a trust. Parenting is important. We enjoy each other. We love each other. I consider issues carefully. I am loving. I allow individuality. I reinforce the good in my children. I care for my children," etc.

innertalk-store.com/products/positive_parenting

Pregnancy (Comfortable Pregnancy) ~ Subliminal

~ Research has demonstrated that attitude plays a significant role in the pregnancy process.

Pregnancy is both a time of great excitement and demanding adjustments. For some, it can also hold special challenges and even fear. Physical and emotional changes, and shifts in hormonal and metabolic processes, together with the discomfort pregnancy can produce, are but some of the many issues that can arise during pregnancy. The good news is that research has demonstrated that attitude plays a significant role in the pregnancy process. Attitude can dissolve the discomfort and replace it with awe and joy. This program will help you to be comfortable during pregnancy.

"I am loved. I love my unborn child. I am comfortable. I am at ease. I experience pleasure. Pregnancy is wondrous. Childbirth is joyous. I relax. I breathe deeply. I sense only comfort. I feel only pleasure. Childbirth is painless. Pregnancy is pleasurable. My body changes are wondrous. I take care of my body. I eat good foods. I drink water. I eat small portions. I eat only at regular meals. I eat leafy vegetables. I eat fresh fruits. I sleep soundly and peacefully. I rest regularly," etc.

innertalk-store.com/products/comfortable_pregnancy

Respect and Good Manners ~ Subliminal

~ Respect and good manners can give your child a head start, while adding balance to your own home and relationships.

Teaching young people respect and manners is more challenging today than ever. Respect and manners begin with a mind-set, with an expectation, with a mental attitude. Parents have reported witnessing the almost immediate effect of this program. Proper respect and good manners are always appropriate and beneficial.

"I am good. I am loved. I like myself. I like others. I respect myself. I respect others. I respect my elders. I respect my parents. I love my family. I am loved. I am safe. I am cared for. I am grateful. I am lucky. I like to respectful. It's easy to be respectful. I can be respectful. I choose to be respectful. I use good manners. I listen quietly. I pay attention. I know when to be quiet. I know when to be still. It's easy to be quiet. It's easy to be still. It's easy to show respect. It's easy to have good manners. I have good manners. I am admired. I treated with respect. I treat others with respect," etc.

innertalk-store.com/products/respect_and_good_manners

School (Freedom from Stress in School) ~ Subliminal

~ Guide your student away from the wrong sort peer groups as well as promote the proper perspective about education.

All students experience some sort of stress in school. It can be stress produced by peers and it can result from a rigorous academic curriculum. This program is appropriate for all grade levels. It aims at guiding the student away from the wrong sort peer groups as well as promoting the proper perspective about education. Balance is the key to successful students and this program is all about not just de-stressing but enhancing the balance in life.

"I do my best. I am happy. I smile. I laugh. I experience joy. I like school. I make friends. I communicate. I am a leader. I make wise choices. I am responsible. School is fun. Learning is exciting. I am relaxed. I am calm. I am confident. I am positive. I learn easily," etc.

innertalk-store.com/products/stress_in_school

School (Joy of School) ~ Subliminal

~ Remove the fear of school and watch your child excel!

School should be fun. Learning should be exciting. The classroom does not always promote these ideas. Indeed, sometimes the pressure that arises in the classroom from both teachers and peers can be so intimidating that the student loses confidence and begins to fear school. Research has demonstrated that a student's attitude toward learning makes all the difference in their experience. Promoting that attitude often falls almost exclusively on the parent. When a child learns to enjoy going to school, they do better in their studies and in their relationships.

"I enjoy life. I love living. I feel good. I am unique. I accept myself. I accept all others. I like myself. I am good. I am capable. I succeed. I do my best. I am happy. I smile. I laugh. I experience joy. I like school. I make friends. I communicate. I am a leader. I make wise choices. I am responsible. School is fun. Learning is exciting. I am relaxed. I am calm. I am confident," etc.

innertalk-store.com/products/joy_of_school

School Phobia ~ Subliminal

~ Help your child become more comfortable in school, gain a sense of security, and add to their self-esteem!

School phobia is a complex syndrome that can be influenced by the child's temperament, the situation at school, and the family situation. Current thinking defines school phobia or school refusal as an anxiety disorder related to separation anxiety. It can vary from outright refusal to attend or stay in school to a more aggressive defensive attitude in school—throwing tantrums, tossing objects, and so forth. Sometimes the unruly child is actually suffering from some form of school phobia and it can go undiagnosed by teachers, counselors, and parents alike. This program has been used successfully to eliminate the school phobia response.

"I am safe. I am liked. I have friends. I am secure. I like being social. I like learning. I like school. I like being top of the class. School is fun. My friends are nice. My friends are kind. I am kind. I am happy. I smile. I am joyful. Being happy is fun. I enjoy life. I look forward to each day. I find joy in everything. My body is happy. My stomach is relaxed. I am relaxed. I am a jovial person. I have a great sense of humor. I am stress free. I am free of anxiety. My nerves are calm. School is exciting. I look forward to school. I like my teachers. School-work is easy," etc.

innertalk-store.com/products/school_phobia

Thumb Sucking (Freedom from Thumb Sucking) ~ Subliminal

~ While thumb sucking may provide security during early years, it eventually becomes socially unacceptable and personally damaging.

Most experts believe that thumb sucking actually begins in the womb. Thumb sucking is comfortable and calming and generally practiced by most infants in the early stages of their life. Unfortunately, this habit can become a means to assuage anxiety, something your child turns to in times of doubt and fear. Thumb sucking can lead to both psychological and physical issues. Teeth can become deformed leading to the need for braces. The habit of comforting oneself by sucking during times of stress can eventually lead to smoking and other oral fixations. Help your child help themselves to break this early habit

"I am free of thumb sucking. I am sufficient. I am confident. I think about my hands. I think about my fingers. I know where my fingers are. I keep my fingers and thumb out of my mouth. My mouth is clean. I like a clean

mouth. I am enough. I am whole. I am secure. I am loved. I am good. I am accepted. I am cared for. I am good to myself," etc.

innertalk-store.com/products/thumb_sucking

Young People (Positive Interactions for Young People) ~ Subliminal

~ Encourage and build attitudes relative to listening, cooperating and behaving patiently.

This title was developed especially for young people, ages 6 through 16. The musical background was chosen for a young audience and combines musical renditions of Techno, Rock and Country (a lot of Techno and a dab of the other). The affirmations encourage and build attitudes relative to listening, cooperating and behaving patiently in addition to those of a healthy self-esteem. If the young person you know tends not to listen, fails to cooperate and/or lacks the patience to wait for anything, you may want to try this program.

"I make a difference. I am good. I develop naturally. I accept myself. I accept others. I am myself. I am okay. All things change. It's okay to be different. I do my best. Happiness is within me. I am happy. I am honest. I do not blame. I am responsible. I make good choices. I can become anything. I am capable. I am patient. I am attentive. I make friends easily. I am a leader. I am confident. I can do anything. I listen to my elders. I learn easily. I am a good student. I enjoy school," etc.

innertalk-store.com/products/positive_interactions_for_young_people

Child Guidance Series ~ Audible/Subliminal

~ Learning was never this much fun!

All the programs in this wonderful series use the patented InnerTalk subliminal technology behind audible stories, adventures and fantasies. The affirmations are self-esteem builders and, while the audible stories are tutorial, learning was never this much fun! The child guidance stories either lead your child to really thinking about what they wish to be, or takes them into a fantasy world, where they see choices they may not have previously considered. Put the program on at bedtime. Let the audible information engage your child while helping them fall asleep at the same time—all while building their self-esteem. Also included in this set is the InnerTalk subliminal program, *I Can: Building a Child's Esteem*.

TITLES INCLUDE:

Why?

Everyone with children knows that the question, *Why?* could be described as a stage young people pass through. This story was created to teach young people to reason, question and think about their questions in a systematic way and integrate their knowledge as a system whole. It has been often stated that genius is a matter of seeing the same thing differently.

Miracle of Life

How can we teach our children the value of life when we live in a world where most of us are protected from the realities of death; where violence in the media is the norm; where games and toys desensitize values; where peer pressure encourages violent tendencies and so much more. This story was written by one mom who wanted her child to see the bigger picture. A fairy tale with a marvelous message!

Leadership and Wise Choices

More than ever young people today are faced with a deluge of stimuli that often leads them down a road of violence, thrill, drugs and other abuses of self and society. Indeed, specialists believe that we have lost a generation to the gangs and unrealistic peer pressure. Our school systems are prohibited from doing much more than educating. The teaching of values is assumed to be the responsibility of parents. Unfortunately, many parents are just not in touch with the pressures young people are faced with. How does one prepare their child to make wise choices in an arena of insane alternatives? This story uses the power of imagination to take a young person on a journey designed to give them a sense of self respect, leadership and wise choices.

innertalk-store.com/products/child_guidance_set

Learning

For our most complete learning related packages, please see:

Brain Power (Maximizing Brain Power) ~ Album

    innertalk-store.com/products/maximizing-brain-power-album

Smart and Sharp ~ Album

    innertalk-store.com/products/smart_and_sharp_album

Learning is Fun-damental ~ Collection

    innertalk-store.com/products/learning_is_fundamental_collection

Exams (Learning for Examinations) ~ Subliminal Set

    innertalk-store.com/products/learning_for_examinations_set

Art (Developing and Enhancing Artistic Abilities) ~ Subliminal

~ Realize a new dimension of skill and express your artistic visions!

Art can add a layer of happiness to your life that you've not previously known. Whether your plan is to become a skilled professional or happy hobbyist, acquiring and advancing your artistic side is an edifying experience. This program was created for those among you who wish to realize a new dimension of skill and express your artistic visions. If you've ever thought you want to be a good artist, now is the time to begin.

"I am creative. I am artful. I love art. I love expressing myself through my art. I practice my art skills. I hone my art skills. I am good. I am a good artist. Every day I improve in every way. My realistic drawing skill is excellent. My constructive drawing skill is excellent. I use my skill to produce harmony in visual elements. I effectively use contrast and tonal values. I excel at the use of symmetry. I am good at human anatomy. My art skill set improves every day. I practice my skills. I study art composition. I study artistic techniques. I am an art lover," etc.

innertalk-store.com/products/artistic-abilities-subliminal

Brain (Using Both Halves of the Brain) ~ Subliminal

~ When the artistic and the linear work in tandem, genius arrives!

When the artistic and the linear work in tandem, genius arrives. Albert Einstein reported that he imagined (visualized) the curvature of space. His spacial abilities integrated with his logical, linear abilities and the rest is history writing itself still today. Bring out the best of both halves of your brain by fully expressing the left-brain (logical and scientific) and the right brain (artistic and creative) simultaneously. Why not integrate both hemispheres of your brain today and add another dimension to your thinking and creativity?

" I choose to use both hemispheres simultaneously. I am able to use both hemispheres simultaneously. I will always find it easy to use all of my abilities. I create my mental habits. I create hemispheric balance in me now. I love my new mental power. My mental abilities improve in every way every day. I have keen mental abilities. I have the use of my entire mental abilities now. I feel words. I see words. I taste words. I hear words. I imagine with all my senses. Numbers have colors. Stimuli are sensory rich. I alternate hand usage. I alternate the leg I put my weight on. I visualize in sensory detail. I visualize dimensionally. I write poetry and rhyme. I sing to myself. I learn new words. I play mental games with mathematics. I color my emotions. I value my learnings," etc.

innertalk-store.com/products/using_both_halves_of_the_brain

Cognitive Enhancement ~ Subliminal

~ Train your mind to want to learn and remember!

Mental training has been proven to minimize cognitive decline and some instances even restore lost abilities. According to Harvard Health, eating right, exercising and tackling new areas of learning facilitate ending normal aging decline. This program was designed to motivate you to learn and remember. There are many reasons for cognitive decline, but there are also lots of things you can do to slow this decline down and even reverse it. There is much truth in the statement, *"Use it or lose it!"* Train your mind to want to learn and remember.

"My memory is strong. I easily remember everything I need whenever I need it. I integrate my learnings. I associate my learnings. I associate my memories. My memory is powerful. I learn easily. I pay closer attention to new information now than ever before. I remember names, places and dates. I make an effort to remember names, places and dates. I am relaxed about my memory. I am a powerful communicator. I am a good public speaker. I am relaxed and comfortable. I deliberately learn something new every day. I add words to my vocabulary on a daily basis. I go out of my way to learn. I practice my memory. I practice my learnings. I find it all easy. It is easy to speak. It is easy to remember. It is easy to share my learnings," etc.

innertalk-store.com/products/cognitive_enhancement

Concentration Is Easy ~ Subliminal

~ Re-train your attention and fine-tune your concentration ability.

The mind can wander for many reasons. Environmental factors and other stimuli can increase the difficulty involved in focusing our attention. This program is designed to facilitate training your attention and thereby fine-tune your concentration ability. If you have ever thought that you lack the ability to concentrate, then this program may boost your powers of concentration with amazing results.

"I think clearly. My mental processes are clear. My mental processes are sharp. I focus attention. I do it easily. I hold related ideas. I network my learning. I concentrate easily. Concentration is focused attention. I do it. I do

it effortlessly. I do it naturally. Concentration is fun. Learning is fun. I love living. Concentration is natural. I am attentive. I concentrate. I am good. I remember. Memory is natural," etc.

innertalk-store.com/products/concentration

Exams (I Excel in Exams) ~ Subliminal

~ Master the art of taking tests and maximize the results of all the work involved in learning.

For many people, no matter how much they study or how well they know a subject, the stress of exams produces anxiety and even mental shutdown. This program will remove these mental blocks and relieve your anxiety so that you can access your store of knowledge easily. Test taking is a measure of what we learned—or it's supposed to be. Why not master the art of taking tests and maximize the results of all the work involved in learning? This program was demonstrated to work in a tight double-blind scientific study conducted at Stanford University.

"I am confident. I am sure. I am relaxed. I like tests. Tests are easy. I remember easily. I am relaxed during tests. I look forward to tests. I study well. I take good notes. I prepare carefully. I associate learnings. I am positive. Tests are fun. Tests are easy. I am smart. I excel at tests. I solve problems. I am capable. I am swift. I remember facts. I find tests easy. My thoughts are clear. My memory flows easily," etc.

innertalk-store.com/products/excel_in_exams

Also Available In:

Exams (Learning for Examinations) ~ Subliminal Set

innertalk-store.com/products/learning_for_examinations_set

Genius Power ~ Subliminal

~ Plug into the genius expectation and release the genius within you!

Research has shown that genius is possible for even those who have been labeled as learning impaired. Indeed, the Pygmalion factor demonstrated this when troubled children were given to a teacher as specially gifted children. A follow up showed that when the teacher believed the child was precocious instead of learning impaired, the child not only improved behaviorally but also showed a vast increase in their learning ability.

Science used to believe that I.Q. was fixed. Today, we know better. When you stop thinking that you are just not smart enough, then you will start reaching your true potential.

"I am a genius. I claim genius. I will genius. I am quick. My mind is keen. I am alert. I am at ease. I appreciate learning. I remember effortlessly. I learn directly. I learn inferentially. I learn literally. I learn in pictures. I learn visually. I learn audibly. I learn through all my senses. I am always calm. My senses are keen. My senses are alert. I am intuitive. I am insightful. I dream solutions. I remember. I question. I am confident. It is easy," etc.

innertalk-store.com/products/genius_power

Also Available In:

Genius (Creative Genius) ~ Video

innertalk-store.com/products/creative_genius_dvd

Learning (Accelerated Learning and Study) ~ Subliminal

~ When our perception regarding learning changes, the task suddenly becomes much easier.

For many learning is a chore—a dreaded struggle with memorizing and understanding. Research has repeatedly demonstrated that this struggle is the problem. When our perception regarding learning changes, the task suddenly becomes much easier. The fact is, the more joy we find in discovering the new, in mastering the learning, the greater ease we find in doing so. As such, learning is largely a matter of attitude and expectation.

"I learn easily. I learn effortlessly. I like learning. Learning is fun. Learning is great. I concentrate. I do one thing at a time. I focus. I perceive clearly. I am confident. I am calm. I am relaxed. I am attentive. I am still when studying. I am alert in class. I listen intently. I associate learnings. Learning comes easily. Learning is powerful. I remember. I take careful notes. I like

to read. I do it easily. I can do it. I do it well. I am a winner. I study well. I read with comprehension. I schedule time to study. Studying is fun," etc.

innertalk-store.com/products/accelerated_learning

Also Available In:

Learning is Fun-damental ~ Collection

innertalk-store.com/products/learning_is_fundamental_collection

Learn Easily ~ Echo-Tech

innertalk-store.com/products/learn_easily_et

Learning (Accelerated Learning) ~ OZO

innertalk-store.com/products/accelerated_learning_ozo

Learning (Power Learning and Memory) ~ Power Imaging/ Hypnosis

innertalk-store.com/products/power_learning_and_memory_pi

Learning Power ~ Power Set

innertalk-store.com/products/learning_power_ps

Learning (Accelerated Learning and Memory) ~ Video

innertalk-store.com/products/
accelerated_learning_and_memory_dvd

Mathematics is Easy ~ Subliminal

~ Math is an essential aspect of music, art, science and life in general.

There is no such thing as life in our modern society without the necessity of mathematics. From balancing checkbooks and paying taxes to calculating gas mileage and the impact of interest rates on purchases, mathematics is essential. Don't let the fear of math stand in the way of excelling in school or on the job. You'll find the fear replaced with a new sense of self-confidence and ability to learn quickly as a result of using this program. Our customers report their children going from 'D's to 'A's as a result of using Mathematics Is Easy.

"Math is an extension of logic. Math has simple rules. Math interprets the world. Math is easy. I learn math rules. I remember math rules. I am logical. Math is effortless. Math comes in steps. I learn math in steps. I learn math easily. Logic is natural. I am natural. I solve easily. Math is fun. Life is wonderful. I am calm. I am relaxed. I am confident. I am good. I am in control. I am good at math," etc.

innertalk-store.com/products/mathematics_is_easy

Memory (Powerful Memory) ~ Subliminal

~ Everyone's memory power can be enhanced!

Short and long-term memory power are both critical to mastering new subjects in the workplace, in school and in everyday life. It's not at all uncommon for memory to dim with aging, but it is also not necessary. As with any skill or muscle, use it or lose it is a truthful mantra. Unfortunately, many people have either never acquired the skill involved to sort memories properly and/or they have failed to use that skill for long enough that the deterioration becomes obvious. You can learn or reacquire memory skills at any age.

"I network learnings. I have a powerful memory. I remember easily. I am relaxed. I am confident. Details are easy. Memory is natural. I make mental notes. My notes flow freely through my mind. I am intelligent. I like remembering. Memory flows effortlessly. I learn easily. Memory is easy," etc.

innertalk-store.com/products/powerful_memory

"The Powerful Memory CD is so good. Despite not managing to listen for the recommended time, it is having an effect. A number of times in the past few days I have found lost items that have defied being found. I had emptied cupboards, drawers, coat pockets, yet they still remained lost. Suddenly they have been discovered exactly where my inner mind remembered. I was truly amazed."

Musical Abilities (Developing and Enhancing Musical Abilities) ~ Subliminal

~ Access the musical zone!

Do you ever wish you could improve your musical abilities? Well, now you can. Perfect for all—ranging from those with limited musical experience to those who have not reached the standard they would like. Music has been shown to be beneficial for mood, stress, brain development, learning abilities and more. Discover a new dimension to your own life by developing the musician within!

"Music has awakening power. I love to create music. I make up lyrics. I assemble new sounds. I practice my music. I love to practice. Every day in every way I improve. I am patient. I am patient with myself. I am persistent. I am determined. Music is a part of the joy in life. Music is one of my joys. I take lessons. I enjoy my music lessons. I look forward to learning more every day. I love learning music. I feel the rhythm. I hear the subtleties in sounds. I learn the technical features of music," etc.

innertalk-store.com/products/developing-and-enhancing-musical-abilities

Reader (I Am a Great Reader) ~ Subliminal

~ Reading is fundamental to success in all areas of life.

Reading is not only important for academic success it can be critical to understanding the job. Vocabulary can be the deciding factor that sways an interview and thereby wins a promotion. Reading is fundamental to success in all areas of life. Reading can also be recreationally rewarding. It can be a get-away from the drone of daily life. Reading can introduce us to other cultures and in many ways enrich our lives.

Whether you are a student or an adult, reading not only gives power through knowledge but it can be very relaxing, adventuresome, and simply fun. Open the door and see what the world of reading can do for you!

"I like reading. I like learning. Reading is fun. Reading is adventuresome. Reading is easy. I learn new words. I read effortlessly. I remember what I read. I read faster and faster. I read with comprehension. I associate what I

read. I read silently. I see paragraphs. Seeing has meaning. Reading is seeing. My thoughts are fast. I am confident. I concentrate when reading," etc.

innertalk-store.com/products/i_am_a_great_reader

Word Power: Spelling and Vocabulary ~ Subliminal

~ One is often judged by their vocabulary.

This program isn't just for students—it's for all of us. Think about what word power means. Did you know that IQ tests are vocabulary weighted? Have you ever tried to communicate something but were amiss to pull up the right words? Do you find yourself reading material and coming across words that you do not recognize? When you listen to the people in the news, do you find some of what they say fails to connect with you? Do you sometimes question how to spell some words? Isn't it time that you changed all of this and built your own powerful vocabulary?

"I have a powerful vocabulary. I like words. I use words correctly. I listen to words. I listen to new words. I look up new words. I look up words. I remember words. Remembering is easy. Remembering is natural. Remembering is effortless. Words are meaningful. I speak well. I write well. I am fluent. Fluency is easy. Fluency is natural. Fluency is fun. I have word power. Words are fun. Words are keys to knowledge. Words are keys to understanding. I have the power and ability. I do it easily. I associate words," etc.

innertalk-store.com/products/word_power

Spirituality

Note regarding our Spiritual Programs:

Many of our programs include a spiritual component. We offer a variety of spiritual programs. We believe the spiritual component of life to be as important, if not more so, than any other component. However, we do not wish to choose the spiritual path for anyone. That is each of our rights, both under God and our Constitution. We, therefore, try to provide a variety of spiritual programs in an attempt to bring something for everyone. We recognize that this is difficult to do while not offending anyone. Nevertheless, we find it a responsibility to use our technology in the spirit of the saying, "As a man thinketh, so is he." Many religious leaders use and have endorsed our programs. Still, if you have a question, please ask your spiritual advisor to review the affirmations in order to ensure that the program you choose is in keeping with your particular spiritual path.

For our most complete success-related packages, please see:

Mystical Mind: A Path to Mastership ~ Library

   innertalk-store.com/products/mystical_mind_library

Meditation (Deep Meditation) ~ Album

   innertalk-store.com/products/deep-meditation-album

Mindfulness (Optimal Mindfulness) ~ Album

   innertalk-store.com/products/optimal-mindfulness-album

Spiritual Connectedness ~ Album

   innertalk-store.com/products/spiritual_connectedness_album

Asclepiad Experience: The Healing Dream
~ Subliminal

~ Discover the answers!

Asclepius, the Greek God of healing, used dreams to heal both physical and emotional ailments, as he believed the answers to all things come from within. Dreams have throughout history revealed information that defies so-called scientific understanding. Everything, from pre-cognitive dreams to miracle healings, has been documented as a result of a dream. This program will not only facilitate enhancing your dream states, it alone is a great meditative device for discovering answering from within. This program includes an audible meditation in addition to the InnerTalk subliminal affirmations.

"God dwells in all. God loves all. God is love. I am a gift. I am whole. I am giving. I am a part of the gift. I am whole as a gift. I am loving. I am caring. I am supporting. I am sharing. I am alive. I am eternal. I share myself. I live an example. I am humble. I am learning. I listen. I care. I am strong. I am honest. I am a miracle. I heal. I help. I assist. I guide. I share. I allow. I accept. I encourage. I facilitate," etc.

innertalk-store.com/products/asclepiad_experience_the_healing_dream

Astral Projection ~ Subliminal

~ Experience the tranquility, openness, and control you can have over your astral travels.

Are you curious to see where your spirit travels unrestrained from your body? Where would you go? What answers would you seek? How would you use your newly found talent? Are you ready to open your mind and soul to experience the astral planes beyond this current physical realm?

Ingo Swann was so successful at remote viewing and astral projection, that the CIA funded his research. He and many others have spent their lives cultivating this skill – and now you can try for yourself! Some believe that we all astral project, but most just can't remember the experience.

"My spirit is eternal. Astral travel is natural. Consciousness is energy. Energy is mass. Energy exists in all. I am energy. My consciousness is pure energy. Energy is unlimited. My energy expands. It's okay to use my energy. It's okay

to expand my energy. It's okay to consciously employ energy. Life force is energy. Astral travel is a natural extension of energy. I extend my energy. I extend my energy naturally. I am conscious of astral travel. I remember astral experiences," etc.

innertalk-store.com/products/astral_projection

Auras (Viewing Auras) ~ Subliminal

~ Explore the possibility of seeing auras with your own eyes.

In parapsychology and spiritual practice, an aura is an apparent field of subtle, luminous radiation that some people say surrounds a person or object. Halos are often depicted in the art portraying Saints. Often it is held to be perceptible, whether spontaneously or with practice: such perception is at times linked with the third eye of Indian spirituality. Reading auras is something we can all learn to do once we come to sense the aura of others.

"Auras are energy. Energy fields exist in all. All is energy. I am sensitive to energy. I feel energy. I see energy. I sense energy. Colors are vivid. Patterns are clear. Coronas are obvious. I see clearly. All things radiate energy. Energy fields exist in everything. I am sensitive to energy fields. I have aura seeing ability. I see auras. I see and sense auras. I am thankful. I am blessed. I am interrelated to all. Perception is natural.," etc.

innertalk-store.com/products/viewing_auras

Awakening ~ Subliminal

~ Are you ready to wake up?

Awakening is all about transitioning from individual mind into the One Mind that underlies all intelligence. In the awakened state, ego no longer controls your destiny. An Awakened individual is free of attachments. In this special state of mind, the universe becomes a part of you. That is, for a moment, or for longer for some, you become one with all that is.

It takes courage to let go and allow the quietness of spirit to overcome the sense of self as an individual, separate from all that is. Are you ready to try?

"I open up. I trust my senses. I trust my impressions. My hearing expands. My sight sees inter-dimensionally. I feel. My feeling expands. I touch. I taste. I am a master. My consciousness senses. I am consciousness. I know. My impressions are clear. My senses are powerful. It is a gift. It is natural. I am a gift. My chakras open. Energy is natural. I vibrate energy. I serve.," etc.

innertalk-store.com/products/awakening

Biblical Wisdom ~ Subliminal

~ The Lord is my Shepherd.

Make these key teachings from The Bible a real part of your subconscious beliefs.

"The Lord is my Shepherd. The truth shall set me free. The Kingdom of heaven is within. Whatever I do unto the least of people, I have done unto Christ. Judge not lest ye be judged. Let ye without sin cast the first stone. All things whatsoever ye pray and ask for, believe that ye have received them, and ye shall receive them. Let every soul be subject unto the higher powers. For there is no power but of God: the powers that be ordained of God," etc.

innertalk-store.com/products/biblical_wisdom

Centering ~ Subliminal

~ Discover the peace, balance and harmony within.

Centering is another word for stilling the outer and becoming harmonious within. It is the place where one quietly seeks peace, balance and harmony within. Remaining centered is an important skill set in today's world of constant stimuli. It can produce a stress free inner-world akin to a duck in storm where the rain is shed without ever penetrating the duck's feathers.

"I am master of myself. I center my thoughts. I observe my emotions. I am lifted by my spirit. I am peace that passeth understanding. I see good in all. I experience good in all. I am eternal. I learn without resistance. I have all I need to be happy now. I am happy. I live in joy. Life is wonderful. Only beauty surrounds me. Love and beauty are all there is. All is us. Everything

is oneness. I am always where I am. That is where I am supposed to be now," etc.

innertalk-store.com/products/centering

Chakras (Opening/Balancing the Chakras) ~ Subliminal

~ Allow the life energy to flow freely through you.

Many spiritual systems refer to the energy centers of the body. According to Indian thought, there are seven major power centers in the body. These seven centers are known as chakras. Some health care professionals have successfully deployed electrophotography to evaluate these energy centers and their meridians to diagnose and prognosticate health conditions. Indeed, many find a correlation between the chakras and the Chinese practice of acupuncture, believing that the meridian system connecting the centers can become blocked, just as the meridians themselves that like blood vessels move energy from place to place in the body, can become obstructed.

"Life energy flows through me. I am creative. My energy is creative. Life is creative. Kundalini energy is creative. My root chakra is open. My spleen chakra is open. My solar plexus chakra is open. I love life. I am a gift. I am grateful. All that comes to me is good. Good exists in everything. I see God's presence in all. I am accepting. I am whole. I am at peace. The Spirit and I are one. My heart chakra is open. My throat chakra is open. My third eye chakra is open. My crown chakra is open. I feel my energy. I am in touch with all life. I am sensitive to all life," etc.

innertalk-store.com/products/opening-balancing_the_chakras

Connecting with the Force ~ Subliminal

~ Explore the possibilities!

What is it that lies behind the curtain and powers so-called psychic experience? What force is it that bends spoons and levitates objects? Is there a supernatural force that can be harnessed to perform great feats as some of those recorded in psychokinesis experiments? Is there an unseen energy that can be tapped into, giving rise to a perception of a deeper level of reality and a power to manipulate certain aspects of ordinary reality? Mystics have long said so. Explore the possibilities with this program.

"I have the power and the ability. I feel life. I live in now. I breathe life. Life and Light are one. I am one with the Light. I am one with life. Life's force flows through me. I sense the Force. Time and space are illusion. All is the Force. I am one with the Force now. The Force contains all. The Force is infinite giving light. I am a gift. I manifest to the glory of Light. I am one with the Force. I see the Force. I hear the Force. I feel the Force. I think the Force," etc.

innertalk-store.com/products/connecting_with_the_force

Conscious Connectedness ~ Subliminal

~ Enjoy a deeper sense of life, discover a special inner meaning and purpose, and experience a greater feeling of peace.

A connected consciousness beholds the miracle of life—all life. It is enabled by the awareness that all life is inherently interconnected. This special state of consciousness recognizes with awe the beauty and balance in nature. It surrenders the independent ego in favor of interdependence. As a result, the consciously connected person enjoys a deeper sense of life, a special inner meaning and purpose, and a greater feeling of peace.

"All life share the same atomic nature. My atoms were the atoms of life's ancestors. All life evolves. All life has consciousness. All life matters. All life is sacred. Life is a miracle. Life is a gift. Living is sharing. Life is all interconnected. The planet lives. The forests live. The flora and fauna all share life with me. We all live in the now. We all share the miracle. I behold the miracle. I am in awe. Absolute awe. Beauty. Miracles. I can create a feeling of connectedness. I can create a deep sense of awe," etc.

innertalk-store.com/products/conscious_connectedness

Also Available In:

Emotional High: Feeling Connected to the All ~ Platinum Plus

innertalk-store.com/products/emotional_high_feeling_pp

Conscious Expansion ~ Subliminal

~ Discover the limitlessness of your conscious awareness.

A particular meditation technique involves expanding your consciousness outwards. Many report mystical experiences when they do this and are generally left feeling very much at peace—in harmony with the world. Discover the limitlessness of your conscious awareness. You'll find the only limits you have are those you impose upon yourself.

"I am a being of the Light. I am a facet of the One Mind. I am One with the One Mind. God created me in God's image. God knows everything. I am one with the Divine. I access the Divine Mind. I am a gift - a gift of unconditional love. I accept the gift. All that I do is in love. I expand and open my mind. I receive from the One Mind. I access the One Mind," etc.

innertalk-store.com/products/conscious_expansion

Also Available In:

Hyperemperia: Conscious Expansion ~ Platinum Plus + Audible Meditation

innertalk-store.com/products/hyperemperia_pp

Dreaming (Awakened Dreaming: The Lucid Dream Experience) ~ Subliminal

~ Use the power of your dreams to assist in manifesting the life of your dreams!

The mind is more than the ultimate frontier, it is also the gateway to worlds not yet fully discovered, comprehended and/or limited by the finite nature of physicality. Awakened dreaming is a state of consciousness where dreamers are fully aware that they are asleep, and that what they are experiencing is a state of reality completely manufactured by the dreaming mind.

Researchers are talking more and more about the benefits to lucid dream states. In a lucid dream, one can enter the dream and literally alter its content and conclusion. This can be both a healing event as well as a significant uncovering. The inner world of dreams does much more than simply vent unresolved conflict and consolidate memories. Why not visit and participate in your dreams?

"I am aware of my dreams. I enter my dreams lucidly. I have the power to change my dreams. I have the ability to generate dreams. The dream state can be conscious. I am aware during my dreams. My mind alerts me to dreams. I remain within the dream in an alert state. My consciousness expands. It is like being awake while dreaming. I enjoy lucid dreaming. I monitor my dreams. I record my dreams. I keep a journal of my dreams. I review my dreams. Dreams have power. Dreams provide insights," etc.

innertalk-store.com/products/awakened_dreaming

Dreams (Using Dreams for Problem Solving) ~ Subliminal

~ Dreams afford a doorway into a realm that knows no time/ space limitation.

Dream petitioning has a very long history. The phrase, "Let me sleep on it," is such a part of our vernacular; we don't often stop and investigate just what it means and why we say it. The fact is, dreams often provide us with important insights. This program was created to assist you in attuning your dreams to answering your questions, bringing forth solutions, uncovering causes and so forth. We recommend first reading the affirmations, for conscious acknowledgment, and then simply play the program, especially while you sleep. Take a problem to bed tonight with our Dream Petitioning program and see if you don't find solutions coming through your dream sleep.

"Dreams are healing. Dreaming is natural. Dreams are a doorway. Dreams provide solutions. Dreams see through time. Dreams access higher levels of consciousness. Consciousness is. My mind is an aspect of the collective mind. Ideas are universal. Consciousness is universal. Mind knows no limitation. My dreams provide solutions. My dreams are helpful. My dreams give me insight. I petition my dreams for help. I petition my dreams for insight. I remind myself at bedtime. I record my dreams," etc.

innertalk-store.com/products/using_dreams_for_problem_solving

Also Available In:

Dream Petitioning: Using Dreams for Answers ~ Platinum Plus

innertalk-store.com/products/dream_petitioning_pp

Healing (Spiritual Healing) ~ Subliminal

~ Call on a higher power to assist in healing.

There are many stories of miraculous healings involving spiritual practices. People in hospices have risen, walked out, and lived long healthy lives. The power of prayer has been shown to influence healing at a distance, even when the patient being prayed for was unknown to those doing the praying. Research literature has begun to proliferate demonstrating the healing power possible when spiritual side of life is called upon.

"I am a gift. I am a creation of the Divine. I am created perfectly. I have power. I have Divine gifts. God has already forgiven me. I forgive myself. I forgive others. Forgiveness is Grace. I live in Grace. I am strong. I am capable. I am powerful. I will this so. My body serves me. My mind serves me. I will health. I am healthy. I am well. Divine Power makes this so," etc.

innertalk-store.com/products/spiritual_healing

Higher Power (Opening Up to a Higher Power) ~ Subliminal

~ Allow a higher power to show you the way!

Opening yourself up to a higher power enables spirit to work through you and with you. Higher power consciousness accepts and loves you just as you are while encouraging the very best in you. Stories abound of people who have saved their marriages, healed incurable diseases, abandoned addictions, and so much more by simply opening up and turning their lives over.

"I am a creation of the Divine. I was created perfectly. I accept the gift. All that I can ever be is a gift. I am grateful. I manifest unto the glory of the giver. Life is a school. I have many learnings. I have had many choices. I accept responsibility for my choices. I am responsible. I am loving. I am forgiving. I am forgiven. I have always been forgiven. I am loved. I have always been loved. I am loving. I am accepting. I am allowing. The kingdom is within me. The still small voice speaks to me from within. I trust. I listen. I turn it over," etc.

innertalk-store.com/products/opening_up_to_a_higher_power

Humble and Powerful ~ Subliminal

~ Humility inspires others because it recognizes their importance and worth.

Truly powerful people who remain humble, are those the world respects and admires. Leaders of all walks of life who head organizations are both powerful and yet humble. Indeed, the wise role of leadership is to always remain humble. Others admire those who remain humble regardless of their success or role in life. The fact is, there is no true respect for others possible unless humility resides in the heart. As such, humility inspires others because it recognizes their importance and worth.

"I am a child of the universe. I am one with the universe. I am in harmony with the universe. We are all children of the universe. I am a gift from the Divine. I am patient. I forgive myself. I was created perfectly. I like myself. I forgive others. All is a Divine gift. I like all others. I accept all. I am one with the life force of the universe. I like life. I attract harmony. Living is a gift of love. I attract balance. Power is unconditional love. I let go. I attract peace," etc.

<u>innertalk-store.com/products/humble__powerful</u>

I AM Presence ~ Subliminal

~ Awaken the powers within!

Most spiritual traditions address the idea of the "Kingdom of Heaven within." Implicit in the idea that in the beginning there was only God, and God divided and created all that is, exist the proposition that within each of us is a particle, a spark, a seed, and so forth of the origin of our being. In other words, there is a higher-self, a god-self, that dwells within.

Awaken the powers within—that God given part of your true being—and experience the doorway to your highest self. It is said, "Thy will be done, for Thy will is my perfect will." Come to know for yourself.

"Father, I call forth into your presence and use your name, God, the Father, knowing that it is the indwelling God principle that raises the rate of vibration of my body and whole being. Your name, God, resonates my being. I think your name at all times. God dwells within me now. I am God's divine plan. These are not my words, but your words, God, coming from

the Christ of God within that is me. God, My Father. The Divine principle flowing through me is all. And all that God is, I am. I am the Christ of God. God/Man," etc.

innertalk-store.com/products/i_am_presence

Love, Light and Life ~ Subliminal

~ Discover how it feels to live in God's light!

God is Love, Light, and Life. This is based on three statements about God made in the gospel of John the mystic apostle. 'God is love' (1 Jn 4:8b, 4:16b); 'God is light' (1 Jn 1:5; Jn 9:5); and 'God is life' (1 Jn 1:2; Jn 14:6). Many believe that these are the most profound words in the Scriptures. A pleasingly alliterative way of expressing these interconnected ideas is light, life and love. Generally speaking, light relates to reality, love to relationship, and life to redemption.

"I forgive others. God's love is unconditional. I give love unconditionally. Love is Light. Eternal Love and Light are my blessings. I am at peace. I radiate peace, balance and harmony. There is no darkness in the Light. I am a child of the Light. I am a child of God. God's Will is my perfect will. I am loved by God. Love cancels all fear, anger and judgment. I love God. Love is powerful. God gifted me with life. I am powerful. Life is Eternal. My thoughts are positive. I am eternal. God's gifts are powerful," etc.

innertalk-store.com/products/love_light_and_life

Manifesting Your Vision ~ Subliminal

~ The magic of your mind exists in expectation and visualization.

This powerful program not only works to assist us in realizing our vision, but it brings our focus to exactly what that vision is. Your mind is truly a co-creator of everything you know or will ever come to realize. The magic of your mind exists in expectation and visualization. By creating an expectation of success—success in all walks of life from prosperity to happiness—and merging that with the crystallization of your thinking (a clear visualized direction and purpose), success is certain.

"I create my vision of success. I create my vision of perfect health. I create my personal vision of my life and work. I hold the vision intently. I visualize my vision daily. I include all my senses in my visualization. My vision is powerful. I manifest my vision in life. I create my own destiny. I have the power. I have the ability. I am successful now. I am admired. I am appreciated. I appreciate myself. I respect myself. I deserve the best," etc.

innertalk-store.com/products/manifesting_your_vision

---

*"I have been using InnerTalk for about 5 years now.
My only regret is not using them more regularly.
My first CDs were **Manifesting Your Vision** and
Building Your Personal Icon. I was a furniture
salesman, now I own my own business with
10 employees."*

Also Available In:

Manifesting (Manifesting Your Vision) ~ Platinum Plus

innertalk-store.com/products/manifesting_your_vision_pp

Meditation (Contact Meditation) ~ Subliminal

~ Regular meditation can literally rewire the brain and increase cortical matter!

More and more people are using meditation for bio-feedback purposes, stress management, pain control and the search for spiritual knowledge/experience. You do not need years of practice and special training to begin to take advantage of this marvelous tool. This program was created to facilitate deep reflective meditation—meditation that is often called contact meditation. At these deep inner levels, many things are possible. The music track on this program was especially selected for its meditative background quality.

"It's time to be still. It's time to center. It's time to let go. It's time to know no time. Relaxed. Calm. Serene. Peaceful. At peace with myself and the world around me. Quiet. Enters the quietness of spirit. Allow. Breathe deeply,

evenly, rhythmically. Trust and let go. Turn within. It's okay. Everything is okay. I am grateful. Life is wonderful. Living is a miracle," etc.

innertalk-store.com/products/contact_meditation

Also Available In:

Meditation (Deep Meditation) ~ Album

innertalk-store.com/products/deep-meditation-album

Metaphysical Oneness ~ Subliminal

~ Immerse yourself in the oneness of all!

Many of the documents considered sacred by followers encourage us to escape the illusion of duality. Imagine an immersion that is so complete that you, as separate from all, disappear. Imagine a state of being free of time and space, knowing no barriers, existing as one drop in a sea of drops indistinguishable from the totality of the ocean. Use this program to immerse yourself in the oneness of all.

"I live in oneness. I live in balance. I live in peace. I am in harmony. I am in peace, balance and harmony. I am Divine Will. I am in control. I am responsible. I can do anything. I release all that is not Divine. I manifest divinity in all things. I express divine thought and action. I am a master. I am one with the Divine. My mind is one with the Universal Mind. The Father and I are one. My perfect will is God's Will. The Mother and I are one. I live in the Light," etc.

innertalk-store.com/products/metaphysical_oneness

Mindfulness (Cultivating Mindfulness) ~ Subliminal

~ Unleash your ability to find peace in a hectic world!

Mindfulness heals the mind and the body. It aids in emotional regulation, reduces stress, improves sleep, enhances the immune system and increases cognitive abilities. Mindfulness can take the sea of harshness and clutter in our world and convert it into the quiet and calm of still waters. Pay attention to your thoughts and select those that support your goals, fortify your health, and enhance the quality of your life. Discover inner strengths you never knew you had. Learn to create joy rather than waiting for it to come to you. Using this program your inner world will become a place of serenity, and with practice, this inner peacefulness will be reflected in your outer world.

"I accept myself. I am non-judgmental. I allow my thoughts to pass without judgment. I observe my mind. I listen and acknowledge. I pay attention to my thoughts. My thoughts are just thoughts. Thoughts are not facts. I can retrain my mind. I rewire my mind. I choose to retrain my mind. I can choose my thoughts. I choose my thoughts. My mind supports me now. My mind believes in me. I choose to meditate often," etc.

innertalk-store.com/products/cultivating-mindfulness-subliminal

Also Available In:

Mindfulness (Optimal Mindfulness) ~ Album

innertalk-store.com/products/optimal-mindfulness-album

Miracle Mindedness ~ Subliminal

~ As our expectation of the world changes, the world seems to magically change.

This wonderful program was created around the *Course in Miracles.* The emphasis is on seeing everyone in the Divine Light. By holding others in our mind as divine beings created by the same Giver who formed our beings, we find ourselves more involved and with a higher sense of caring and empathy than most experience. Everything around us seems to transform. As we see the good in others, they see it in us. As we radiate love and acceptance, it is reflected back to us. The more we give of our inner most treasure, that of love and acceptance, the more we reap. What's more, as our expectation of the world changes, the world seems to magically somehow change. It is then, when we least expect the miracle that it often arrives.

"Within me is the power. The power flows through me. I am the power. The power was given me. The power is mine. Miracles are natural. There is no degree to miracles. I am a miracle. Life is a miracle. I appreciate the miracle. I live in grace. I am humble I am that I am. The I AM presence is in me. I accept the power. I accept the gift. I have the ability to will miracles. Illusions

are not real. The real is eternal. I am eternal. I invest belief in the real. I see past illusion. I see God in all. I recognize good in all. I acknowledge God in all. Minds communicate. I allow my mind to notice God in all," etc.

innertalk-store.com/products/miracle_mindedness

Miracles ~ Subliminal

~ When you open your mind to miracles—miracles seem to happen!

More than one giant thinker has acknowledged that science moves the marker for miracles and scientific knowledge has advanced the creations of the gods. There are also those miracles that cannot be explained by science—indeed, the very fact that some apparent intercessions occur defies the principles of science. Miracles of this nature also occur every day to people around the world. Miraculous events ranging from unexplainable cures to giant hands lifting a small child from an automobile collision occur all the time. There simply is no shortage of miracles.

"God loves me. I am eternal. I love God. God forgives me. I forgive all. I am love. I am a miracle. I am a gift. God's presence resides within me. I am. I express God's love. I emulate the Divine. I love unconditionally. I am grateful. I am humble. I am a vessel of God's love. I share. I give. I am a healer. I am a leader," etc.

innertalk-store.com/products/miracles

Now (Living in the Now) ~ Subliminal

~ It is in the moment that our lives take on the richness that is life in its fullest!

You can't live in another time space and live in now. What's past is past and whatever may be in the future has not yet arrived—therefore now is all any of us ever have! Still, many choose to dwell on the past or future, allowing worries and regrets muddle their lives so the now passes into another regret. The only way to live in now is to fully cherish the moment. In doing so, live is fully enlivened and each moment is as infinitely divisible as infinity. It is in the moment that our lives take on the richness that is life in its fullest.

"Now is all there is. Living fully in the moment is living in the Now. Each moment is as infinitely divisible as all time. Each moment is eternal. In the now, all things are possible. In the now, I have everything I need. The eternal Now is now. My mind is fully in the now. My body is fully in the now. All of me is fully in the now. Now is all I need. Now is bliss. I live in bliss. Now is balance. I am balanced. Now is harmony. I live in harmony," etc.

innertalk-store.com/products/living_in_the_now

Prayer (The Lord's Prayer) ~ Subliminal

~ The Lord's Prayer has comforted many through the darkest of hours.

The Lord's Prayer has comforted many through the darkest of hours. Vietnam POWs frequently report using this Biblical classic throughout their internment. Senator John McCain tells us that church to prisoners in Vietnam included reciting the Pledge of Allegiance, the Lord's Prayer and the 23rd Psalm.

The Lord's Prayer is used in many Christian churches for purposes of worship. This is the prayer Jesus taught. Using this prayer encourages children to participate in worship. This prayer brings comfort to many and reminds us of our dependence on the way of the Lord.

This version is taken from the King James version of The Bible.

"Our Father, who art in Heaven. Hallowed be thy name. Thy Kingdom come. Thy will be done on earth as it is in Heaven. Give us this day our daily bread," etc.

innertalk-store.com/products/the_lords_prayer

Psalm 23 ~ Subliminal

Taken from the King James version of The Bible.

"The Lord is my shepherd; I shall not want. He maketh me to lie down in green pastures: he leadeth me beside the still waters. He restoreth my soul: he leadeth me in the paths of righteousness for his name's sake. Yea, though I walk through the valley of the shadow of death, I will fear no evil: for thou art with me; thy rod and thy staff they comfort me. Thou preparest a table

before me in the presence of mine enemies: thou anointest my head with oil; my cup runneth over," etc.

innertalk-store.com/products/23rd_psalm

Also Available In:

Psalms 23 and 91 ~ Subliminal Set

innertalk-store.com/products/psalms_23_and_91_set

Psalm 91 ~ Subliminal

Taken from the King James version of The Bible.

"I will say of the Lord, He is my refuge and my fortress: my God; in him will I trust. Surely he shall deliver thee from the snare of the fowler, and from the noisome pestilence. He shall cover thee with his feathers, and under his wings shalt thou trust: his truth shall be thy shield and buckler. Thou shalt not be afraid for the terror by night; nor for the arrow that flieth by day; Nor for the pestilence that walketh in darkness; nor for the destruction that wasteth at noonday," etc.

innertalk-store.com/products/psalm_91

Also Available In:

Psalms 23 and 91 ~ Subliminal Set

innertalk-store.com/products/psalms_23_and_91_set

Quintessential Self (Connecting with My Quintessential Self) ~ Subliminal

~ Connect with the Source of your being and find the guidance that leads you to your higher purpose!

This program was intentionally designed to help each of us know more fully the consciousness that animates all life—the companionship of the Divine. Holding thoughts of love, dedicating some time every day to acknowledging the Divine presence within, and praising the Divine intelligence that is the all that is, connects you to the spirit that defines your real higher purpose.

*"I sense my connection with the all. In the quiet of my soul, I sense all that
I need. My soul expresses its true purpose. I hear my higher self. I feel the
guidance being given to me. I hear the quiet. I feel the interconnectedness
of life. The interconnectedness of life fills me with joy. Peace and joy are in
the heart of my being. It is easy to know my higher calling. I heed my higher
calling. Peace, calm, and quiet enter my being. All is oneness. I connect to
oneness. Oneness brings me joy. My soul is content," etc.*

innertalk-store.com/products/quintessential-self-subliminal

Reincarnation (Reincarnation: Exploring Past Lives) ~ Subliminal

~ Investigate reincarnation for yourself!

Would you like to be able to remember past lives? Are you interested
in investigating reincarnation for yourself? There are many stories of individuals who remember their lives and are able to recount with specificity
names, places, and events they lived in prior lives.

Use this program during meditations or while you sleep and see if
memories surface for you. Our customers have reported some truly interesting experiences as result of using this program, so why wait?

*"I am eternal. Life is school. Living provides opportunities. I remember
my lessons. I sense my eternality. I sense my growth. I sense my evolution.
Experience is evolving. I have learned much. I review all experiences. I learn
from experience. I grow from experience. I release any negativity. I remember
my talents. I incorporate love and acceptance. I am honest. I honor myself.
I observe learning opportunities. Evolution is learning. My learnings teach
Divine. I am aware of the Divine within. I am a gift," etc.*

innertalk-store.com/products/exploring_past_lives

Sixth Sense (Developing the Sixth Sense) ~ Subliminal Set

~ Awaken your inner abilities!

The latent psychic ability within all of us is usually extinguished when
we're children. According to the world's most studied Psychic, Ingo Swann,
awakening this latent power is a matter of remembering our senses and

changing our beliefs. This program is designed to aid you in awakening the psychic power within.

THIS DUAL INNERTALK SET INCLUDES
1: Awakening and Using the Force (in music)
2: Developing Psychic Abilities (in nature)

"I open up. I trust my senses. I trust my impressions. My hearing expands. My sight sees inter-dimensionally," etc.

"All is the Force. I am one with the Force now. The Force contains all. The Force is infinite giving light. I am a gift. I manifest to the glory of Light," etc.

"I fix my thoughts and attention steadfastly on God and His Divine perfection. My body vibrations are raised so as to blend harmoniously with those of Divine perfection. We are absolutely one. I am divine perfection. I am one with God. I see God in all things. I know God's love, life and wisdom," etc.

Also Available In:

Sixth Sense (Opening the Sixth Sense) ~ Video

innertalk-store.com/products/opening_the_sixth_sense_dvd

Spirit (Power of the Spirit) ~ Subliminal

~ Feel the spirit run through you.

Living in the power of Spirit means living in the Spirit of God. Living in an elevated state of consciousness—raising above the mundane. Allowing the spirit of God to direct you is living according to the will of God. Your perfect will is the will of God. Accepting the Spirit of God and living out of this perspective can be very challenging yet still more rewarding.

"I fix my thoughts and attention steadfastly on God and His Divine perfection. My body vibrations are raised so as to blend harmoniously with those of Divine perfection. We are absolutely one. I am divine perfection. I am one with God. I stand steadfastly with my being fixed on God. I see God in all things. I know God's love, life and wisdom. God's spirit is my spirit. God's Divine spirit pervades me always. God's spirit surrounds me and abounds within me always," etc.

innertalk-store.com/products/power_of_the_spirit

Spiritual Awareness (Increasing Spiritual Awareness) ~ Subliminal

~ Fully awaken and enliven your spiritual side!

The brain is wired with a spiritual center that when electrically stimulated gives rise to a deep religious experience. Every culture in the world shares a certain religiosity and spiritual framework. Emerging research tends to suggest that one lives longer and is happier and healthier when they hold a spiritual awareness, a sort of connectedness, to the spiritual side of life.

It would seem that we are born with this innate spiritual quotient—but for many, it is never developed. Indeed, it is often pushed aside as something we do in our sixties, or superstitious non-sense, or so-called unscientific, and so forth. This program is designed to fully awaken and enliven our spiritual side.

"Christ Consciousness fills my mind and being. I am vital energy. I am connected to the Mind of God. We are all One. From the One we all are. I am a creation of God. God's perfection is who I am. The All Wise knowing intelligence flows through me. I am awakened. I remember, I am enlightened. My consciousness expands. My being is unlimited and eternal. My awareness is open and receptive. I am in harmony with all life. Joy and Love are my being. I am a creation of LOVE. I am a gift of Love. All that I can be is a gift. I see God in all people and all creation," etc.

innertalk-store.com/products/increasing_spiritual_awareness

Also Available In:

Spiritual Connectedness ~ Album

innertalk-store.com/products/spiritual_connectedness_album

Inspirations: The I Am Presence ~ Video

innertalk-store.com/products/inspirations_dvd

Synchronicity ~ Subliminal

~ When you're ready the message comes!

The universe abounds with information. When we are alert and aware, prepared to listen to both the message and the messenger, we find many answers. Our clients have reported such things as searching for an answer in their business only to receive an unsolicited magazine with a feature business article that seemed to be written just for them and about them. The key to accessing this information is in becoming aware and alert to its presence.

"The Universe is purposeful. Everything comes to me for some reason. I am a gift. All that I am is God's gift. All that I become is my gift to God. Consciousness flows through me like energy. I am consciousness. I am aware of consciousness. Minds communicate. I accept and acknowledge the communication. I invest my thoughts in Peace and Love. My environment is rich with information," etc.

innertalk-store.com/products/synchronicity

Yoga Meditations ~ Subliminal

~ Yoga is a way of thinking and living!

The benefits of yoga regarding health and wellness have been repeatedly demonstrated. Yoga is not just a form of exercise; it is also a way of thinking and living. Learn to enjoy yoga and the significant health and spiritual benefits it brings. This program was created with the direct input and approval from Dr. Vijayandra Pratap, the founder and director of the SKY Foundation in Philadelphia, PA.

"I enjoy yoga. I visualize yogic poses. I learn the meaning of poses. I sense and feel meaning. My body is an expression of LOVE. I accept the gift. LOVE is truth and wisdom. I am a gift of LOVE. I am LOVE. Becoming— perfecting—younging. Health is mine. Physical and mental are one. Yoga integrates the mental and physical. Yoga is a tool. I use the tool. I visualize and feel the poses. Peace flows through me," etc.

innertalk-store.com/products/yoga_meditations

Power Imaging

Power Imaging is a very special guided imagery program. It is assumed that there is a reason why you have not been as successful in the past as you would like to be. It helps you discover the reasons behind your behavior, and once you know that, success is much easier to achieve. ***Power Imaging programs should be used with headphones and require you to take time out, close your eyes, and put your feet up.*** Power Imaging programs should not be used when conscious attention is required like with driving a vehicle or operating machinery.

What you can picture with your mind, you can make a reality

Enter a State of Deep Relaxation

Power Imaging guides you into a state of deep relaxation called "Alpha consciousness," in which your mind is open and receptive to suggestion. In this state, the positive self-images and goals you visualize - whether to let go of anxiety and stress - or to see yourself slender, confident, or successful - are programmed into your subconscious mind. The changes you desire begin to unfold in your life without conscious effort. After each session, you feel relaxed and renewed, as if you have been on a mini-vacation.

Each of the Power Imaging programs combines discussion with guided visualizations, music, and InnerTalk messages.

NOTE: Power Imaging must be used with headphones and should not be used when conscious attention is required, such as when driving a vehicle or operating machinery. These programs can be used once or twice a day!

Titles Available

(Sample affirmations can be found under the
appropriate titles in the first section of this resource guide.)

Creativity is Natural ~ Power Imaging/Hypnosis

innertalk-store.com/products/creativity_is_natural_pi

Esteem (Well-Being and Esteem) ~ Power Imaging/ Hypnosis

innertalk-store.com/products/self_esteem-pi

Health (Pain Relief and Health Imaging) ~ Power Imaging/Hypnosis

innertalk-store.com/products/pain_relief_and_health_pi

Learning (Power Learning and Memory) ~ Power Imaging/Hypnosis

innertalk-store.com/products/power_learning_and_memory_pi

Peace (Personal Peace) ~ Power Imaging/Hypnosis

innertalk-store.com/products/personal_peace_pi

Relax Now ~ Power Imaging/Hypnosis

innertalk-store.com/products/relax_now_pi

Smoking (Stop Smoking Forever) ~ Power Imaging/ Hypnosis

innertalk-store.com/products/stop_smoking_forever_pi

Sports Hypnosis ~ Power Imaging/Hypnosis

innertalk-store.com/products/sports_hypnosis_pi

Stress (Free of Anxiety and Stress) ~ Power Imaging/ Hypnosis

innertalk-store.com/products/anxiety_and_stress_pi

Weight (Optimal Weight Loss) ~ Power Imaging/ Hypnosis

innertalk-store.com/products/weight_loss_pi

OZO and Echo-Tech

**Advanced sound technologies create the most
mind-expanding experience you may have ever had!**

It has long been known that meditation and biofeedback techniques can alter your brainwaves from the everyday Beta state into deeper Alpha and Theta states where a sense of utter wellbeing, intuition, and creativity are triggered. With OZO and Echo-Tech, you don't have to spend years of practice in meditation or expensive biofeedback training to reach these heightened states.

Recorded with InnerTalk's neuro-entrainment matrix of special tones, echo effects, and brainwave frequencies delivered to each hemisphere of your brain with the use of headphones, OZO and Echo-Tech automatically synchronize your brain waves in the Alpha/ Theta range.

OZO's Command Coaching or Echo-Tech's Gentle Suggestion?

The OZO programs are recorded with authoritative verbal coaching, reinforced by affirmations to imprint both your conscious and subconscious mind with positive commands. The Echo-Tech series takes a more gentle, supportive approach. The beautiful music of renowned composer Steven Halpern soothes you into a highly receptive state to absorb gentle verbal coaching.

What do OZO and Echo-Tech programs sounds like?

On both programs you hear a voice telling you that you are capable, it's okay to succeed, you can do it, etc. On OZO, the voice is very commanding and authoritative, stirring you to action. On Echo-Tech, the voice is gentle and supportive. In the background you'll hear relaxing music containing our patented InnerTalk subliminal messages. The presentation on both is uniquely dramatic and fun, making it seem like you are in an echo chamber, surrounded by encouraging and/or commanding words, sound tones, and soothing music. The three-dimensional echo effects, combined with alternating sounds going from one ear to the other, help balance the right and left hemispheres of the brain and create a lasting impression, even from the very first listening. These powerful programs are an ideal complement to InnerTalk subliminal and Power Imaging programs.

OZO and Echo-Tech are sister technologies in that they both consist of InnerTalk affirmations, tones, and frequencies. The tones and frequencies help you to relax by altering brainwave activity and thereby increasing your ability to absorb the affirmations. Both OZO and Echo-Tech also contain audible coaching. The resulting effect is that the InnerTalk affirmations change the way in which you talk to yourself, and the audible coaching makes you feel as though you are surrounded by people encouraging you. The difference between the two is that the audible coaching on OZO is forceful and authoritarian and the tones and frequencies are energizing, whereas on Echo-Tech, the audible coaching is gentle and supportive while the tones and frequencies are relaxing and calming.

Note:

Both OZO and Echo-Tech should be used with headphones and should not be used when conscious attention is required (like when driving or operating machinery).

*"Your OZO and Echo-Tech recordings are fantastic.
They work so fast! I'm seventy-three years old and felt like I
was dying on the vine. In listening to the recordings, I now
have so much get up and go. I use these recordings to get
my batteries charged!"*
~ M.L., OR

Titles Available

(Sample affirmations can be found under the
appropriate titles in the first section of this resource guide.)

OZO Titles Include

Addictions (Overcoming Addictions) ~ OZO

innertalk-store.com/products/overcoming_addictions-ozo

Confidence (Soaring Self-Confidence) ~ OZO

innertalk-store.com/products/soaring_self_confidence_ozo

Fitness (Optimum Fitness) ~ OZO

innertalk-store.com/products/optimum_fitness_ozo

Health and Healing ~ OZO

innertalk-store.com/products/health_and_healing_ozo

Joy (Boundless Joy) ~ OZO

innertalk-store.com/products/boundless_joy_ozo

Learning (Accelerated Learning) ~ OZO

innertalk-store.com/products/accelerated_learning_ozo

Motivation (Maximum Motivation) ~ OZO

innertalk-store.com/products/maximum_motivation_ozo

Peace (Inner Peace) ~ OZO

innertalk-store.com/products/inner_peace_ozo

Procrastination (End Procrastination) ~ OZO

innertalk-store.com/products/end_procrastination_ozo

Smoking (Stop Smoking Now) ~ OZO

innertalk-store.com/products/stop_smoking_ozo

Sports (Excel at Sports) ~ OZO

innertalk-store.com/products/excel_at_sports_ozo

Success Power ~ OZO

innertalk-store.com/products/success_ozo

Weight (Optimum Weight Loss) ~ OZO

innertalk-store.com/products/weight_loss_ozo

Echo-Tech Titles Include

Co-Dependent (End Co-Dependent Patterns)
~ Echo-Tech

innertalk-store.com/products/codependence_et

Esteem (Powerful Esteem) ~ Echo-Tech

innertalk-store.com/products/powerful_esteem_et

Have It All ~ Echo-Tech

innertalk-store.com/products/have_it_all_et

Learn Easily ~ Echo-Tech

innertalk-store.com/products/learn_easily_et

Self-Destructive Patterns (Ending Self-Destructive Patterns) ~ Echo-Tech

innertalk-store.com/products/self_destructive_patterns_et

Smoking (Stop Smoking) ~ Echo-Tech

innertalk-store.com/products/stop_smoking_et

Stress Free ~ Echo-Tech

innertalk-store.com/products/stress_free_et

Weight Loss ~ Echo-Tech

innertalk-store.com/products/weight_loss_et

Power Sets

Power Sets on include one OZO or Echo-Tech program and one InnerTalk program using a nature soundtrack. Power Sets get you started with that right now *"I feel it"* response from using program 1 and back it up with our patented and proven InnerTalk technology to reinforce and sustain the change.

Titles Available

(Sample affirmations can be found under the
appropriate titles in the first section of this resource guide.)

Co-Dependence (End Co-Dependence) ~ Power Set

innertalk-store.com/products/end_codependence_ps

Confidence (Strong Confidence) ~ Power Set

innertalk-store.com/products/strong_confidence-ps

Esteem (Soaring Self-Esteem) ~ Power Set

innertalk-store.com/products/self_esteem-ps

Fit and Athletic ~ Power Set

innertalk-store.com/products/fit_and_athletic_ps

Joy (Living in Joy) ~ Power Set

innertalk-store.com/products/living_in_joy_ps

Learning Power ~ Power Set

    innertalk-store.com/products/learning_power_ps

Motivated ~ Power Set

    innertalk-store.com/products/motivated_ps

Peace and Serenity ~ Power Set

    innertalk-store.com/products/peace_and_serenity_ps

Procrastination (End Procrastination) ~ Power Set

    innertalk-store.com/products/end_procrastination_ps

Sabotage (Stop Self Sabotage) ~ Power Set

    innertalk-store.com/products/stop_self_sabotage_ps

Smoking (Freedom from Smoking) ~ Power Set

    innertalk-store.com/products/freedom_from_smoking_ps

Sports: Mentally Fit ~ Power Set

    innertalk-store.com/products/sports_mentally_fit_ps

Stress Free Living ~ Power Set

    innertalk-store.com/products/stress_free_ps

Success Power ~ Power Set

    innertalk-store.com/products/success_power_ps

Weight Loss Now ~ Power Set

    innertalk-store.com/products/weight_loss_ps

Younger and Healthier ~ Power Set

    innertalk-store.com/products/younger_and_healthier_ps

Platinum Plus Series

This is one of our most complicated technologies—complicated to explain but not to use. Our Platinum Plus programs are designed for headphone-only use. They have been called a shortcut to the years and years of training normally required in order to obtain states associated with advanced meditation. They are an experience that will take you to new insights and adventures within. Platinum Plus includes the best of the best of cutting-edge tools. As a quick overview, this series incorporates the following:

1. The Proven Whole Brain InnerTalk patented method to insure the best results.

2. New PHI ratio-generated sound signature to facilitate coherent emotional and brain states. (Recursive Golden Mean geometry).

3. Patterned mantra intonations to assist in producing a peaceful state of relaxation and balance.

4. Neuro matrix sound patterns to entrain brainwave activity, bringing it within the optimal learning range. (Alpha brainwave pattern).

5. Radionic rates encoded via computer-generated signals believed to assist in training or refreshing nervous system memories. (Sympathetic resonance).

6. Direct pathway commands: I can, I will, I choose, I have, I love, I create, I enjoy...

7. Egoless and neuro-emotional affirmations.

8. Special healing soundtrack and more!

Phi is a magic number in physics. The ratio of phi is both the ratio of creation as seen in the toroidal donut and the ratio of the DNA molecule. The sound of phi is a ratio of chords graduating in mathematical proportion. Many believe that this sound can resonate with the being in such a way as to optimize mind and body states.

Patterned mantra intonations are the sounds of geometry. The geometry of sound has led many scientists to conclude that the mind somehow intuits sound, often leading to higher meanings. For example, the intonation of ohm produces a circle with three triangles within it and Handel's "Hallelujah Chorus" produces a five-pointed star—the star of Bethlehem.

Neuro matrix sound patterns to entrain brainwave activity means bringing brainwaves within the alpha and theta brainwave pattern. These brainwave states are those associated with increased learning, hypnosis, meditation, biofeedback, and so forth.

We often deliver tones and frequencies 'out of phase' which simply means one speaker is pushing while the other is pulling, and this process alternates, enhancing the deepening effects of the neuro matrix patterns.

Titles Available

(Sample affirmations can be found under the
appropriate titles in the first section of this resource guide.)

Bliss: Coherent Emotion ~ Platinim Plus

innertalk-store.com/products/bliss_coherent_emotion-pp

Creativity (I am Creative) ~ Platinim Plus

innertalk-store.com/products/creativity_pp

Dream Petitioning: Using Dreams for Answers ~ Platinim Plus

innertalk-store.com/products/dream_petitioning_pp

Emotional High: Feeling Connected to the All ~ Platinim Plus

innertalk-store.com/products/emotional_high_feeling_pp

Icon (Building Your Personal Icon: Finding Your Path in Life) ~ Platinim Plus

innertalk-store.com/products/personal_icon_pp

Manifesting (Manifesting Your Vision) ~ Platinim Plus

innertalk-store.com/products/manifesting_your_vision_pp

MLM (Living the MLM Dream) ~ Platinim Plus

innertalk-store.com/products/living_the_mlm_dream_pp

Passion (On Fire with a Passion for Life)
~ Platinim Plus

innertalk-store.com/products/passion_for_life_pp

Younging (Fountain of Youth: Remembering Youth to be Young) ~ Platinim Plus

innertalk-store.com/products/fountain_of_youth_pp

Hyperemperia: Conscious Expansion ~ Platinum Plus + Audible Meditation

innertalk-store.com/products/hyperemperia_pp

Platinum Plus (The Complete Platinum Plus Collection) ~ Platinim Plus

innertalk-store.com/products/platinum_plus_complete_collection

Video Entrainment

Taking the advanced InnerTalk technology one step further, we also offer a line of video titles that use geometric visual patterns to produce a dramatic response.

Form is believed to be as important, if not more so, than any other element in every science. Shape, not chemical bonds, may even drive DNA synthesis, new research shows. Form is geometry . . . and InnerTalk videos put geometry to work like you've never seen before!

This tantalizing multi-sensory experience mesmerizes the senses and induces the bliss of an eyes-open altered state of consciousness. It is a wonderful new method for positive change that will affect your mind power in a way most people don't believe is possible—let alone have ever experienced.

As you relax in front of the colorful, ever-changing geometries on your television screen, your subconscious mind perceives the hidden visual affirmations within the patterns.

And while your eyes are immersed in the kaleidoscope of colors, your ears are bathed with pleasant, easy-listening music containing powerful InnerTalk audio affirmations.

This incredible technology, known as Video Entrainment, slows down brainwave activity, producing a pleasant altered state of consciousness. Reduced brain activity is positively associated with deep states of relaxation and increased endorphin levels. Frequency signals actually pace brainwave activity for maximum results.

These programs have been described by some as *"like watching stillness in motion."* They produce powerful responses on a very deep level and add a whole new dimension to the patented InnerTalk technology

Our Video Entrainment programs have been described as *"an experience that is indescribable."* They have also been referred to as *"a technology so advanced that its power may not be comprehended even by those that use and love them."* We simply describe the video series as *"a right use of light and sound."* This technology will simply mesmerize you while filling you with a strong sense of wellbeing. You will not only enter an altered state of brainwave activity, but find yourself so relaxed, at ease and comfortable, that it may be how you both start and end every day.

Special note: The video titled *Cardiac Care* was developed by Eldon for patients who were recovering from open heart surgery.

Titles Available

(Sample affirmations can be found under the
appropriate titles in the first section of this resource guide.)

Addictions (Freedom from Addictions) ~ Video

innertalk-store.com/products/freedom_from_addictions_dvd

Anger and Fear (Freedom from Anger and Fear) ~ Video

innertalk-store.com/products/freedom_from_anger_and_fear_dvd

Blood Pressure (Relaxed: Lower Blood Pressure) ~ Video

innertalk-store.com/products/lowered_blood_pressure_dvd

Cardiac Care and Recovery ~ Video

innertalk-store.com/products/cardiac_care_and_recovery_dvd

Children (Successful Children / Family Dynamics) ~ Video

innertalk-store.com/products/successful_children_family_dynamics_dvd

Coherence: Brain/Body Balance ~ Video

innertalk-store.com/products/coherence_dvd

Dental Anxiety (Freedom from Dental Anxiety)
~ Video

innertalk-store.com/products/freedom_from_dental_anxiety_dvd

Depression (Freedom from Depression) ~ Video

innertalk-store.com/products/freedom_from_depression_dvd

Genius (Creative Genius) ~ Video

innertalk-store.com/products/creative_genius_dvd

Golf Like a Pro ~ Video

innertalk-store.com/products/golf_like_a_pro_dvd

Healing (Accelerated Healing and Pain Relief) ~ Video

innertalk-store.com/products/accelerated_healing_dvd

Immune (Psychoneuroimmunology: Powerful
Immune System) ~ Video

innertalk-store.com/products/powerful_immune_system_dvd

Inspirations: The I Am Presence ~ Video

innertalk-store.com/products/inspirations_dvd

Learning (Accelerated Learning and Memory) ~ Video

innertalk-store.com/products/accelerated_learning_and_memory_dvd

Relaxation and Esteem Building ~ Video

innertalk-store.com/products/relaxation_and_esteem_dvd

Salesperson (Powerful Salesperson) ~ Video

innertalk-store.com/products/powerful_sales_dvd

Sixth Sense (Opening the Sixth Sense) ~ Video

innertalk-store.com/products/opening_the_sixth_sense_dvd

Stress and Anxiety (Freedom from Stress and Anxiety) ~ Video

innertalk-store.com/products/stress_and_anxiety_dvd

Success (Ultra Success Conditioning) ~ Video

innertalk-store.com/products/ultra_success_conditioning_dvd

Weight Loss ~ Video

innertalk-store.com/products/weight_loss_dvd

Younging (Quantum Younging) ~ Video

innertalk-store.com/products/quantum_younging_dvd

Further Education

Books and DVDs by Eldon Taylor

It is not what a book says that matters, but rather what it does!

Eldon Taylor is the author of numerous best-selling titles, including the New York Times best-seller, *Choices and Illusions*. For more than thirty years, his books, audio and video programs, lectures, and radio and television appearances have approached personal empowerment from the cornerstone perspective of self-responsibility, forgiveness, gratitude, and service.

Choices and Illusions (Revised edition) ~ Book

"Read this book! We are living at a time when people are searching for answers to fundamental questions in their lives. This book can be, if applied, a road map to personal enlightenment and empowerment. I believe it can 'tune in' the frequency you are currently operating on. More important, it helps you see that you can manifest change." — *John Edward, psychic medium and author of* After Life.

How would you like clarity in your life? What could you achieve if you no longer had to juggle conflicting beliefs or desires?

True peace comes when you know clearly 'who' you are. Clear out the clutter and make it possible for yourself to grow and achieve your highest goals and dreams. Become the person you were meant to be, living a life that is meaningful and satisfying.

**Eldon Taylor's New York Times Best-Seller,
Choices and Illusions.
Now revised, expanded and updated!
Comes with a free InnerTalk program entitled
Unlimited Personal Power (a $27.95 value).**

Choices and Illusions tells the story of one man's journey into the workings of the human mind and our reason for being. The adventure is every bit as exciting as the best scientific discoveries. Eldon Taylor's approach is pragmatic, and his conclusions are inspirational and soul enhancing. Along the journey, you'll hear fantastic stories of divine intervention, see why you think and do what you don't wish to do, and understand the very clear message that it's never too late to be happy and succeed, regardless of your past actions.

Eldon says,

> *"Many believe that self-help and self-improvement is about rags to riches, failure to success, and so forth, when indeed it's the beginning of a journey into self-discovery. Inside every human being is an eternal truth and a life purpose. Using our mind power is simply starting the engine on that path toward highest self-actualization."*

innertalk-store.com/products/choices_and_illusions_r_book

Exclusively Fabricated Illusions ~ Book

This book is not for those with dogmatic beliefs. This is a marvelous book for showing you the fallacies in modern thinking. Reading *EFI* could open up a whole new world for you. If you have ever felt disappointed by spiritual or religious systems, questioned orthodox beliefs, resisted the so-called institutionalized approach, and/or just thought seriously about the reality of spiritual inquiry, this book is for you! (Not light reading, but light shedding).

innertalk-store.com/products/exclusively_fabricated_illusions_book

Gotcha ~ Book

> *"Eldon Taylor is so spot on. Gotcha! tells it like it is and it isn't what we want to happen!"*
> — *George Noory, Host of Coast to Coast AM*

In *Gotcha*, Eldon Taylor explores the 24/7 bombardment of information designed to win the hearts and minds of the public. He demonstrates how new sound bites are championed into personal awareness, becoming memes of the culture. All of this results in framing and re-framing classical positions thereby causing adjustments to personal values and history itself. Your very decision process is being managed and manipulated, and the quest for discovering your real self becomes exponentially more difficult if not impossible as a result.

innertalk-store.com/products/gotcha_book

I Believe ~ Book

> *"I Believe is one of those special books to be experienced and contemplated not just read and the information recorded. Enjoy the journey . . . I did."*
> — *Lindsay Wagner, actress and author*

What's the foundation underpinning success in all areas of life? Is there a blueprint? What if you learned that your beliefs were the very cornerstones that supported success, and that some could give rise to success in certain areas but complete failure in others? Would you choose to build a stronger overall foundation? *I Believe* is a book that will not only inspire you, it will also highlight the kinds of beliefs you hold that may be causing you to fail. In the process, it will provide you with the opportunity to choose, once again, what will drive your life.

innertalk-store.com/products/i_believe_book

Just Be: A Little Cowboy Philosophy ~ Book

"Eldon Taylor's investigation of the "guide"
phenomenon is very moving and humorous. It deals with a
variety of metaphysical topics in a novel way. Throughout,
one gains new insights and I would recommend this book
to all readers of self-help and metaphysical books."
— Peter Uys, Johannesburg, South Africa

While *Just Be* began as a spoof on channeling, it quickly takes a trickster twist into the exploration of being and reality. Dr. Taylor says this is his favorite book and was fun to write, although he is not sure how much was actually written by himself . . . This book will tickle the funny bone, cause you to pause and reflect, lead you into the depths of the mystery of creation and inspire and excite you . . . all while entertaining in a "I couldn't put it down" way.

innertalk-store.com/products/just_be_book

Mind Programming ~ Book

"Brainwashing and marketing are big business; and
your precious mind is a coveted commodity. In this book
Eldon Taylor exposes all and tells you how to take your
power back and be free to become your own best self. Eldon
is really a master!"
— Joan Borysenko, Ph.D. Author of Minding the Body.

It is the 21st century and we have experienced a technology explosion that has granted us a cornucopia of luxuries and opportunities. At this point, virtually anything seems possible. However, along with the positive developments are ominous collaborations designed to deprive us of an inherent birth right—the power of a free mind.

Mind Programming is a riveting expose on the plethora of research that has been carried out simply to discover ways to control your every thought and desire. What you will learn will both shock and horrify you.

Tweaking your psyche has become big business. Never again will you be able to ignore the truth—your very thoughts are not your own.

Mind Programming provides the tools to take back control and reprogram your own mind. Eldon Taylor provides the insight, information, and easy-to-use methods that will empower you to realize the life of your dreams. You were not meant to be the product of another's manipulation, whether in attitude and mood or in ambition and consumption.

innertalk-store.com/products/mind_programming_book

Self-Hypnosis and Subliminal Technology ~ Book

"Don't wait another day to achieve your dreams and goals! Eldon Taylor's guide for self-hypnosis and subliminal messages will show you how to liberate the creative power of your mind to realize success, self-improvement, health, happiness, and well-being. Create your own program with Eldon's proven tools for easy use at home, on the road, anywhere!"
— Rosemary Ellen Guiley, author of Develop Your Miracle Mind Consciousness

Self-hypnosis and subliminal communication have long been mired in mystique, urban legend and disinformation. The truth is that both of these techniques are backed by extensive research demonstrating their efficacy and more importantly, once learned, both tools can be customized for any situation and can be used almost anytime and anywhere.

Join Eldon Taylor as he unravels the truth behind these technologies and demonstrates how they are invaluable tools in your self-help armamentarium.

innertalk-store.com/products/self_hypnosis_subliminal_technology_book

Simple Things and Simple Thoughts ~ Book

If thoughts are atomic, then *Simple Things and Simple Thoughts* is nuclear energy compacted into a few words that set off chain reactions in the reader's mind. Sometimes emotionally penetrating, sometimes thought provoking, it always succinctly states what we often need to say to ourselves. Topics include friends, consciousness, problems, education, victims, death, forgiveness, and much more.

innertalk-store.com/products/simple_things_and_simple_thoughts_book

What Does That Mean? ~ Book

"I love this book! There is something about the
energetics of Eldon's languaging that breaks open my heart.
It's very vulnerable, but if one possesses the courage to fully
let it in and respond to it, there is great power involved."
— Anita Rehker

Enlightenment is not something that can just be handed to you. The closest thing to it that you can receive are thoughts and questions that can lead you inward in the search for meaning. *What Does That Mean?* is full of thoughts and questions that do just that. Some insights you may have thought of and then forgotten, and others you may have experienced but simply haven't appreciated.

Throughout these pages, Eldon shares life experiences that will lead you to revelations about your own life. Perhaps this book's greatest value is that it assists you in remembering who you really are and thereby places you firmly back on the path to personal enlightenment.

innertalk-store.com/products/what_does_that_mean_book

What If? ~ Book

"Few are the authors who turn you inside out, who blow up your preconceived notions and cause you to become honest with yourself through and through. That's precisely what happens when you read What If? I highly recommend this book to those spiritual warriors who are unflinching in their journey to the Authentic Self."
— *Dr. Michael Bernard Beckwith, founder of Agape International; author of Spiritual Liberation*

What if you awoke tomorrow with amnesia—no memory of who you are, what you like and dislike, and so on. Would you be the same person? What if, as in the movie *The Matrix*, you discovered that everything was a simulation and you were just a programmed component? What if everything you believed was false? Who would you be then?

What If? is a very personal book. By using everyday situations and guiding you through numerous thought experiments, Eldon does an excellent job of peeling back the layers and revealing the dissonance in much of your thinking, beliefs, desires, and choices—contradictory beliefs held at the same time with no apparent awareness. Once you have seen your own mind with the filtered lenses removed, it is impossible to remain the same.

innertalk-store.com/products/what_if_book

Change Without Thinking ~ 3 DVD set (full day workshop)

"I can't say enough about the masterful way Eldon Taylor leads you through the massive amount of information gathered from years of training and perfecting the programs he develops to inspire and motivate others towards discovering their greatness. He has a loving and down to earth approach that instantly draws in the viewer.

I was glued to the TV hanging on to every word!
— Laurie Carty, Cognitive Skills Practitioner,
Hypnotherapist

For one full day, Eldon spoke to a packed audience and a number of dignitaries including the former First Lady of Malaysia. He taught them of the inner workings of their own minds, told them of the process by which he developed his patented InnerTalk technology, revealed glimpses of his past that shaped the man he became, but most importantly, gave them the real tools to live a truly successful life. Now you can see this presentation for yourself. Available on DVD - the *Change Without Thinking* seminar that formed the basis of his New York Times best seller, *Choices and Illusions* and that cost several hundred dollars to attend in person.

innertalk-store.com/products/change_without_thinking_dvd

Mind, Meaning and Mysteries ~ DVD

The phenomenal stories Eldon shares will bring tears to your eyes and a warm glow to your heart.

Join Eldon as he takes you on a journey through the workings of your mind and beyond. Share in the systematic approach he undertook in order to discover the purpose and meaning to his own life, and then apply the same principles to your life. The process is fascinating, and the outcome is life-changing.

This three-part video course addresses those areas that we all need to take into consideration if we are ever to achieve our highest best. This holds true regardless of your goals, whether your priorities are success and prosperity, building better relationships, or spirituality and personal peace.

innertalk-store.com/products/mind_meaning_mysteries_dvd

Frequently Asked Questions

InnerTalk Guarantee and Disclaimer

Please Note: Our offices are open Monday through Friday
from 8:30 a.m. to 5:00 p.m. Pacific time.
Any email enquiries will be answered during those times.
Most email responses are sent out within twenty-four business hours.

Caution and Disclaimer

As with any powerful modality, one should use common sense in their application. For example, the use of the Whole Brain InnerTalk program for relaxation while driving a vehicle or operating dangerous equipment could create a hazard. The products in this catalog are sold as educational properties only. No claims are made regarding any medical or psychological condition or impairment. As always, in the event of any serious symptom, seek the advice of a physician or psychologist. The programs are NOT intended to replace proper health care. The use of these programs by those who have serious emotional or medical conditions requiring that they be closely monitored by a physician, should not be undertaken without the professional's consent.

Our Guarantee and Return Policy

We know our products work, but they must work for you. Unlike the majority of manufacturers of pre-recorded audio materials (music, audio books, etc.), we want to make sure that you are fully satisfied with your purchase. As such, your first order for CDs comes with a full thirty-day satisfaction guarantee. Simply try it for yourself in the comfort of your home for thirty days, and if you are not satisfied that the technology works to prime your self-talk, simply contact us for return authorization. We will issue you a full refund for the cost of the product (not including the shipping and handling charges) once we have received your return. For all subsequent orders, we allow a two-week period after receipt of your order for you to check your order and to request any exchanges. Only your first order is refundable. We retain the right to refuse to do business with anyone for any reason at any time. Prices and shipping costs are subject to change. (Please note: Our downloadable products are non-returnable/non-refundable. If you wish to make sure that the technology works for you before purchasing, please try our free downloadable *Forgiving and Letting Go* program first).

Also, should your CD break, tear, or wear out we will replace it for $7.50 plus the cost of shipping for the first year after the original purchase. You will also be asked to return the damaged CD and we must have record that you purchased the item directly from us.

We recommend that you keep a copy of downloadable orders in a safe place such as on a flash drive. If you need to request replacements for downloadable orders (due to issues such as computer failures or phone changes), there will be a charge of $5.50 per program. If you need to request fresh download URLs for lost files, please e-mail innertalk@innertalk.com. We must also have a record that you purchased the InnerTalk downloadable programs directly from us.

Please note: There are no return or exchange privileges for downloadable orders. However, if an item is defective, please contact us and we will send you a replacement.

Contraindication Statement

As with any powerful modality, there can be both relative and absolute contraindications to the use of our programs. For example, a relative contraindication may be the use of a peaceful sleep program while driving. Absolute contraindications may exist for persons under the supervision of a professional health care provider. If you have a serious health care issue, seek the advice of your health care professional before using one of our programs.

Educational Purposes

All products are sold as educational properties only. No medical benefits are either claimed or implied. There can be both relative and absolute contraindications to the use of our products. Nothing in this offer is a substitute for proper health care. Whereas many health care professionals use our programs as a take-home care modality for support purposes, this is not to be confused with health care per se. If you have a serious physical or mental condition, see your health care provider before ordering any of our programs. We are in the business of helping people help themselves. We believe you deserve the best in mind-training technology, and we do our best to bring it to you.

You Decide!

Within you is an absolutely incredible and awesome power. It is yours to do with as you choose. It has been said that all that each of us may ever be is a gift, and all that we become is the only way we have to express our gratitude for the gift! We sincerely wish that you enjoy the best of you in all that you experience!

Thank you.

Downloadable Products

How will I receive my order?

As soon as you finalize an order containing a downloadable product, you will be taken to a page with your personal download URLs. Simply click on the link and the file will automatically download for you. An email is also sent to you with the personal download URL.

Can I download to my smart phone/tablet?

It is easiest to download your order to your computer and then move the files to your preferred devices. You will receive a zipped file, which your computer should easily be able to unzip. A zipped file is sent so that, in addition to your audio file, we can also send you a PDF containing the affirmations included on the program.

When downloading your order to a smart phone or tablet, you will need to use a download manager app. There are many free ones available in the app store. If you attempt to download to a smart phone or tablet without using a download manager app, your device will not know what to do with the file, but our shopping cart will register the fact that you have already downloaded your order. If this happens to you, please contact us and we will be happy to provide a fresh download URL. For more details instructions on downloading to smart phones and tablets, please click here.

It says I have exceeded my 'download limit' but I do not have my files. What should I do?

Each downloadable order can be downloaded twice. We make this possible just in case you have an Internet problem and the download is interrupted. Download URLs are good for six months. If there was a problem with your download and you do not have your files, please contact us. We will be happy to provide you with a fresh download URL.

Do I need special software to open up your downloadable files?

Our download files are provided in a zipped format. Most computers come with an app to unzip the files automatically. If your computer does not have this, there are a number of free utilities you can find on the Internet.

General Questions

When will I receive my order?

Please see our shipping schedule.

What's the difference between InnerTalk programs and so-called 'subliminal' programs?

By definition, a subliminal program is recorded at a sub-threshold level of awareness. Our messages are recorded at a perceptible level of awareness and disguised in what is best described as an audio illusion. (You will hear words from time to time.) By "blending" the affirmations in with the music or nature sounds in this way, we are able to bypass normal conscious awareness, yet still ensure that the affirmations strongly register in the mind.

How often should I play the programs and how quickly will I see results?

We recommend listening a minimum of once a day for thirty days. Results can often be noticed in as little as a few days to a few weeks. Listen as much as you can day and night and watch for the change in your self-talk!

Why is bypassing conscious attention necessary?

Experts have described InnerTalk as a "powerful new technology that uses our natural human ability to absorb information even when we're not thinking about it." Scientists have proven that the key to changing our state of mind is to do it with the least amount of conscious effort possible. Conscious thought interferes with and even prevents proper mind stimulation. Yet InnerTalk® programs are able to produce life-changing mind stimulation without the interference of conscious thought. They bypass the usual resistance in the mind and go right to work at the subconscious level, producing change "from the inside out."

How did InnerTalk technology develop?

Early research by Eldon Taylor and others proved that auditory stimulation is one of the most effective ways to change a state of mind. Eldon Taylor theorized that by using verbal stimuli just below the threshold of awareness, he could have a positive effect on the moods and behavior of the listeners. His theories were proven correct and thus was born the InnerTalk method.

What role does the subconscious mind play?

Eldon Taylor's programs are effective because they permit positive messages to reach the subconscious mind, where they can produce positive results without conscious resistance. This is important because the human subconscious is indiscriminate with the information it accepts over a lifetime. All the statements we have ever accepted are present in our subconscious minds, and for most of us that is negative programming. So, an individual's current behavior is based on all the information their subconscious has decided to accept over the years.

To change current behavior, you first have to change the information stored in the subconscious. It sounds easy, but you can't just tell your subconscious to think differently and ask for life-changing behavior modification. You must find a way to counteract those subconscious thoughts and introduce different thoughts for your subconscious to use. The InnerTalk method will help you control the introduction of stimuli to the subconscious and therefore control behavior modification.

Do other methods work just as well?

There are other methods available to modify your behavior without the use of mind technologies, but they often fail, and all for the same reason. Most motivational and self-help programs fall short because they attempt to appeal to the conscious in order to change behavior. It's often wasted energy. The conscious wants to change, but it's the subconscious that is controlling and overwhelming any effort to change. Every time someone tells us we are good our subconscious sends a thought to the conscious: *"Really! Good at what?"* In order to conquer the harmful effects of the subconscious mind we must attempt to change it on the very same level. Only then can you successfully disarm it and reverse the damage that has already been done.

The positive InnerTalk messages overtake the negative information contained in the subconscious. They literally re-script our own "inner talk," thereby creating positive self-beliefs that begin the cycle of self-fulfillment. When this happens the subliminal beliefs that formerly were self-limiting begin to change. As they change, so do we!

What are the principles behind InnerTalk?

The powerful results may seem like magic, but the principles behind the programs are pure science. As you know, the human brain is composed of two halves or hemispheres, the left brain and the right brain. These two hemispheres work together or independently to help process information and control our bodies.

The left brain is most commonly referred to as the *analytical brain* and is thought to control such things as mathematical and language skills, organization, logic, reason, observation and analysis. The left hemisphere also includes defense mechanisms such as rationalization built around logic and reason.

The right brain is also known as the *spatial brain*. It is thought to be responsible for creativity, emotions, athletic ability, intuitiveness, relaxation, and visualization. Many scientists believe the right hemisphere is associated with emotional and subconscious learning.

How do InnerTalk programs actually work?

The InnerTalk mind technology is unique in that it appeals to both hemispheres of the brain, according to their function, to achieve "whole brain" stimulation. For example, it is believed that the *left brain* views language literally and according to the rules of language while the *right brain* views language spatially and emotionally, tumbling the words in a process called subconscious cerebration and even seeing the words as our eyes see the world—upside down.

The brain halves work together to understand language both spatially and literally. The InnerTalk technology has been specifically designed to involve both the left and right brain according to their unique specialties using an entirely new and patented electronic encoding process.

What is this encoding process all about?

On one channel, accessing the left brain, meaningfully spoken, permissive affirmations (such as, *"It's okay to succeed. It's okay to do well."*) are delivered. On a second channel, accessing the right brain, directive messages (such as, *"I am good. I succeed. I do well."*) are delivered in reverse, to be recognized by the right brain's unique spatial understanding.

The channel-differentiated messages shadow each other from conscious recognition. But on the subconscious level, where the perception takes place, the mind understands and receives these affirmations. The analytical left hemisphere cannot argue with the permissive *"It's okay"* statements and the non-analytical right hemisphere simply accepts the directive *"I am"* statements.

What other techniques are used?

Most affirmations are delivered in a round robin manner by a male voice, a female voice, and a child's voice. Research has shown that individuals may respond more favorably according to their preference of male, female, or child voices. Research also has shown that an individual is more likely to remember a round robin like *"Row, row, row your boat"* rather than a simple song, even if the song is heard many more times. The round robin affirmations are recorded in echo-reverberation, giving rise to a *singing* effect. The affirmations are of a positive nature and are electronically synchronized with the volume level of the primary audio track (music or nature sounds) to ensure that your subconscious perceives the entire message.

No other mind technology compares to InnerTalk, which has been patented with the U.S. government and scientifically proven effective in leading universities around the world.

Some Programs Are Also Available in Other Technologies Besides InnerTalk. Which Technologies Should I Choose?

With any of our programs, the more you use them, the better the results. Technologies should therefore be chosen according to your lifestyle. Also, great results have been reported using the different technologies at the same time. For this reason, we have put together collections and albums of complementary titles and technologies, available at great savings!

Why do some of your programs include statements about a higher power and the divine? Are these programs religious?

Many of our programs include a spiritual component. We offer a variety of spiritual programs. We believe the spiritual component of life to be as important, if not more so, than any other component. However, we do not wish to choose the spiritual path for anyone. That is each of our rights, both under God and our Constitution. We, therefore, try to provide a variety of spiritual programs in an attempt to bring something for everyone. We recognize that this is difficult to do while not offending anyone. Nevertheless, we find it a responsibility to use our technology in the spirit of the saying, *"As a man thinketh, so is he."* Many religious leaders use and have endorsed our programs. Still, if you have a question, please ask your spiritual advisor to review the affirmations in order to ensure that the program you choose is in keeping with your particular spiritual path.

There is one common denominator in all our programs: forgiveness. It is our conviction whether in school violence or matters of government; it is never okay to get even. We believe it is so important that we offer our *Forgiving and Letting Go* program free of charge to those who ask for it (mailing charges do apply).

I received my last order very promptly. The programs were shrink wrapped together. Why don't you shrink-wrap all the programs individually?

The programs are shrink-wrapped together for shipping. This eliminates damage. Individual programs can be shrink-wrapped at no charge by simply asking for it. We do not shrink-wrap, unless requested, simply because the material is not environmentally friendly. Indeed, duplicators must be instructed not to shrink-wrap and there is no cost break by not wrapping. It's all about our planet.

I just received one of your double InnerTalk sets (music plus nature). It does not mention how it is to be used. Should I listen to it daily? When should I expect to see results?

- Listen a minimum of one hour per day.
- Listen initially for thirty days.
- Most people will notice changes or see results in the first two weeks. However, people are different. Some people may notice changes in the first few days, others may take longer.
- Our double sets were created for maximum use and enjoyment, one program with a music soundtrack and the other with a nature soundtrack. During the day, surround yourself with the uplifting music. At night, sleep to the soothing ocean. The ocean soundtrack is also ideal in the background while you work or watch television.

How can I find the affirmations for a particular title?

Sample affirmations are available in our shopping cart. The samples are listed with the product description. Each product we sell comes with the complete affirmations printed on a small card or on the CD cover.

I used to be able to listen to several different soundtrack samples and now I'm unable to find them. Where did they go?

We used to offer a variety of soundtracks on every title. This led to a lot of confusion and increased our inventory requirements substantially. We carefully analyzed our sales and decided to offer a choice between nature and music, so that you could select one for evening or background play such as when watching television and another for driving or background music. We used our most popular soundtracks and hope you enjoy them. Since our business is "change," we simply couldn't continue to try and deliver music that fit everyone's preference. We hope you understand. Thank you.

You have similar instances of products ending with different terms. Accelerated Learning & Study ends with "—InnerTalk," "—Echo-Tech" and "—OZO." I need an explanation as to what those ending terms mean.

This question is asked frequently.

InnerTalk is our original, patented, and proven subliminal technology. This utilizes a set of positive affirmations masked behind a music or nature soundtrack. You will not consciously hear the affirmations . . . all you will hear are the music or nature sounds.

Echo-Tech and OZO both utilize the same InnerTalk technology. However, they also include an audible version of the affirmations. Echo-Tech is the more supportive verbal coaching and OZO contains more authoritative coaching. Mixed in with this are a combination of 3D sounds, tones, and echo effects that stimulate positive and highly receptive brain states. These programs do require listening with headphones.

For further explanation of our different technologies, please refer to our Technology Guide.

Can I import InnerTalk CDs to my iPod or MP3 player?

Remember, your InnerTalk programs are for personal use only. According to international copyright laws, sharing, copying, broadcasting to a large audience or any other such use, may be criminal. For personal use only then, yes, you can transfer InnerTalk programs to your iPod, smart phone, iPad, etc., but care needs to be taken to ensure no loss in quality. For complete instructions on importing InnerTalk programs to your iPod or MP3 player, please see the online instructions:

www.innertalk.com/faq-import.html.

Further Information

Speaking Engagements

Dr. Eldon Taylor and Ravinder Taylor are available for public speaking and book store engagements. For details, please call 509-299-3377.

Motivational Training

Our team is available to train your business staff and provide them with the customized tools necessary to accelerate their motivational skills. For further details call 1-800-964-3551.

Contact Information

Progressive Awareness
P.O. Box 1139
Medical Lake, WA 99022
Toll Free (US and Canada): 1-800-964-3551
Int'l: +1-509-299-3377
E-mail: innertalk@innertalk.com
Informational website: www.innertalk.com
Online Store: www.innertalk-store.com

www.ingramcontent.com/pod-product-compliance
Lightning Source LLC
Chambersburg PA
CBHW032039050726
47590CB00001B/65